ALAN ROUSE

A MOUNTAINEER'S LIFE

ALAN ROUSE

A MOUNTAINEER'S LIFE

compiled by Geoff Birtles

UNWIN HYMAN
London Sydney

First published in Great Britain by Unwin Hyman, an imprint of Unwin Hyman Limited, 1987.

UNWIN HYMAN LIMITED
Denmark House, 37-39 Queen Elizabeth Street, London SE1 2QB

and

40 Museum Street, London WC1A 1LU

Allen & Unwin Australia Pty Ltd
8 Napier Street, North Sydney, NSW 2060, Australia

Allen & Unwin with the Port Nicholson Press,
60 Cambridge Terrace, Wellington, New Zealand.

British Library Cataloguing in Publication Data
Alan, Rouse,
1. Rouse, Alan 2. Mountaineers
England — Biography
I. Birtles, Geoffrey
796.5'223'0924 GV199.92.R6
ISBN 0 04 440075 6

Designed by Julian Holland. Typeset by Pickards, Sheffield.
Printed and bound at the University Press, Cambridge

Acknowledgements

These acknowledgements are my thanks to the many people, mostly Al's friends, who have given their help and support, not just with this book but for everything else which had to be done. The list is in no particular order and, of course, my apologies to anybody whom I have inadvertently omitted. To: In particular, all the contributors in this book whose names appear elsewhere; Deborah Sweeney, Connie Austen-Smith and Barbara Fuller, Pam Davies my long suffering secretary, Ian Smith, Peter Minks, Andy Parkin, Al Burgess, Sue Carrington, Alan and Sandra Elliott, Pat Coleman of Sheffield City Library along with Mike Surr and Edwin Speight, Sir Jack Longland, Helen Geddes, Jim Perrin, Dennis Gray, Cameron McNeish, Mike Richardson and Laraine Curran, Pat Lewis and Leslie Bolton, the Rev. Wilfred Hudson, Phil Burke and Julia Rodwell. To those journalists who, after three weeks of seige, when all was lost, telephoned just to say 'sorry'. And finally to my wife Jackie and our children; Alexander, Oliver and Elizabeth.

Contents

INTRODUCTION

Alan Rouse is presumed to have died on August 10 1986 at Camp 4 situated at 8,000 metres on K2, the world's second highest mountain. He had been at this unholy altitude for too long, first by choice preparing for a summit bid, then after becoming the first ever Briton to climb K2 he became trapped by a storm with six other climbers of which only two survived.

He was 34 years old and had had a glittering career as a climber only outshone at times by the sparkle of his social life. He had done more daring deeds than most of us and on many a late night he relished in the retelling of dashing climbs and Keystone Cop-style sprints round the streets of Chester. On more than one occasion it was suggested to Al that he write his candid biography, tell the whole truth, the countless climbs and censored fast living. He would always grin knowingly at the very thought. What would they all say if only they knew? And what of his friends, how would they feel in clean-pressed middle age to see it all in print? No, Al would never have done it that way. He was set on making a career in a fast and efficient manner and a bridle of hippydom would just get in the way. 'K2 will be my last big climb,' he said. 'I can set myself up with that.'

The truth was that he was so bright and able that he could have set himself up anyway and nobody ever believed he would resist another big hill. However, what had changed in his life, apart from impending middle age, was the expected birth of a first child with his girlfriend Deborah Sweeney. He had recently moved up market to a larger house and domesticity was now on his mind. In the event, Deborah gave birth to a daughter, Holly, three weeks after Al perished.

Following Al's death, some close friends arranged a Memorial Service which packed St. Andrews church in Sheffield's leafy Nether Edge which had been home to Al for several years. Rab Carrington paid his tribute to a close friend and climber, Chris Bonington read a short passage and Jim Curran concluded with a modern tribute. The services of the Rev. Wilfred Hudson, the church and its choir were donated free of charge, caught up as they were with a genuine public distress. Press and television blocked the doorway and it was a crowded Byron pub which took the strain for the evening. Food was laid on by many friends who delivered their plates for old friends who had travelled from as far away as France. This was a family affair in the widest sense and with the exception of him not being present, Al would have thoroughly approved.

What made him so popular is difficult to explain. His character was not particularly one type or another, not always the amusing raconteur, nor ever out of conversation for long. Malice was not in his nature and he tended to suffer the failings of others with great understanding though he could quite easily if the occasion demanded cut deeply with a sharp wit into a person's insecurity. He was not one to hold grudges preferring to build and maintain bridges. At his best he could entertain for hours, laid on the floor propped against a cushion telling some never to be repeated stories though some were pure farce such as the slight-handed but short-sighted snatching of a pair of socks from outside a shop in Grindelwald only to find that they were attached by string to many other pairs which then trailed behind down the street and had to be swiftly abandoned.

There was an element of university rag week about Al's life which began before he went to Cambridge, probably about the time he met the Vagabond Mountaineering Club and continued until he was about 30, after which he began to gather round him some stable trappings of life such as his own house and the ensuing responsibilities. From a comfortable middle-class upbringing with outstanding scholarly achievements, he made a classic rebellion away from swotting to experiencing life in the raw. His survival at Cambridge was tenuous. In the end he achieved an Ordinary Degree though he had reached the required Honours standard which was denied him for non-attendance.

I don't need to repeat here, in chronological order, what is in the Summary and the book itself. It stands to reason that along with the other contributors Al was held in high regard, primarily as a friend. All that was asked of the writers was that they write the story as it was (within reason) taking a period theme in order to avoid too much overlapping, to allow some structure, and this they all readily agreed to do. In the end we have a loose biography. All the royalties from the book will go to the 'Alan Rouse Memorial Trust Fund' which with Sheffield City Libraries, will jointly administer a climbing library, called the 'Alan Rouse Collection' which is now open and housed in the reference section of Sheffield's Central Library.

Finally I dedicate this book to Holly, Al's daughter, whom he never saw. When, one day, she reads this she will know of her father that he was a fine man.

(Geoff Birtles. Sheffield.)

BIOGRAPHICAL RECORD
Alan Paul Rouse
Born: 19th December 1951
Died: August 1986
Age: 34

Personal: Born in Wallasey, Merseyside. Won a scholarship to Birkenhead School where he excelled academically winning a place at Emmanuel College Cambridge and gained a degree in mathematics. He subsequently worked as a school teacher periodically before making his living as a professional mountaineer via lecturing writing and as a consultant to the outdoor trade.

Climbing Biography:

1968: Began climbing at the age of 16 with Nick Parry at The Breck which was close to his home. Here he developed a finger strength and wall climbing technique at which he excelled throughout doing 6a problems even before he started climbing proper. He progressed to Helsby soloing up to 5a and top-roped the classic but unled Beatnik at 6a. Began frequenting North Wales achieving leads of Vector and Cemetery Gates. Joined the local (Birkenhead) Gwydyr Mountaineering Club.

1969: Established a solid list of Extreme leads particularly in North Wales including Suicide Wall at Ogwen, Winking Crack on Gogarth, Left Wall and The Thing in the Llanberis Pass. Visited the Alps for the first time and with Fred Heywood made an ascent of the Menegaux Route (TD) on the Aiguille de L'M, Chamonix.

1970: At the age of 18 exploded in climbing significance with an audacious solo ascent of The Boldest on Cloggy, considered to be one of the hardest routes in North Wales at that time; this was after meeting Eric Jones who had introduced him to solo climbing. Made the first ascent of Gemini on Cloggy which had a bold and fearsome reputation and repeated Afreet Street on Gogarth. Made second visit to Alps and attempted with Leo Dickinson the difficult South Face of the Fou an ED with a substantial reputation which they failed on for various reasons. Climbed North Ridge of Peigne in six hours and retreated from 90m diedre on West Face of Dru in bad weather; both with Geoff Tabner. Climbed West Face of Blatiere with Geoff Birtles. Other rock climbs in Britain included Great Wall on Cloggy and further soloed many routes apart from Boldest including Suicide Wall and the first pitch of Vember (on sight). Started at Cambridge in October and led Our Father in November. Joined the Vagabond MC which gave him a base in North Wales.

1971: In February made second ascent

of Wee Doris and first ascent of Matrix at Stoney Middleton. Climbed Point Five Gully in very good time with Geddes, Higham and Gillespie. Made first lead and solo of Beatnik at Helsby in March along with first ascent of Positron on sight at Craig Gogarth regarded as one of the best UK routes of this year. Soloed Vector at Tremadog with Pete Minks. Made first ascent of Sheaf Direct on Cloggy with John Cardy. Met and began climbing with Rab Carrington in April so starting a long and successful climbing partnership and lasting friendship. Soloed the North Ridge of Piz Cengalo in four hours. Repeated with Pete Minks, Hemmings/Robbins on West Face of Dru continuing up Magnone Route. Also with Minks climbed North Face of Triolet. Attempted to solo the difficult South Face of the Fou breaking an ankle in a short fall when a piton came out. He executed a diagonal abseil self-rescue to regain the gully and descended alone until 300ft from the bottom. Others assisted him down to the glacier from where a helicopter took him down to Chamonix. Got back to climbing in October with a solo of Nea and was back to leading such as Rat Race by December and soloing Raeburns Gully as the year closed.

1972: With Mick Geddes made third ascent of Don Whillans's Direct Finish to Carnivore on Craig a Bhancair, Glencoe. Made an early ascent of Adjudicator Wall in Dovedale, Staffs. Began serious Scottish winter climbing with second ascent of Orion Face Direct on Ben Nevis with Mick Geddes. Climbed Kellett's Right-Hand Route on Minus Two Buttress and first ascent of South Pillar on Creag Meaghaidh. In Summer Alpine season with Carrington made the first ascent of a route to the right of the Direct Route on the NE Face of the Gletscherhorn and did Walker Spur. He followed his Alpine season with a visit to Yosemite where he broke his ankle again after a short fall five pitches up the North Face Direct on Half Dome.

1973: Went on International Meet at Ecole Nationale at Chamonix. Again with Carrington he went to Patagonia but a sequence of bureaucratic hold-ups restricted their time in the hills and the trip was without great mountaineering achievement though they managed a route on the East side of Mojon Rojo and tried the West Face of Fitzroy. This trip sowed seeds for a Super Trip in the future. Visited Vercors and Shawangunks. Made second ascent of Zappelli/Bertone route on Mont Maudit with Mick Geddes.

1974: After returning from South America, lived in a cottage near Bangor. Climbed first ascent of Wonderwall at Gogarth.

1975: In January he made his first winter visit to the Alps with Rab Carrington. They climbed the Gervasutti Pillar with two bivouacs and made the first winter ascent of the Rebuffat/Terray route on the North Face of the Aiguille des Pelerins which has since become a classic winter climb. They also made an ascent of the North Face of the Col de l'Aiguille Verte. In Britain he maintained his rock-climbing form with an early ascent of The Leech on Cloggy. In the summer with Carrington he made an eight hour ascent of a variation on the Bonatti/Zapelli on the Grand Pilier d'Angle, an early ascent of the Sandri/Stenico/Chiara/Perenni route on the Aiguille Noire, Pointe Bich SE Face, and Cecchinel/Nomine route in a fast time and a second ascent of the Lesueur Route which crosses the North Faces of the Petite and Grande Dru, they found 'the climb to be very hard and very good; a forgotten masterpiece that was very advanced for its time', a good piece of research.

1976: With Carrington made a fine first winter ascent of Left Edge Route on Gardyloo Buttress, normally a 700ft VS in summer.

1977: His idea of a 'Super Trip' to South America came to fruition in the company of Brian Hall, Rab Carrington, John Whittle and the Burgess twins as well as several girlfriends. With Carrington he climbed new routes on: Aiguille Poincenot, Nevado Rasac South Face, Nevado Rondoy West Face, Nevado Yerupaja South Face and an attempt on the 7,000ft West Face of Fitzroy. They also climbed some small unclimbed summits and visited the Paine region. This was a major successful expedition rounded off with a visit to Yosemite on the way home combined with some guiding work in the Palisades.

1978: In March (winter) with Carrington made a one day ascent of the North Face of the Col de Peigne and a three day ascent of the North-east Spur (Tournier Route) of Les Droites. Went to Himalayas for the first time in the post-monsoon season with Carrington, Hall and Roger Baxter-Jones and made a very fine Alpine-style ascent of Jannu (25,294ft).

1979: In February made the first winter ascent of Pointe du Domino NW Couloir with Aidrian Burgess and American Carlos Huber. In the summer had a successful trip to the Cordillera Huayuash, Peru and with Brian Hall and Frenchman Nicholas Jaeger made first ascent of West Face of Tsacra Grande Oeste and SW Ridge of Trapecio. Climbed West Ridge of Ninashanka with Hall. Made a post-monsoon visit to Nepal attempting a new line from the Dudh Kosi side of the lower summit of Kantega with Hall and Carrington which was aborted low down. With Hall continued to Everest Base Camp and joined-up in October with Doug Scott and Frenchman Georges Bettembourg to climb the first ascent of Nuptse's North Face from the Western Cwm.

1980: Joined Bonington in a reconnaissance trip to China where they prospect Mount Kongur and climb first ascent of Sarakyaguqi (6,200m).

1981: Winter 80/81 led a British expedition to attempt Everest by the West Ridge via Lho La without oxygen or Sherpas in the severest conditions. The expedition consisting of Paul Nunn, Pete Thexton, Joe Tasker, John Porter and the Burgess twins made a high point on the West Shoulder but were defeated by an assortment of problems. In the summer he joined Bonington, Tasker and Boardman to make a successful first ascent of Mount Kongur (7,719m) in China.

1982: With Paul Nunn, Brian Hall and Andy Parkin made attempts on three separate routes on Baintha Brakk 2 (Ogre 2) 6,960m in Pakistan.

1983: Major visit to Karakoram with ultimate goal of K2. International team comprising from UK of Doug Scott, Don Whillans, Pete Thexton, Andy Parkin; plus Frenchman Jean Afanassieff, Australian Greg Child and American Steve Sustad. With Parkin, Thexton and Child climbed the first ascent of a training peak of 18,000ft close to Lobsang Spire. Attempted but failed on both another small peak (Pt.5607) and a route on Lobsang Spire (18,724ft). Climbed Broad Peak Alpine-style with Parkin, RBJ and Afanassieff. Attempted a new line up the South Ridge Direct on K2 with Parkin and Sustad.

1984: With new vigour for domestic rock-climbing at E5 and putting up the odd outcrop route such as Reagent (E4,6a) at Stanage, and Quality Street (E5 6b) at Millstone Edge with Phil Burke. Visited Jersey over Easter holiday and climbed a number of new routes, three of which have since become classics of the island, Perihelion (HVS) Citizens Edge (E2) and Tax Exile (E5). Went to Pakistan with Bonington and two Pakistani climbers and attempted Karun Koh (7,350m) but failed primarily due to bad weather.

1985: Mainly pusued domestic climbing but took opportunity while on a lecture tour of New Zealand to climb in the NZ Alps. Elected Vice-President of the British Mountaineering Council.

1986: Went to K2 as Joint leader of a strong British team attempting first ascent of NW Ridge; failed due to bad weather and the difficulty of the line. Stayed on with Jim Curran after rest of team returned and attempted Abruzzi Spur amidst an ad-hoc group of four Austrians, Englishwoman Julie Tullis and a Polish girl. Reached summit of K2 on August 4th to become first Briton on top. Left ill but still alive on August 10th at Camp 1V at approximately 8,000m and is presumed to have died there.

A slightly shorter version of this biographical summary appeared in the October 1986 edition of High Magazine and was prepared with the assistance of Rab Carrington.

1

Formative Years

SUSAN ROUSE

ALAN PAUL ROUSE was born on the 19th December, 1951. As a baby he was blessed with blond curls, and an angelic countenance and his quiet gentle appearance meant that he was occasionally mistaken for a girl. Our mother, Eve, was just 19 and Alan was a 'honeymoon baby', born exactly nine months after her marriage. Father, John Arnold Rouse, was employed as a clerk by the Mersey Docks and Harbour Board. The family home was a semi-detached house in Wallasey on Merseyside. Grandparents lived near, a dog slept in front of the fire, and Alan grew up surrounded by all the traditional trappings of family life. I appeared on the scene two-and-a-half years later. He surrendered his teddy bear to his little sister and accepted the addition to the family philosophically enough, for he was not jealous or possessive by nature. As we grew up together we played and argued; he was always very much the older brother to me, someone to look up to and follow.

We all said that he seemed to have been born lucky and that when he fell, he landed on his feet. Success in an unlikely sphere came at a very early age. The photographer who had been commissioned to take Alan's portrait sought permission to enter the photograph in a national competition. It reached the final stages and became part of an exhibition to be held by the National Portrait Gallery as an example of 'British Childhood at its Best'. This was an achievement to which Alan referred in later years with amusement and some ill-concealed pride.

As Alan grew up, he developed a deep-rooted wanderlust. No sooner had he learnt to walk than he would wander off on his

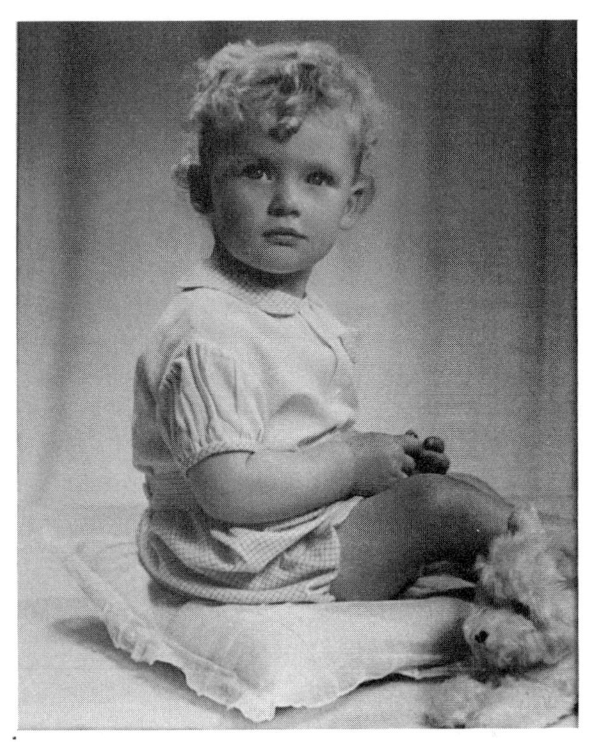

Photo of Alan that reached the final stages of a competition and became part of the National Portrait Gallery exhibition "British Childhood at its best".

own exploring the local streets, too young to know any fear and with too strong a sense of self-preservation to come to much harm. He horrified grandparents by being seen all over Wallasey before school age. Although superficially shy and retiring, he had an innate inner confidence and, perhaps more significantly, the ability to inspire confidence in others. Family rows were, more often than not, caused by his apparent inability to appear for meals at set times; his safety never in doubt. Perhaps there was less to worry about in those days, or perhaps our mother, being so young herself, was happily unaware.

Explorations on foot were, after a few years, superseded by bike rides; first Parkgate, West Kirby and Chester, and then, by the age of seven, further afield to North Wales. Even the long walk home necessitated by a puncture one night did not deter him. He enjoyed freedom. Given that, he was cheerful and happy to endure almost any physical discomfort. If restrictions were imposed, however, he would become restless, and although never bored, he would lose some of that spark, that enthusiasm for life which was so much part of his character.

Not everything in life was made easy for him. He inherited the family stammer which had so affected the lives of both our father and grandfather. Even pronouncing his own name became a major obstacle and source of embarrassment. It made the first few years at school difficult, but fortunately we were able to ignore it and it grew less obvious in time. Indeed, he spoke well as an adult and there remained no hint of his early struggles. Physically he looked pale and far from robust. Although of an independent nature, he was gentle and quietly spoken and suffered rather badly from the childhood illnesses of measles and chicken pox. A further weakness, that of shortsightedness, came to light in the classroom. His glasses were to become a virtual trademark, a constant source of irritation when climbing, frequently broken and held together with sellotape. It was only during the last few years of his life that he came to terms with contact lenses.

These inherent weaknesses, together with a lack of real talent or interest in any of the conventional sports, helped to create the impression of a retiring academic and his early school career served to reinforce this. He showed a clear-sighted approach to solving puzzles of a mathematical or logical nature and a fine skill in playing the childhood games of Risk and Monopoly. He enjoyed practical science, and from a small commercially produced chemistry set he graduated to buying large quantities of chemicals and apparatus from the local chemist's. He connected his Bunsen burner to the gas cooker and performed a wide variety of experiments with differing degrees of success. Indoor fireworks were a particular favourite of his, rather than my mother's. He filled saucepans with a sticky mess, 'cinder toffee', as a demonstration of the effect of carbon dioxide, I believe, and made his own toothpaste with soot. Meccano was another favourite. He produced a far greater number of intricate working models from the metal plates, nuts and bolts than those listed in the instruction manuals. He liked to know how things

Alan aged 3.

worked, and when he received a long-awaited electric motor one Christmas morning, he took it apart, a spring shot out and he never did manage to get it working again. He was a strange mixture of ingenuity and impracticality. As he grew a little older he designed and began to build his own computer. He scoured rubbish tips for old televisions and radios and spent his pocket money on 'bits' for it. His bedroom became more like a laboratory than ever. The apparatus, for want of a better word, never did quite work; the reasons sounded very convincing at the time.

Money always proved somewhat of an obstacle for Alan; he never seemed to have enough of it. It wasn't that he wanted it for its own sake, his bank balance would never have borne very close scrutiny, but there were so many things in life which he wanted to do. And so he devised a number of money-making schemes which were elaborate and original but somehow never really got off the ground. There was the selling of frogs and toads which almost strained our mother's patience to the limit, particularly when a rather large and cumbersome specimen hopped on to her foot whilst she was hanging out the washing. Others included cleaning neighbours' cars (too unimaginative to last), clearing snow in winter, and, perhaps one of the most successful, emptying slot machines in the New Brighton Amusement Arcades. In those days it was possible to devise systems of winning which really did work and he would often come home with a saddlebag full of pennies. Eventually he was banned, unfairly he always thought, but as his agent I could carry on; they were less suspicious of a little girl. Even in later years, as desperate as ever for cash, he could always reckon to make some money by 'playing sensibly'. At least it was more fun than working, and he was never a strong believer in that particular ethic. I remember once, many years later, expressing some surprise that he had managed to secure a mortgage. He regarded the matter philosophically: since banks make money out of lending, the best customers are those who borrow money. Alan borrowed as much money as he could, *ergo* he was one of their most favoured customers.

At the age of eleven, Alan won a place at Birkenhead School. It was the nearest direct grant school in the area and it had a good academic and sporting reputation. Father was disappointed by his lack of interest in rugby and cricket, but he had inherited the same interest and ability in mathematics and seemed all set to pursue a course of academic endeavour. He won a number of school prizes and further developed a long-standing interest in chess. From about the age of seven he had represented his junior school and played in local chess congresses. He later joined Wallasey Chess Club, became the Wallasey under-eighteen champion and did on occasion play for the Cheshire senior team. In those days, when he was not hoping to become a second Einstein, he dreamt of being a Grand Master of chess. He enjoyed success and was constantly striving to become the best in the world at something. Strangely, some of the outward changes in his attitude and approach to life — from the quiet, thoughtful conformist to the, at times, outrageous rebel of the late sixties

Alan and Susan, 1957.

and early seventies — can be traced back to the unlikely venue of a British Chess Congress in Hastings. Alan was about 15 and keen to pit his wits against the best on his first major trip away from home. He won a few matches but did not achieve the outstanding success for which he yearned. He did, however, learn to drink a pint in one and much more besides.

From that time onwards he started to question openly all the values on which he had hitherto based his life. It sounds like a cliche, a classic story of adolescence. Perhaps Alan had more intelligence, confidence and daring than was good for him, and they created a dangerous combination. He began to discard convention, grow his hair longer than either his school or his father thought desirable and generally become involved in all the subversive activities of youth. Such changes were reflected in his school reports. The once 'quiet and conscientious pupil' had become arrogant and intolerant of subjects which did not interest him. Later in life he confessed to having intercepted one report so that it never reached our parents. They were not pleased, but despite all, Alan seemed very much more in control of his life. His rebellion was measured; he was experimenting, playing games. He knew just how far he could go and in no way wished to jeopardize his future.

He started to drink, smoke and listen to Jimi Hendrix. I remember my mother, on one occasion, going to wake him for school only to find that his bed had not been slept in; he had not returned from the revelries of the night before. On other occasions his floor would be littered with strangers who had stayed the night whose unexpected appearance at breakfast was often a little disconcerting.

Although a rebel in appearance and philosophy, Alan was never guilty of rude or offensive behaviour. At home he remained as cheerful and polite as ever and did not believe in worrying or upsetting people unnecessarily even if this meant not always being strictly honest. He strove to avoid rows and confrontations and sensed that his mother was happier not knowing everything that went on. Of course, she was more aware than he realized, but she had sufficient faith to let him sort out his own life. For instance, she did not particularly like smoking, and so, even many years after he had left home, he never once smoked in her presence. Yet nothing was ever said.

He had by this stage already passed the necessary O Levels without really trying and there was never much doubt about the area in which he would specialize. He took the Maths, Further Maths and Physics A Levels in his stride, and an extra O Level to keep him occupied. Underneath his childish spidery writing and frugal diagrams lay a keen perception and understanding of mathematical concepts. He continued to enjoy the subjects and was drawn to the more esoteric topics of Nuclear Physics and Relativity. He would discuss their philosophical implications at length and had he really turned his energies in these directions then he could, I am sure, have made a fine research scientist. His interest and enthusiasm inspired me to follow such a course.

Alan aged 9.

I remember the games that we used to play on long car journeys; the Nuclear Quiz where we would ask each other questions in turn and score a point for each one that the other person could not answer. I did score one point once. Also there was the Chemical Elements Game. We would begin with the letter A and try to name elements starting with that initial alternately. The first person unable to think of one lost a point. Then we went on to B, and so on. Bonus points were achieved for correct estimates of atomic weight and atomic number. Our mother adjudicated with the help of a book. She was far from being a scientist herself, and, in retrospect, I don't suppose she enjoyed it very much. Perhaps this early interest was later reflected in the naming of one of his new climbs, 'Positron', the name of one of the more elusive subatomic particles.

One of Alan's hobbies from his early teens was pot-holing and we spent many family outings sitting at the mouths of caves, his estimated time of exploration always falling far short of the real thing. They were situated in the bleakest parts of Yorkshire and Derbyshire, and we all got cold, wet and muddy on numerous occasions. Alan's obvious enjoyment and enthusiasm made it seem worthwhile, and indeed each of us was, on different occasions, persuaded to accompany him through the narrow and seemingly endless passages. He looked forward with eager anticipation to his fifteenth birthday when he could join a proper club. Even after he had embarked on his climbing career, he retained an instinctive interest in pot-holing which had been his first passion.

I have already mentioned various hobbies of Alan's: chess, pot-holing, chemistry. There were many others and each he pursued with the same single-mindedness and enthusiasm. Our father had the beginnings of a good stamp collection and together they added to it. Alan not only developed an extensive knowledge of all aspects of the subject but was also able to utilize his persuasive powers to the full when it came to swapping stamps and 'getting a good deal'. One of his undoubted talents was the ability to influence people. He could persuade someone to part with their most treasured possession and at the same time appear to be doing them a favour. It was the typical challenge that he enjoyed. He also started a rock and mineral collection and his bedroom became the home for many exhibits. Then there was an electronics craze and his bedroom changed from museum to a laboratory. Our mother despaired of ever cleaning it again. Certainly, Alan was never bored with life.

In Wallasey we lived near a small area of common land with the remains of a sandstone quarry called The Breck. This acted as our playground where I could take the dog for a walk and Alan could climb. Most of the local children spent time scrambling up and down those rocks. In retrospect, Alan outstripped all the others. Although far from athletic in inclination, he had shown an agility in climbing ropes and trees as a child and possessed a remarkable sense of balance. As a toddler he would walk happily along the tops of walls and from there graduated to the rails at bus stops. He displayed little fear of heights: any that he had he was able to rationalize, and the risks that he took were calculated ones. Thus the seeds of an obsession which was to so dominate the rest of his life were sown.

Family days out and holidays were centred predominantly on walking in the hills. North Wales, Derbyshire and even the Lake District and Yorkshire were readily accessible from Merseyside. At weekends we would set out early in the morning with picnic, dog and, in the early days, grandparents. Alan was the map-reader and in charge. He would be full of ideas and although his planned expeditions, or 'exhibitions' as I called them as a child (perhaps, on looking back, not totally misguidedly!), tended to be over-ambitious, we were, nevertheless, indebted to him for the discovery of a wealth of interesting and enjoyable scrambles. Holidays allowed us to travel further afield, and Scotland was the destination for several years. Based at a Bed and Breakfast in Fort William, we explored much of the Glencoe and Ben Nevis regions. I well remember the long days walking in the sun and snow of late March. On those holidays we were joined by Dick, a close family friend who was later to become our stepfather. He was around 30 and a good match for Alan in physical fitness. The midnight rambles that they planned together never quite materialized, but they did try to outdo each other with press-ups and pull-ups on the door frames (it was just as well the landlady never knew), out walking he and Alan set the pace. The dog wore her paws down until they bled in a frantic effort to keep in contact with us all, running between us and never quite sure who to stick to. We regarded our ascent of Ben Nevis in snow a particular achievement, especially as Alan was the only one with boots and ice-axe. The descent was not elegant; we sat down and slid, or 'glissaded' as Alan preferred it to be called. Our mother wore a hole in her trousers but was too tired to care. It would have worked out fine if Alan hadn't wanted to explore the north face. We trudged round, lost shoes in bogs and were generally very relieved to see the distillery many hours later.

A Levels came in 1969. Alan seemed sublimely unconcerned and was reluctant to forego his regular weekend climbing activities in the pursuit of academic success. He was also a realist as far as his own ability was concerned and consequently confident of high grades in all subjects. Our father was unconvinced and felt that he was not taking his school career sufficiently seriously. They could not readily agree to differ. Alan, however, seemed to thrive on exams and to produce his best work under pressure. Indeed, he even surprised himself on occasion. He was so impressed by one of his own comments in a General Studies exam that he inserted inverted commas and added the epithet 'as the great Newton once wrote'. He was rewarded by three grade A's, one grade B and two top grades in the Special papers.

He was still only seventeen and by this time well immersed in the climbing world. He had joined the Gwydyr Mountain Club and was making a significant impact on the climbing scene. Still too young to drink (officially) he required parentental permission to go to meetings which were always held in pubs. It remained a characteristic of Alan throughout his life that he had a large number of friends of vastly differing ages and from different backgrounds. Status was of little consequence and the generation gap hardly existed. He began to talk and live for climbing. He had found an activity for which he had an outstanding talent and one which, as he himself wrote 'suited his personality'. Other interests, both social and working, became peripheral to this main theme.

At the same time he was finding the restrictions of school life more and more inhibiting. He felt ready to tackle the world but instead was obliged to conform to the seemingly pointless ritual of a school day. Cambridge was now the ultimate goal. Our father was desperately keen that he should realize his academic potential through university; Alan was not so sure. He had no ambition to work in the conventional sense, life was too short for that, but at the back of his mind he still had a hankering for the benefits and prestige that such a traditional university could confer. Also, he continued to enjoy maths, more as a spare time activity by now, and regarded Cambridge as the best, and so in his eyes the only, place in which to study it. The entrance exams were held in November. He knew exactly how much preparation he could get away with, and set aside sufficient time. At the same time he made sure that his climbing did not suffer. Again he was confident of success and by Christmas he knew that he had secured a place at Emmanuel College. It coincided with his eighteenth birthday. And so began a few months of long-awaited freedom. He painted the house both inside and out to earn some money and took up almost permanent residence in 'Brigham's' climbing shop in Liverpool. He talked a great deal, planned and climbed, and was very happy.

He was, at this time, continuing to lead a very active social life, going to parties and pubs every night. At seventeen he had shown little inclination to learn to drive, but father encouraged him by giving him lessons and allowing him to practise. He surprised himself by passing his test first time after just one professional lesson. It was then that our parents began to doubt their own wisdom for he borrowed the car at every conceivable opportunity. His friends lived in diverse areas on the Wirral and he was seeing a girfriend regularly. An accident was, perhaps, almost inevitable in those reckless days and so it happened. No-one was injured but the car was almost a write-off. Long after the event he admitted that it was probably his own fault. When he was sufficiently well-established to run his own car he was quite firm in the conviction that he would never lend it to an irresponsible 18-year-old.

I found it strange when Alan left for university. Although latterly he had not been around the house very much, he was always there in the background and his influence was strong. He was ready to talk and express an opinion on most topics, and I missed our late night philosophical discussions (or rather monologues since he did most of the talking and I was a willing listener). He enjoyed relating his adventures with all the appropriate embellishments to make 'a good story'. The first time he returned home was for his grandfather's funeral. He confessed to finding the academic work far more demanding than he had anticipated and he made few friends within the rather introverted mathematical circles. Climbing was his safety valve. By the second term he had, by all accounts, built up a good social life, established his reputation in the Cambridge Mountaineering Club and made many friends. His hair grew even longer, he wore his mother's fur coat to lectures and his general appearance was an embarrassment to our parents.

Until this time life had gone well for Alan. There had been no major events to disturb his equilibrium and he had been free to pursue all his own interests. When father fell ill in 1971 it came as a great shock. After a few months of prolonged suffering, he died on July 3rd. We were together at the hospital and we knew it would happen. At forty-seven and with a grown-up family, he was denied the kidney machine which he needed to survive. Some experimental treatment was tried but without success. Such an experience causes one to re-evaluate life and to adjust to new principles. We all have our own way of coming to terms with the inner turmoil that the death of a close person brings. We were not good at displaying emotion and, superficially, we coped well. The pain, however, went deep and the scars remained.

Alan continued to climb and we saw less of him. It was many years before he had a permanent base of his own and so, although his climbing exploits took him off round the world, he would always return home at intervals, usually when he was least expected. He wasn't perfect and if one were to look for his faults then it is not difficult to detect an element of selfishness in the single-minded pursuit of his interests, and certainly there was a grain of roguish dishonesty in his character. Nevertheless, to us he always remained the same. He came home with an unlimited repertoire of stories and anecdotes; he was like a breath of fresh air in the house. He often returned ill, injured or without money, but never with his spirit dulled. I shall remember him not only as a brother, but also as a happy companion, an eternal optimist and someone who made me feel glad to be alive.

2
Early Climbing

NICK PARRY

I FIRST REALLY met Alan when he was moved into the sixth form at Birkenhead School a year early because he was of the chosen few likely to advance to a Cambridge Scholarship. That was in September 1967 and he was a most unlikely candidate to become a mountaineer; a thin, bespectacled, puny and a very studious and scientifically minded lad. His main interest, apart from maths, was chess which he played to a very high standard. He disliked virtually every type of sport but was a passable gymnast.

We first developed a friendship in the school's new sixth form library, where some far-sighted master had purchased several mountaineering books. We had both done a fair bit of hill-walking and were enthralled by the illustrations and romantic ideals in Gaston Rebuffat's 'Between Heaven and Earth', and poured over the techniques in 'On Snow and Rock' at breaks and lunchtimes. It was the excitement generated by those two books which led both Alan and I to become mountaineers.

Al was extremely shy in those days but he announced he had seen people rock-climbing at The Breck, a small sandstone quarry about 100 yards from his home in Wallasey. Together we plucked up the courage to ask them about climbing and to try our first efforts at the easier short problems. From the outset, we were hooked, and began to go to The Breck several times a week. Alan purchased a pair of kletts from Brigham's and between us we bought a polypropylene caving rope, a couple of slings and krabs. The rope was cheap and okay for top roping problems.

In the evenings and at weekends we would climb at The Breck

and it was there that we met two older lads, Maurice Ewing and John Beamer, who told us about a new climbing club that had started on the Wirral — the Gwydyr Mountain Club. Despite the fact that it met in a pub and we were only 16 or 17, we turned up and joined and the older members would go downstairs to the bar to buy our drinks.

This was the time of the foot and mouth epidemic and while the Lakes and Wales were out of bounds our first real climbing on named routes was at Helsby in January 1968, where we soloed five or six Diffs and top roped Z Route at V.Diff. In February the end of the foot and mouth restrictions were announced and we persuaded our parents to let us go to Snowdonia with John Huxley, an older friend from the Gwydyr Club. We hitched to Wales on Friday and were introduced to the delights of Willy's Barn, which at the time cost a shilling a night. The straw was filthy but the outside gents has the best view in Wales. It was here that we discovered that Al had few of the usual Boy Scout camping capabilities, or was extremely unlucky. He knocked our stove over, pitched our dinner in the straw and then poured the rice pudding over his sleeping bag. Anyway, although there was snow still on the ground, it was rock-climbing we were after and climbed Monolith Crack and Zig Zag on the Gribin, together with Milestone Direct and some slab routes.

This was the life for us. Alan went out and acquired his first guidebook, Llanberis North, and I encountered for the first time Alan's lifelong habit of compiling the 'list of things to do'. This first list included Cemetery Gates, the Corner and The Thing — quite impressive for a lad who had done about two V.Diffs.

By this time, we were well and truly addicted to climbing and used to ride our bikes for fifteen or so miles to Helsby and back on Sundays, as well as climbing on The Breck after school. We worked our way up the grades at Helsby and in May, with me in newly purchased Masters boots and Alan in his battered kletts we top roped our first VS there, the 5a Flake Crack. In June, again at Helsby, we met and chatted to Hugh Banner and Jim O'Neill, and talked with growing excitement about climbing on Cloggy. I think this fired Alan's imagination as the next time we went to Wales, in July, we went to Tremadog and Alan decided it was time to try our first Welsh VS's. A new 100ft hawser-laid rope was acquired and tested with Y Broga, Shadrach and Grim Wall.

Birkenhead School had lessons on Saturday mornings and games in the afternoon and we began to develop mysterious injuries and illnesses so that we could hitch to Wales on Saturday afternoons rather than play rugby or cricket.

By now, we were established members of the Gwydyr Club, drinking illegally on club nights and acting as club librarians; that way, we could take the guidebooks home. Newly acquired friends from Wallasey would take us to Wales and Helsby in the back of their mini van, where we were crammed in with four rucksacks and a labrador dog. Our bible was 'Rock Climbers in Action in Snowdonia' which we used to borrow alternately from Birkenhead Library so that no-one else could get it, and Alan used to speculate about how hard the climbs really were. Our climbing level improved with practice and we were soon top roping 5b and 5c problems at Helsby and The Breck. Alan was undoubtedly a natural, and the short technical problems were very much to his liking because, like a vertical chess game, he could work out a series of moves in advance.

Longer climbs in Wales were, however, different to top roping Helsby problems and in August 1968 we did the Nose Direct on Dinas Mot, then struggled up to the Cromlech and did Sabre Cut. While on it, we watched a party having trouble on Cemetery Gates and looking across Alan reckoned he could see some holds, so it must be okay. By the time we got to the bottom to collect our sacks, the leader had taken an impressive fall from just below the stance. Al persuaded them to let him have a go, but somewhat unexpectedly, they asked him to lead. Despite the large floppy kletts he was wearing, he managed to get up the pitch, but the effect of the exposure was suddenly brought home when his second fell off and he was pulled off the ledge to dangle, legs flapping, from the belay.

The experience had a slightly salutary effect because we went back to easier routes for at least six weeks, until on a cool day in early October 1968 we went down to Tremadog. Training at The Breck had built up Alan's confidence again and he decided to have a go at Vector. After all, it was still reckoned to be one of the classic harder routes in those days, and a definite top priority in the 'list of things to do'. He managed the main pitch slowly but comfortably and took a stance in the cave. Unfortunately, his seconds were not quite up to the task and both Fred Heywood and I failed to make the moves on to the Ochre Slab. Alan was marooned in the cave for about three hours before we could discover a second elsewhere on the crag to follow him.

Back at school on the Monday, the P.E. master, Jones the Gym, who did a little climbing up to V.Diff standard, asked what we had been up to. Imagine his face at the reply. He could not believe it, and thought it was just a case of schoolboy exaggeration.

At the end of that October came a lesson which slowed Al down a bit. We spent a weekend at the barn at Tremadog and had completed the Plum and Leg Slip and Al wanted to try First Slip as well. In the thin groove, without the peg which was usual in those days, Al managed to get himself crossed up and ended up bridged across the groove facing outwards. He took off, with the groove acting as a slide, and shot off down and outwards severely damaging his buttocks, and ended up swinging back and forth in front of me at the stance. Standards were again reduced for a while.

In the winter of 1968/69 we had our first winter climbing experiences with Parsley Fern Gully and Crib Goch Ridge our first introduction. This winter coincided with the Club's acquisition of a hut in Llanrwst, about which some epic tales could be told. Several over-zealous pub sessions led to some exciting nights out and I can remember midnight tobogganing down the bottom 100ft of Idwal Slabs with a run out to the lake. Alan led me up one of the Trinity gullies that winter and I remember him being so tired on the way back that we had to carry his ice-axe for him.

1969 had for us a slow start, but then experiences came fast. Alan climbed with Fred Heywood as well as myself, but I remember some epic failures on Slape Direct and Hangover, in the wet. That summer was our A Level year so things slowed down a bit in the middle and Al concentrated seriously on developing The Breck. Over several months he managed to put together the girdle of Bluebell Wall, a continuous series of 5c moves, and made the first continuous traverse that summer, although it was not long before he also made the first double crossing there and back. Also that summer, I held the top rope while Al completed a route up the centre of the Overhanging Wall at the back of The Breck, with some specially difficult moves in the overhanging centre which he reckoned were easily 6a or more, even then. I never did manage it myself. As far as I remember, it was during this spell that Alan first top roped Beatnik (6a) at Helsby, which he was later to solo in 1971.

With 'A' Levels over, it was back to Wales at the end of June and Al celebrated with an ascent of Left Wall which was rarely climbed in those days. He managed to use two or three nuts for aid rather than the usual half dozen. Rain stopped play, no-one could follow, and a dawn start had to be made to retrieve the gear left on the crag overnight.

We used to go over to Liverpool for the afternoon on non-climbing Saturdays, and sit on the floor of Brigham's shop, gossiping and making a nuisance of ourselves, and offering free advice to unsuspecting customers. It was there we met Pete Minks, Brian Molyneux and Leo Dickinson and others in the Vagabonds with whom Alan was to climb a lot during the next year or so.

In July/August 1969, four of us set out for Chamonix for the first time. We had no idea what to expect and took all our food with us in tins. We camped in squalor at the Biolay, until the Gendarmerie came and closed it down for public health reasons. We were up in the mountains at the time and came back to find a notice pinned to the tent. After that, we made the shepherd's hut at Montenvers our base. Alan and Fred began with the Ménégaux Route on the L'M, which took about 10 hours rather than the guidebook six. Maurice and I sat on the top waiting for hours having done the NNE Ridge. Next we all climbed the Requin from the Mer de Glace side by different routes. Then we had a severe shock which stayed with us all for several years. On the way up the Nantillons Glacier, to climb the Charmoz-Grépon, we heard a shout and saw a party of English lads, with whom we had shared the hut the night before, fall from the Spencer Couloir. We were the first on the scene but despite numerous attempts were unable to reach them where they hung on the rock face. Two were dead but the third hung upside down alive and bleeding. He died later after the rescue team arrived. Alan was deeply affected by this and despite the fact that we did some more climbing, his heart was not in it. However, we were all impressed by Alpine climbing and it was this first experience which whetted Alan's appetite for the experiences and excitements of larger mountains.

In September 1969, I went to Leeds University whilst Alan stayed at school to do Cambridge Scholarships. Despite problems with his school reports, Alan was still a bright mathematician and eventually passed. During this time, he began to climb with friends from the Vagabond Club in Liverpool, particularly with Pete Minks and Leo Dickinson. We still climbed frequently together, squeezing in Park Lane, Winking Crack and Strand in one day at Gogarth in September 1969 and celebrating Christmas with a trip to Tremadog for Grasper, Pellagra, Tensor, Zukator and Diadic. We got our own back on First Slip; no problems this time, and also on Vector.

By now, Alan was becoming ambitious. He had his eyes on various new routes, but decided to try some second ascents first. Falls Road at Gogarth was selected and at Easter 1970 in good weather, we had a go. All went well until a hold came off in his hand about 20ft from the top of the last pitch, and Alan took a long fall, about 40ft, hitting the stance at the bottom. Despite the shock and a stiff shoulder he did not forget the important things in life, and forced me to prusik up the rope to rescue his krabs and runners before I was allowed to shepherd him off.

This episode did not put him off for long and 1970 was a great year for Alan. A number of hard routes at Gogarth, including Mammoth, Quartz Icicle etc., and at Tremadog led to a blitz on Cloggy, with many routes including Great Wall, Scorpio, Boldest and a new route Gemini. It was also the year when he took up soloing for a short period. In one weekend he soloed Suicide Wall and Suicide Groove on the Saturday and Boldest on the Sunday.

In these days, Alan was a regular visitor to the house in Leeds which I shared with Brian Hall. Although the main purpose of the visits was the rock concerts for which Leeds University was famous at the time, we did plenty of climbing on Yorkshire gritstone and limestone. I remember Alan being preoccupied with a second ascent of Alan Austin's Wall of Horrors at Almscliff, but being beaten to it by John Syrett. We also used to hang a top rope over a famous problem, The Goblin's Eyes, which Al eventually top roped, but never risked leading.

We climbed in the traditional garb for those days, long hair with headbands, brightly coloured bell-bottomed trousers, with fur coats and RAF greatcoats and were usually accompanied by a cassette player to encourage us with Pink Floyd or the Rolling Stones.

As Alan's standards at both rock and ice grew harder and more exacting, and my interests turned more to parties and rock music, we climbed together less often but remained close friends.

The last climb we did together was at Easter 1971 when on a beautiful sunny day we climbed White Slab on Cloggy. We left our girfriends to sit in the sun by the lake and strolled to the bottom of the cliff. As usual, Alan was disorganized and we discovered he had left his half of the double rope at the lake, so he had to scramble back to get it. But it was a lovely day and we took the long slabs slowly, enjoying every moment. Our first attempt at the lasso failed and Alan could not be bothered to have another try, and we did Alan Austin's direct variation instead. Alan was in his element on the technical, delicate climbing of the upper slabs and we climbed slowly, taking in the atmosphere of the cliff, and the exposure. We climbed out into the sun at the top to end what he always remembered as one of the best days.

3
After School

FRED HEYWOOD

THE GWYDYR MOUNTAIN Club had been formed just before the great foot and mouth epidemic of 1967. During those dark days, when the hills were often veiled in black smoke from the farmyard funeral pyres, the members kept themselves amused bouldering at the local quarry. Al Rouse and some of his school friends began to attend the regular weekly meets. I had been invited to the club by one of the founder members just as the foot and mouth outbreak was coming to an end. Alan cornered me on the first night, full of youthful enthusiasm.

It was very difficult talking Al out of attempting The Fang as our first climb. I had no decent boots although I did have a brand new Viking No.3 rope. Al was the proud owner of a pair of Masters boots and a Moac chock on 9mm line. In truth I was a trifle unsure of Al's ability as his only previous experience was Lockwood's Chimney, on a communal rope.

In the Golden Fleece pub Al presented his views on climbing. He was an avid reader and collector of climbing books and guides and didn't agree with my view 'that guides spoiled the adventure of climbing'. We both agreed, however, that pegs and artificial aids were often unnecessary. He remained a purist, disliked those who 'desecrated' rock with pegs and disagreed with the fashion for top-roping new routes, gardening routes or abseiling to place runners prior to an ascent.

We ticked off One Step In The Clouds, Shadrach and Merlin on our first day climbing together. We climbed in Wales on every available weekend. Using the graded list at the back of the Tremadog guide, Al planned sustained progress through the

A motley Cambridge crew at the Roaches. Left to right: Al after his fou accident, John Robinson who went on to a successful financial career in the City, Mick Geddes who tragically died so young from cancer and Nigel Lyle who lost a leg following an accident on the Bonatti Pillar. Photo: Rab Carrington collection.

grades. Where we came to a route that had a peg for aid he simply refused to use it.

I recall that on our first climbs together Al was slow and steady but I suppose with only one runner this was understandable. He selected the routes and persuaded me that each was the logical next step. On the cliff his feeble calls were often unheard by me. Following a complete breakdown of communications on Slape, Al decided we should concentrate on vertical wall climbs. My preference for crack-climbing fell on deaf ears. I tried the logical arguments that we could use the Moac occasionally, that vertical walls were hard, that I liked to have nice safe cracks to crawl into when frightened. All arguments foundered when coming up against Al's enthusiasm for holdless vertical rock faces.

As the summer of 1968 arrived we had collected together a selection of runners, a pair of Masters each and I had a healthy overdraft. We found ourselves in competition with other climbers in the Gwydyr Mountain Club. Plans were made in secret, false trails were laid. Other partnerships changed as teams tried to establish themselves. Rouse, the schoolboy chess champion, had all the moves planned out. We loved it, Al more than me as I was the butt of sarcastic comments, from Nick Parry in particular, over my role as 'professional second'.

The GMC provided an audience for some of our climbs. Suicide Groove which Al only climbed to have a look at 'The Wall', Grasper with Nick Parry in the middle. Al climbed the top pitch free and Nick thought it only fair that I should do likewise. He encouraged me in this by letting the rope out as I approached each runner. This incentive certainly had the effect of speeding up my ascent. Bonfire night on Vector had Al's progress on the Ochre Slab inspired by having bangers hurled at him from the stance. Al was still not keen on getting too close to any cracks so having stepped right at the peg repeated the move and climbed the slab by the far right-hand edge. The holds he used were not apparent to us mere mortals. The bloke on Meshach, who fell off when the bangers were being thrown was a trifle irate. Following my treatment on Grasper, I thought it only fair to leave Al in the cave to contemplate the error of his ways.

As the climbs got harder I was developing a fine technique at jumping for holds, the intermediate grains of sand which Al used never seemed suitable. Al observed these subtle climbing techniques and filed them away for future use. He told me he used the jump technique in his first ascent of Gemini a few years later, but his second that day had not developed the technique and could not follow. Al was always keen to learn about the art of climbing. He carefully reviewed each new piece of gear as it arrived in Brigham's shop. Al had a theory that Super Gratton boots had a better grip than Masters and that his TUF industrial boots were superior to both — 'After all the Tuf Boot soles were guaranteed not to slip on oil and PA's are the very devil when muddy!' The only problem with the TUF boots was that he had no laces for them.

Inevitably Al began to search out the most difficult climbs. He bought each new edition of the New Climbs magazine and would issue forth on the perceived merits of each route; never shy to comment on those who placed pegs. He had shunned such tricks himself at his training ground of The Breck. There he would secretly work on each area of rock face until, after many hours, he had perfected the ascent and then he would demonstrate it to us as a new party piece. His application of the numerical grading system was always harsh. Certainly, Rouse 6a's were all but unclimbable but was this siege approach ethical in Al's terms?

Al's plans for our trip to the Alps in 1969 meant that I was forced to climb in boots. His view was that using Masters had made our technique sloppy. We climbed with rucksacks and boots a lot that year. The other feature of our 'training' was that Al felt the need to place runners more quickly and climb faster. This would be essential to avoid spending over-long on the face and risking the thunderstorms. Al thought that one day would be plenty of time for any 'foreign' climb.

I was talked into buying a 300ft 9mm rope for the trip. Al tried it out on Left Wall. After borrowing every sling and karabiner in the GMC he proceeded to practise nut placement. He spent five hours climbing the route free and placed 36 runners. We lost communications so he tied the new rope to a tree at the top of the wall and soloed off. The rain started and we were forced to leave everything in place overnight. Imagine it. We were back with our retriever (Nick Parry) at first light. Nick prusiked up the rope to retrieve everyone's gear. Nobody lent us anything again.

No story of Al's early climbing could be complete without mention of his great friend and mentor John Beamer. John owned a Mini van but at the time could not drive so Maurice Ewing drove us all out to the hills. Maurice drove on a par with Stirling Moss. We could always guarantee getting to the cliffs in rapid time. Al spent many hours at John Beamer's house in Wallasey. They were very close soul mates and Al put great store on John's advice and friendship. John was the friend he turned to whenever he was troubled.

Alan took delight in baiting the older members of the GMC. In particular he regarded it as great sport to wind John Huxley up in the pub on Saturday nights. John had been a keen climber when at Aberystwyth University. We had once got hold of one of his old guidebooks and were intrigued at the shorthand notes of the climbs he had done. Quite often the note RTF appeared. Al determined to crack the code and finally forced John to admit that this meant Retreat Through Fall. Al used this knowledge to great effect when John began reminiscing about his climbing days. John was an extremely competent mountaineer but fell every time into Al's traps and would often set off to prove a point, usually drunk. We had him leading Superdirect one day (RTF) and another memorable winter's night at Llanrwst Al got John going by questioning his navigation skills. Unfortunately for Al he could not extricate himself from a midnight crossing of the Southern Carneddau. They set out, both drunk, with no torch, for Capel Curig. They made it and spent the night both huddled together in a 'phone box.

Al became very fond of the evil drink and was extremely competent at bumming booze. He could not always manage to keep up with the pace in the early days and was often ill. He was unable to recognize that large quantities of alcohol increase self-confidence but affect balance and strength. One lunchtime session in the Golden Fleece very nearly cut Al's climbing career short. After six pints we all went soloing at Tremadog. After a short time Al decided to take Nick Parry up Merlin. Not content with the ordinary route, Al decided to try the direct finish. He got into trouble and called for assistance. Fortunately, John Beamer had just climbed Oberon and was on hand to throw him a rope. Al tied on and fell off much to Beamer's chagrin and my intense amusement.

Inevitably, as the summer holidays of 1970 approached Al wanted to go to the Alps for the whole season. He had been selected for Cambridge. We spent a couple of weekends at the Vagabonds' hut, guests of Pete Minks, who Al had become friendly with at Brigham's shop in Liverpool. Al went to the Alps for the season and I met up with him for a couple of weeks.

Slowly we drifted apart, although Al still made occasional visits and called on old friends. One occasion resulted in his first lead on sight of Suicide Wall Route with Alan Cowdray. Another, when bored with organizing his trip to South America in 1977, gave John Huxley much pleasure when they climbed Longlands together. Al could give and take pleasure from even the easier graded climbs, especially when he did them with old friends.

A leader on Aries also had reason to be grateful to Al who soloed to give assistance that day. There were many other such visits, he kept in touch.

When he took to climbing with a cassette recorder and headphones blaring out heavy rock music, I began to wonder how this fitted into his purist 'never desecrate rock' views. Al's answer - 'It's the natural pairing of two rocks.'

4

In Our Hey-Days

DENNIS HAY

HAY, PARRY, ROUSE...three of this school's biggest troublemakers, were the immortal and oft repeated words (amongst ourselves anyway) of our esteemed headmaster, John A. Gwillian, the great Welsh Rugby International and Methodist. In the best imitation of his gentle South Wales accent that we could muster, these words would invariably find their way into our every session of reminiscences or story-telling, to our great amusement. We had certainly been no angels. Fortunately the misdemeanours of teenage public schoolboys go relatively unpunished, and although they nearly always got us in the end, we did at least achieve a certain degree of notoriety. The normal exuberance of that age apart, our peers must share some of the responsibility for our behaviour; for our exposure to some of the older and more experienced hands of the climbing fraternity at such an impressionable age surely had an influence upon us. Perhaps they were content to sit back and let the younger generation take their turn on centre stage. We learned from them to be extrovert, which gave us confidence, and to exaggerate. We soon learned, for example, the strategies of the climber's real art, quaintly known as 'taking the piss', which is probably the most important form of protection in a climber's repertoire. We learned to take swift and ruthless advantage of any misfortune, particularly if someone had nose-dived off a climb or, better still, was just about to, to be especially inhumane where relations with a woman were concerned and once a crack in the armour had been exposed to exploit it mercilessly. These, then, were the formative years for me and my two climbing friends, Nick Parry and Alan Rouse.

I recall a moderately shy, bespectacled schoolboy who stammered terribly and turned a deep shade of lobster whenever called upon to answer some searching, but actually pointless, question. Pointless because the answer was always known, even if it took a painfully long time to emerge. At games too, where heroes at public schools are found and worshipped, there was an embarrassing absence of any sense of co-ordination, or of apparent speed or stamina. And so quite often he would be the object of some derision. In maths or physics lessons, however, an unlikely disruptive liaison had formed between us — complete boredom on the one hand combined with (where I was concerned) not the faintest notion nor understanding of what the master was talking about. Trouble was usually the outcome but it was also here that I discovered climbing.

Impressed by the great tales of adventure, I was eventually taken to The Breck in the centre of Wallasey to give this rock-climbing a go — surely it couldn't be difficult? But it was soon apparent that on all routes except those that grubby little kids were swarming all over, there was little chance of my getting off the ground. My companion, however, had no difficulty in going where he pleased with seemingly effortless ease. I suppose it was mainly competitiveness that took me back to The Breck on countless future occasions, but there would never be any victories over Al, although I did get marginally better and learned from him the basic rules and some of the tricks of the trade. But it was only in later years that I appreciated the real irony of his co-ordination, grace and power off the ground compared to his inelegance upon it.

About this time, however, other distractions came along — alcohol, cars and, of course, Girls. There were girls in the Gwydyr Mountain Club, or so Alan said, who also went to Gwydyr Mountain Club parties. These parties were apparently conducted mainly in the bedrooms and so logically I wandered down to the Club Night to see what it was all about. It was true, there were a couple of real Girls there, but they were not the nymphettes I had been led to expect despite the fact that the remainder of the company assembled all appeared to be chatting them up simultaneously. This 'remainder', however, comprised an assortment of the unsung stalwarts of mountaineering who, although they do not aspire to the great heights of the cult figures, are to be found each weekend seeking their pleasures or frights in the hills. The Gwydyr Club took us to Helsby and for weekends to the dizzy heights of Wales. These were the people who took this combination of prodigious talent and remarkable drive under their wing and pushed him gently in the right direction. John Huxley and Roger Hughes who quickly looked for less ambitious partners, Fred Heywood and Maurice Ewing, who belayed when they weren't writing off their mini-vans, and John Beamer with his great beard who climbed with us, drove us everywhere but was always womanless.

In the early days in school holidays or at weekend we would hitch-hike to Tremadog for a week in the barn or to the Gwydyr hut in Llanrwst and in the evenings, Al would tick off harder and harder climbs in his guide books, most of these done with Nick or Fred. The shy, bespectacled image of school was soon replaced by concerted attempts to emulate or outdo the bizarre and outrageous behaviour of our elder statesmen, whilst the talk would no longer be of chess or mathematics but would be third-hand recountings of so-and-so's exploits or the near misses of the day described in graphic detail with hands, arms, and sometimes legs, re-enacting the crucial moves. But, as Al would have been the first to admit, you always had to 'divide by the bullshit factor'. Al, of course, was one of the prime exponents of this other of the climber's art: bullshitting. Although he would always express interest in what you had done that day no matter who you were (unlike many of the top climbers who do not even condescend to speak to you), he was in his element recounting his latest epic or adventure. This could develop, if you allowed it, into a monologue on techniques or equipment, or on grading systems, or on some other aspect of climbing. His knowledge grew rapidly as his interest and achievement progressed and he could soon discourse at length on any aspect of climbing. There was, however, none of the asceticism practised by some exponents of mountaineering: alcohol was consumed in appropriate quantities with the customary consequences the following morning, although climbing can often cure a hangover remarkably rapidly, whilst the rock music and sexual revolutions of the late sixties further fuelled our hedonism. The Concise Oxford Dictionary not surprisingly concisely sums this word up: — 'Doctrine that pleasure is the chief good or the proper aim; behaviour based on this.'

Then, as it is today, Ellis Brigham's shop in Bold Street in Liverpool was a popular meeting ground for local climbers although the darts board has long since gone, and soon other characters began to have an influence on Al. Not least the infamous Peter Minks, Brian Molyneux and Jim O'Neill. These three were leading climbers of different generations of the Vagabonds Club and it was not long before Al's horizons were raised to a yet higher standard of rock-climbing and Llanberis replaced Llanrwst as the centre of the real world. The off-the-pitch exploits of these notorious individuals matched their achievements on it and we were soon treated to blow by blow, often quite literally, descriptions of yet another weekend of desperate climbing, extreme behaviour and alcohol poisoning. Through these liaisons, Al's climbing developed at a rapid pace culminating later in 1970 in the solo ascents of Suicide Wall and the Boldest — two of the hardest routes of the time and pushing Al straight into the headlines. I suspect that there was quiet

Alan on the first ascent of "Supercrack", Craig Gogarth.
Photo: Leo Dickinson.

satisfaction in reaching the top echelons considering his earlier experiences at school.

By the summer of 1969 we had left school, our last term having been spent forging letters from our parents and going climbing. We had by then fallen out with authority by trying to climb the school clock-tower and accidentally destroying a flagpole which we had to pay for out of our meagre resources. Nick was already at Leeds University, as too was Brian Hall, and that summer Nick and Al had their first visit to the Alps. Although a brilliant rock-climber, the attractions of bigger challenges and of snow and ice obviously took a hold. That is not to say that Al had no prior experience on snow, for our very first weekend with the Gwydyr Club had included a fine day on ridges and in gullies on Snowdon in winter. Thereafter, summer trips to the Alps became a regular feature including an invitation one year to Al and to Cliff Phillips to an international meet at the 'école' (ENSA) in Chamonix. Their room in the school soon became almost as crowded as Snell's field. Chamonix, of course, has traditionally been the great outlet for the excesses committed by the hordes of British climbers who visit every summer. Quite often, but not always, the harder the climber, the greater the excesses.

It was not unusual to climb at Helsby or The Breck with the Rolling Stones or Pink Floyd as accompaniment from the Chamonix tape recorder which had been acquired, as McNaught Davis would say: '...following the Chancellor of the Exchequer's instructions to conserve foreign currency by not paying.' The tape recorder would however invariably be sold for peanuts to help finance the next climbing trip or settle debts incurred in the pub. Apart from the need to prolong the holiday and stay alive, the practice of 'liberating' goods owes more to the need for excitement, kicks and competition away from the mountain than to greed — although that of course is no justification. The image of duvet-clad climbers paying a visit to Cob Records in Portmadog on a scorching summer's day does, however, still linger on in the memory.

Back at home, we indulged in a new sport of trying to take particular corners — in our parent's cars — at ever increasing speeds. Al's record attempt failed when he turned the wheel and the car went straight on and only succeeded in wrecking his father's car and demolishing the wall of the local girls' school. This did however have the unintended effect of raising our status immeasurably with the older pupils — into any of whose knickers we'd all been trying to get for years. Although we were now at different universities we would still meet up in Liverpool during vacations or in Wales or in places in between. The adventures and escapades continued apace, especially when Minks or Brian Molyneux were involved, and there was a non-stop supply of laughter and outrageous behaviour. To the cognoscenti of climbing this is nothing unusual and many climbers revert to a seemingly normal existence of respectability during the week following a weekend of concentrated debauchery in the mountains. Al was no exception to this, and could adapt to any situation and be equally at home whatever the circumstances or whoever the company.

Although I saw less and less of Al during the 20 or so years that I knew him, we would meet periodically in some far flung corner of the earth, often by accident for that is the nature of climbing. I make no apology when I say that directly or indirectly, he was the greatest single influence in my life for he gave me the mountains and the people that go with them. Over the years I have had the privilege of meeting and befriending many of Al's climbing partners and indeed even occasionally climbing with some of them. As only a moderate climber, this speaks volumes in itself. But such is the nature of mountaineering that these people encompass the greatest diversity of ages, occupations and values imaginable and like the mountains themselves, they represent infinite variety and interest. The memories will remain forever, for there was never a dull moment with Alan Rouse. It is a sad loss and there is a tear in my eye as I write this. But I am proud to have been his friend.

5

Early Chamonix

ALAN ROUSE

THANK GOD IT'S getting cooler,' I mused as I plodded up the Mer de Glace in the fading light. A heavy pack was my only companion and hardly a commendable one at that. I tried to keep up external appearances by not resting and forcing myself on, as if to fool myself. Always in my mind an adrenalin producing fear bubbled away, not letting me relax for even a moment. I consoled myself with the fact that fear usually disappears in the face of difficulties which do not need to be met actively. Nearly dark now, but not to worry for the lights from the Envers hut aren't far away.

'Quelle course faites-vous?'

'Face Sud du Fou,' I replied to the inquirer, presumably the guardian. I invested in what would be my last brew for several days, as I had ruthlessly thrown out the stove in Chamonix after feeling the weight of my sack, and the chewing of a few cold frankfurters passed the time until I decided to leave at eleven o'clock. The moon elected not to show its face, so I stumbled about finding my way through what seemed endless crevasses. Eventually I came across the entrance to a couloir guarded by a large ice wall. The pack seemed too heavy to climb with, so I sat it on the edge of the bergschrund. The right wall provided a nerve-racking pitch; twice my light went out and all my pegs were in my rucksack. I continued groping about, often sideways, sometimes upwards, until it was possible to free a hand to replace the wire and create my small oasis of life. Stop at a spike to haul the sack which has been patiently waiting on the glacier, surveying the snow slope pitted with numerous fallen stones.

A short abseil off the spike led to the main part of the couloir. Hanging off the abseil I fitted my crampons and stepped off on to the ice. Pack the rope back in the sack — I shouldn't need it for the rest of the couloir. I continued up, front pointing on good ice. Bloody hard work, but at least you get somewhere. Dawn caught me where the couloir splits at the foot of the face. 'Follow the left branch' read the guide. Grotty chimneys led to a pleasing delicate wall and the foot of the route proper. A flake was surmounted to give access to a small but good ledge. A brief rest was in order under the shelter of a large roof about 40ft above, which was obscuring the rest of the face. I sorted out the pegs and tied both ropes to a belay.

One rope I tied directly on to my waist to form a 150ft loop of no.2; in the other I tied a figure of eight, about 10ft from the belay, which I then clipped into my waist line. I planted a peg and started up. It was very hot already despite it only being 8am but I felt too committed to think about retreat, so I slowly pegged up the corner crack. I made occasional free moves only to find the 9mm rope, which was clipped through the pegs to act as a safeguard, was coming tight at a crucial point, and I often found myself lunging back for the last peg to rearrange my knots before continuing, I reached a belay directly under the roof and pulled the no.2 rope tight between the two belays. Tying off the 9mm rope I abseiled back down the no.2 and then jumared up the 9mm removing all the equipment. The sack decided to come along with me on the jumaring but I cursed its weight on overhanging stuff.

I seemed to be on the next pitch for an eternity. The placements were interesting, however, being in discontinuous little cracks and behind flakes. A few incredible warped pegs testified to the difficulties of this sort of pegging using only mild steel equipment. An inverted ring peg without its ring provides an exciting tie off with quarter inch tape. It moved as well, about four inches, but didn't seem willing to be dislodged from its home. Angle followed blade as I slowly progressed over the roof, tired from the night's effort. All things end eventually and so did the roof, but only after consuming two precious pegs clumsily dropped while being unclipped from a krab. Two pegs were worrying; one maybe, but how stupid two, and I had never dropped any in Derbyshire. The stance supported a couple of pegs and a welcome foothold, very useful to a man who would soon be able to bend his foot through 180°. Still, at least it didn't slope too much. I pulled the no.2 rope tight and slid back down to find myself 15ft feet from the belay and several feet below it. I pulled up the rope and arrived at the belay point. Swinging my sack on to my shoulders I had a horrifying thought of a sack plunging down the couloir, pausing only to bounce and perhaps spew forth some of its contents. 'My life depends on that sack, that strap, the cotton holding the straps — Christ, this game is too dangerous for me; mud on boots, a flake of rock...'

The clattering of a small rock interrupted my thoughts: I forced myself back to work, and it did seem like work, no pleasure left, just the vague expectation of finishing shining through a haze of doubts and keeping me going.

The sun got hotter and the sack became heavier as the belt, cutting into my waist, added to my discomfort. The stance at the top of the overhang was reached and passed to continue up a beautiful crack in a steep wall, mainly on pegs, but with occasional free sections. I was reluctantly beginning to enjoy the climbing again; two pitches passed and led to the superb diagonal crack. By now it was about 5.30pm and I felt too tired to continue, so a 100ft abseil took me to a small ledge. The sun was now less hot, and I relaxed into a non-thinking stupor.

The sudden temperature drop as the sun set encouraged me to don bivvy gear. I forced some chocolate down but couldn't eat much because I was too dehydrated. My mind floated apart from my body as I drifted into sleep. The ledge was none too comfortable to sleep on and after my initial tiredness had worn off I tied the no.2 rope on to the end of the other rope and abseiled down to its extremity to look for water. I penduled back and forth in the pitch dark, eventually finding a drip, so I banged a peg in and hung from it. Twenty minutes produced about a pint so I set off up the rope, and by the time I had arrived back at the bivvy ledge it was nearly light, so I collected the gear and continued jumaring back up to the long diagonal crack.

I was more than a little apprehensive this morning: even Boysen and Estcourt had thought the route hard, so it must be bloody hard.The first pitch increased my confidence a little though, and the climbing was certainly good. The second pitch provided some impressive climbing and a rurp in place. Now, seeing a peg in the Alps inspires an automatic clipping in and usually a quick pull: but a tiny rurp in place? It would go free okay but it looks strenuous; give the rurp a pull — of course it's okay should use them more often. So I stand on the Rurp. 'Crack', the familiar sound of a peg moving. Christ that was frightening. I am sure rurps can't move far without coming out. The sudden disengagement of the peg from the rock rather spoils my action and I land 15ft lower.

My foot seemed to be growing out of my leg at a rather peculiar angle and a quick prod revealed a certain amount of pain, so putting two and two together I decided my ankle was broken. Some English lads were doing the East face of the Pointe de Lepiney and I asked them reluctantly to get a rescue.I reached the peg and abseiled diagonally; not too easy but easier than I would have imagined, down a few abseils to a ledge, clouds began to shroud the sun. Bad weather and a broken ankle wouldn't really be my scene I decided, so I set off on the descent again. I'll bet I got the abseil fixing record for a man with only one leg on the first abseil off that ledge. Abseils led to more abseils and a jammed rope massacred to a meagre 60ft. Ethics went to the wind as I pegged across easy ground to reach a new abseil point. 'Fancy, pegging on Moderates Rouse.' Rock made way for snow and even a red vulture, hovering and then returning to Chamonix, made occasional appearances. Diagonal abseils on snow finally took me to the rock walls of the couloir. Axe in, kick a step, axe in further over, axe out, 50ft pendule, axe in, kick a step; this will definitely be my last climb. Near the bottom of the couloir the rescuers reached me and I relaxed, glad to be still alive.

Beware those sunny days in Chamonix which lure you to the mountain; do yourself a favour and stay in the valley!

Note: This article first appeared in the 1972 Cambridge University Mountaineering Club Journal.

6

Heavy Mettle

BRIAN MOLYNEUX

AFTER ANOTHER OF the now legendary all-night Al Harris parties, Alan Rouse and myself, still very hung-over, hitched a ride to Anglesey. As we walked across to Wen Zawn my enthusiasm started to wane. Last night we reckoned we were the best of a small close-knit group of climbing friends but Pete Minks did not agree and said he thought that he was the best. We therefore decided to go and do Tyrannosaurus Rex as it was rated one of the hardest climbs on Anglesey. We chose Anglesey as we figured the walk over to the climbing area and the sea air might help with our then anticipated hangovers.

By the time we reached the top of the Zawn, I was losing interest rapidly and having abseiled down to the sea-level start, the beer from last night was on its way back up. There is nothing less likely to turn you on to climbing in the state we were in than sitting on a pile of seaweed and the rest of the stuff that the tide leaves behind on its way out. I did not think Al was feeling any better and in fact I did not not think he could have looked any worse had he tried.

To reach the start of the climb you had to make a hop, skip and a jump over the boulders between the tide swells. Al had made the hop and skip but blew the jump on a large piece of kelp and landed in the sea.

'Is this my end of the rope Al?'

'Yeh' he said.

'Well pass us the gear then'

'What do you mean, pass us the gear? Who said you were leading?'

'Well why not, you're soaking wet from the arse down. It'll take you a pitch and a half at least dry out and that is just on the outside.'

'Bollocks, we'll toss for it the same as ever.'

The same as ever meant that Al tossed a coin, a stone or whatever was at hand. If he lost he made it the best of three and if he lost that, it was the best of six or 10. Anyway this time, much to my relief, he won first time. The 'give us the gear' bit had been a bluff on my part so Al led off. Pausing only to throw up, I followed.

The route was okay with us sharing the leads. It was a good climb with some hard bits, some okay bits and some good holds for puking from. This route, climbed as we had done it, was not out of the norm for our group, pretty good climbers but very good drinkers and party people.

Al had joined the Vagabond Mountaineering Club through a good friend of ours, Jim O'Neill, a hotshot from the Frodsham sandstone with a lot of good first ascents to his name, such as Beatnik and Jimmy's Crack. After a short time Minks and myself noticed that Al was getting up some pretty sharp routes so, as one does, we made him the 'apprentice'. Well it didn't take long for that apprentice to start showing the masters how it's done.

Leo Dickinson was another member of the group who was making a name for himself as a climbing photographer. He would climb with Pete Minks or myself and take photos and then a month or so later the pics would be in one of the climbing mags; great bullshit material and it didn't do any harm when trying to chat up the lasses.

Around this time, solo climbing was becoming popular. We would go off to a crag with the portable stereo. Finding a good place for the music was quite a job as you wanted to hear it anywhere on the cliff and solo some good routes, then bullshit to each other how your route was better than anyone else's. The climbs that we were soloing started to get harder, and we began to solo extreme routes.

After we came down from the crag, Alan and Pete would be looking for something else to solo and I was starting, no, not starting. I had decided that I was looking for a way out. I mean you can't just stand up and say 'Hey, I'm getting scared.' If I had a rope on I could climb okay. Even if there were no runners you had the psychological crutch of the rope — it might just snag on something if you fell. Anyway, Al and Pete didn't seem to need this as much as I did, so I stopped soloing.

Alan and Pete seemed to go from strength to strength soloing routes like Cenotaph Corner on Dinas-y-Cromlech, Vector at Tremadog and then that magic day on Cloggy when Alan soloed the Boldest. A very fine difficult route, the hardest British climb ever to be soloed up till then.

At the end of the day, there wasn't all that much time spent solo climbing. We were still the close-knit climbing group with all the inter-rivalry that went with it. One day out on Cyrn Las, Minks and Rouse were having a go at each other. There had been this picture on the front cover of Mountain magazine which showed Pete spread out on the first pitch of the Skull. I must have seen it a dozen times and noticed nothing, when Al pointed out that Minks was clipped on to the peg and there it was for the climbing world to see and on the front cover. To add insult to injury, he had failed on the route.

Well here we were at the bottom of the Skull. The air was blue with Minks telling Al what he thought about him telling me about the sling. 'Well Pete, the whole world knows you can do it with the sling, let's see if you can do it without.'

Pete was so pissed off with this that he flew across the pitch; I mean he did it very quickly and in good style. He was trying out some new boots which were a rigid vibram-soled rock-boot, great for edging, which was good for that pitch. Leo was his partner for this climb as he took the picture and they were sticking together. Leo hardly had time to tie on when he was yanked up. Pete was mad and Al was just taking the piss more and more. Everything went okay until the last pitch. We had started the route late, which was usual after a Friday night session and late night party at the Vag's cottage, so for the last pitch we tied on together as it was getting dark. Al led this pitch, I followed. Leo was up next and Pete, with his new boots, was coming up last and the light was going fast. There was quite an awkward move on the last pitch, a sort of smear step out to the right. We had all had a rough one on it with our EB's but Pete with his rigid boots, well. Al was waiting for it. I was belaying

Rab Carrington (left) and Al at the Fitzroy road-head in 1973. Photo: Mick Geddes.

Pete, then the rope came tight. Pete had stopped. We reckoned we knew where he was, just around that smear area.

'Are you OK Pete?'

'Yes'

Five minutes later: 'Are you sure?'

'Of course I'm f...... sure.'

'Well Brian, if he is that sure, you'd better give him a bit of slack.'

Well Pete was completely stuffed. When Al led this pitch he had put a sling in just about the smear move. When I came up after Al, I pulled on it and I knew Pete was in for a hard time with those boots so I took the sling out. So there he was; it was now dark, there was no handy sling and he had a slack rope. Eventually up through the darkness came

'Take it in you * * '

I took in the rope and Pete came up. We could not see his face in the dark but every other word was blue. It was so funny that Al nearly fell off laughing. It took a long time to get down that night but it was fun. Al had the bit between his teeth and there was no letting go. By the end of the night the whole pub was laughing and so was Pete. It was like that. You could get as mad as hell but you never went over the top, not with each other.

On other Saturday nights in the Padarn Lake pub, there were lots of times when you were crowded at the bar and you smacked someone, or someone jumped the queue in the chippy or accused you of jumping it. It was just the same, you lashed out anyway. In all honesty that was mainly me. Al would just laugh and take the piss and Minks would shake his head and walk off (but never too far in case I got out of my depth). Then it was off in Leo's car to a party. You never scrapped at a party, most of the time it was all mates and if someone was out of order, well it was time to join in. Why should they have all the fun.

The pecking order was about to be sorted, on rock that is. Al had his eye on a line on the main cliff of Gogarth, a route he eventually called Positron. It was a very fierce line which Pete was being a bit laid back about. On Al's first attempt he had made good progress up to the second stance on Rat Race where Minks established himself in fine style with lots of cigarettes and the stereo which he reckoned was necessary for his concentration on the rope as he thought Al might be pushing it a bit.

Al made the same bold moves above his last runner. He was making a long push to a good flake but needed a Moac nut to rest on. That nut was on the second stance of Rat Race with Pete. Al was shouting to Pete but Pete was away with the sounds. After a short time Al ran out of muscle power and screamed to Pete that he was going to jump off. The first thing Pete knew about this was the reduction in the stereo volume. It was not that the stereo had fallen off, but that Pete had been plucked away from the music as Al plummeted seaward in a 40ft arc. At this point Al called it off but only for a day. Again his determination was coming out.

Next day he was back on the hard pitch with the Moac nut between his teeth. He completed the pitch and so created Positron. Pete had to climb without the music. (You cannot blame the sounds two days on the run) Pete did okay until the Moac moves and then came off — even with the rope in front of him it was still a very hard task. The pecking order was sorted, for some. But hell we weren't going to agree over it; just one lucky day on the rock.

7

The Apprentice

LEO DICKINSON

WHEN ASKED FOR these reminiscences, it was said in the conversation that Rouse was always kind to those of lesser intellect than himself. He must have been a very kind man.

Some of these facts may not be facts but may be a poor memory, moulding a story to make the facts fit. It doesn't matter really because he's dead, we're alive and we all miss him.

I'm sure it was Minksy who first found Alan, somewhere in Birkenhead on a small crag called The Breck — I never saw The Breck, so I speak from images conjured from conversations.

'He's 16 and my apprentice,' as Minksy put it. 'He's going to be very good.' I didn't agree with Pete about much but he was right about Alan. We picked him up in Liverpool in my mini-van. He was shy and grateful and laughed. He curled up in the back, the front seat obviously taken by the 'boss'. If Brian came along then whoever got in first sat in the front seat. If either of them could have driven (legally that is), then I'm sure I would have sat in the back. Alan bided his time.

We went to Wales every weekend, to Helsby occasionally. Alan wanted to climb but, above all, wanted to be one of the lads — so did I. He played chess, for Cheshire I think, and was very good. Minksy played for himself and wasn't so good. They taught me and I was worse. Alan once played both of us in his head at the same time — he said to me: 'You've got three or seven moves left depending upon whether you are smart or not'. I moved and Alan laughed 'I hadn't thought of that move,' he said, 'You're mated'. Minksy refused to play after a while as he hated losing — it wasn't good for the image, and after all Minksy was still king.

It was his fingers that accounted for it, Minksy told me. They were terribly strong; he could pull up on holds that really weren't holds and certainly not in fashion in those days and he trained on his stupid Breck. 'They're not climbs,' Minksy pronounced, 'not in the real sense, they're only 20ft high.'

Minksy went there once or twice and failed to get more than a few moves up or even off the ground on some routes. This provoked the first of what everyone else in the climbing world who bumped into Alan would remember as his humour. 'I had to quickly re-grade them,' Al joked. 'They are mainly 6a but obviously I've mis-graded the ones that Minksy can get off the ground on.' Pete was only vaguely amused. He couldn't do much about it anyway and resorted to other tactics like taking Alan to the pub first. Pete could laugh it off as after all he had taught Alan to climb hadn't he? 'Well not exactly,' according to Alan, 'Rather he taught me how not to climb.' You could never win with Alan.

Helsby tempted Minksy out occasionally. It was a little higher than The Breck and anyway it must be OK as Colin Kirkus trained there. I used to go there in the evenings with Steve Suthorn from Preston and we would *do* Frodsham; first solo all the guidebook climbs twice, apart from the unled roof, adding a couple in the process, then move on to Helsby proper. Alan preferred Helsby as there was thin wall climbing. Steve and I top roped Brush Off a few times, then soloed it — there were no runners anyway. Alan hadn't done this climb before and seeing Steve and I solo it, assumed it must be easy. It was for him. He soloed Beatnik, Jim O'Neill's horror wall and it was obvious to anyone who watched that Alan was good, very good. A top rope didn't make much difference to me as there weren't enough holds.

Minksy had this theory that Martin Boysen thought he was competition and therefore wouldn't talk to him in the Padarn. The alternative pub the Vaynol, was naturally Minksy stomping ground being so near to the Vagabond hut but the 'in crowd' drank in the Padarn. It came as a big shock to Pete when it later turned out that Boysen had never heard of him. Alan wanted Martin's head; he was the one climber that Alan respected, perhaps the similarity in height and size, both wore black thick-rimmed glasses, and both were very, very dry. It was Martin's sarcasm and psyche that I think attracted this adulation — Crew was never put on this pedestal although Alan naturally had to knock his routes off.

I did a lot of climbing with Alan, Pete and particularly Brian. They were all different. Alan was one of those rare rock geniuses who seem able to move up nothing. The trick of course was that the few holds he did find were fed into his analytical brain and used in the best possible manner. Pete on the other hand was the more natural climber but refused to accept training, liked his beer and was very lazy. I know more than most that Pete had an ability second to none. If anything he was too heavy, but his footwork was superb and his confidence in himself like none other. If Pete had only trained... Brian was a mixture of the two but a far better actor than either. Doing Big Groove one day with Lou Brown and myself, Brian moved around on to the crux pitch 7b. The rope moved ever so slowly upwards, then down, then up just a little but more... this was interspersed with a running commentary from Brian with words like 'Watch me...watch me...I'm nearly off...watch me...almost there...no I'm off...watch the rope...watch the rope...urgh'. Suddenly there was a tremendous laugh from lower than we expected and Brian's head popped round the corner. 'Thought I was off then...didn't ya..'. He had sat around the corner pulling in the rope ever so gently just for the fun. Lou and I were sweating with the display but Brian had the ability of making the easiest move look difficult and difficult moves look even harder, as many of my photos at the time would demonstrate.

You could always tell what a pitch was like following Brian or Pete but Rousey was different. All you could tell was that his jokes were fewer and further between, or worse, that he became silent. He always assumed that you were paying attention and would never question your support role, perhaps he would say that it looked difficult, then having done the move, correct himself in case word got out that he had found a route hard. If Pete asked if the belay was good it meant he was about to fall off, if Brian asked it was because he wasn't sure if he was going to fall off.

Cliff Phillips, Alan, Pete and I went to Ogwen one day to

practise filming for our Eiger climb — we wanted some slabs I suppose to resemble the ice-fields. After the filming, Alan said: 'Have you any film left? I'm going up here.' Here was Suicide Wall and Minksy was about to see his crown disappear. He told the apprentice to be careful and watched with a mixture of admiration and perhaps a little envy. Alan quickly reached the half-way ledge and turned for a breather. 'Let me get further up the scree,' I yelled. He waited. He was in complete control. 'It's only one move really,' he said to no-one in particular in an effort to increase his psyche. Then he went quickly and confidently upwards. The roll of film was 100ft long and two and a half minutes, but it got lost with all the rest of the film that Yorkshire TV did not use in our Eiger film.

His flowing bellbottom jeans, lanky arms and black glasses in the underexposed shadows of Idwal are only vague images deep in my imagination — perhaps the others remember better but you still can't telecine your brain. That's barely 20 years ago. How could Professor Odell be expected to keep looking for more details on Everest 70 years ago.

Alan was now firmly on his way to the top of the ladder of Welsh rock. We did some routes on Anglesey together, but I think he was looking for new lines. He was out to impress not only others but himself and he did so frequently. There was one memorable day on Cloggy with a kaleidescope of images. I can't remember the routes I did as they paled into insignificance alongside other events.

In the late sixties there were two distinct schools in Welsh rock circles. There were those who sought out new routes such as Brown, Crew, Boysen, etc., and those who soloed the existing routes at the very top of the scale. Richard McHardy was definitely one of the latter. He had soloed quite a few hard climbs in Llanberis Pass then made everyone gasp by soloing Overhanging Arete on Cyrn Las. I had done it with Steve Suthorn and knew the tremendous exposure it involved apart from its sheer technical merits. Then there were Cliff Phillips and Eric Jones who more or less soloed the Llanberis North guide. These were often referred to as 'unroped ascents' and not true solos by Ken Wilson editor of Mountain magazine at the time due to them being able to talk to each other and presumably help each other if they fell. As an example Cliff would solo Cenotaph and Eric the Gates, more or less in synchronization, then they would run down and swap routes.

Then Cliff had his dreadful accident on Black Foot when he fell from the second pitch whilst soloing. He hit the ledge after 90ft, bounced again into freefall and landed on the boulders at the bottom. He crawled to his van at the roadside, somehow managed to drive it downhill to where Eric was staying and collapsed. He should have been dead. Some weeks later he discharged himself from hospital and started climbing again solo but much easier routes. He did after all want to climb the Eiger within a couple of months so getting back to normal fitness was important to Cliff. Richard McHardy also had his share of accidents soloing, which prompted Pete to come out with one of his immortal lines: 'If you fall off soloing you had no business being on the route in the first place' which provoked Alan into questioning how you knew until you fell off whether you should be on the route. To which Pete replied with irrefutable logic that he only did routes he knew he would not fall off.

It started with Richard who had just soloed Woubits. He started to come bounding down the Western Terrace naturally elated. This was clearly going to steal the show for the day and without further ado Alan set off up The Boldest. Minksy engaged Richard in small talk when he arrived saying how impressed he was but if he wanted to see something really impressive just look up there. Alan was almost on the crux — ropeless. It was audacious at the time and Richard's face was a picture. Tut and Paul Nunn were higher up the route and Tut looked worried. Paul was also affected as he had recently witnessed Tom Patey's fatal accident. Alan seemed to linger on the crux, working it out, but the slight breeze whipped his trousers and hair adding to the illusion of insecurity. Everyone held their breath. He did the hard move turned and laughed. Everyone else relaxed too. It was a moment of worry, the aspirant's time had come.

Half an hour later Alan, Richard, Cliff, Pete and myself went up Great Slab solo. Those four ran up it — I walked. Halfway, there was a roped party whose day had just been destroyed as four climbers treated it as a race track. I paused at the belay halfway up. 'Who were they?' he gasped in a state of shock.

'Oh just four climbers,' I replied. 'But why were they in such a hurry?' 'The pub's open of course' and left him to join the others who by now sat on top shouting abuse at me to hurry.

The route that Crew proclaimed would not be repeated for 20 years, the route that Drummond took three days to repeat and then offered to guide, had now been soloed. Crew laughed when he heard of Alan's exploit. He knew the climbing scene was moving on.

8

Vagabonds

MICK COFFEY

THE BBC WORLD Service News was droning on as I slowly cruised the project in a four-wheel drive. Just another Saudi day awakening as the sun rose over the desert haze. The bulletin was about to conclude when the laconic announcer dropped the bombshell. There had been an accident on K2, Julie Tullis dead and Alan Rouse missing. I woke from my reverie in an instant. What's he mean, Al Rouse missing? No way man, no way. Al had taken knocks before but he's paid his dues. Al always came back with a big smile and a wild tale. Al just always came back.

I guess I first met Al at the Vagabond Hut above Nant Peris in North Wales. There were no formal introductions, you just got to know a guy as a good hand, a good climber or both. I'm not even sure if he was a member, as the Vags Hut was used as a doss if Jim O'Neil wasn't around. I was living in a disused chicken hut at the time along with Smiler Cuthbertson, Dan Pierce (Big Dan) and Gordon Caine.

After a day on the crags and a night's drinking at the Vaynol or Padarn we would adjourn along with others to the Vags for the crack with the carry out. Invariably Al would be there if we had not already met in the pub.

He was a young baby-faced lad then with short hair, spectacles and a big infectious grin, taking in all the antics of an aspirant macho crew. He was in good company: Minks, Molyneux, Dickinson, Whitehead to name but a few. These were the start of some pretty good times. Pete Minks was just perfecting his party piece — dancing around naked with blazing newspapers stuck up his backside.

Al had arrived in Wales with a pedigree of some renown having wiped off all the top routes at Helsby including something called the Beatnik. I could never figure out how a skinny kid like him could do such routes. We had yet to enter the era of brown rice and serious training. A night on the ale was followed by egg, chips and beans down at Wendy's cafe and to hell with the training.

The competition on the rock increased, the social scene was getting even better — the crack was mighty. The after-hours partying moved to Bigil, a house in Dinorwic owned by Al Harris and with it moved the hard core from the Vags including Al Rouse. Bigil was almost the high altar of its time for this new rock generation. Anything went, everything did; they let it all hang out. Some bright spark at Sheffield Education Committee had the brilliant idea to send a bunch of sixth form school girls on a rock-climbing course at Bigil. 'Climb with Harris...' read the advertisement. I don't know how much rock-climbing, if any, was done but they sure learned how to climb in and out of bed.

Then Harris went to California and returned with a completely re-vamped set of values for La Dolce Vita set: 'Go for it'. We did; joints were consumed, in amazing quantities with an equally amazing amount of booze. Even more startling was the high standard of climbing consistently maintained. Friday and Saturday night at Bigil would start usually after the pub. Hi-fi speakers situated in the ceiling would blast the sounds of some raunchy rock band while the North Wales hard-core would mingle with the week-end pleasure seekers. Stoned conversations in the kitchen would plan expeditions and trips to far flung parts of the earth.

Al was a central figure in the kitchen crew, usually emerging from the wild gyrating throng with a joint and a big grin and a tale to tell. Marriages and relationships were made and lost with the peel of a zip in that place.

Morning would see Al and the crew down at Wendy's cafe before a mad drive to the chosen crag of the day. Al was instrumental in introducing me to the infamous Aleister Crowley — The Great Beast. From then on Crowley influenced our social habits as we strove to shock and outrage the establishment (or so we thought).

Over the next few years our climbing experience grew and horizons widened; the pillage of the Alpine resorts began; climb hard, play even harder, always one short step ahead of the law, (some of us not even maintaining that), retreat eventually to the fast-living of Bigil in North Wales like the 'Hole in The Wall Gang' of yore, to carouse and party. The crack was great as tales of conquest and daring both in and out of the mountains were retold. Some were legal, some illegal, all counted on the points system. Through it all Al always had a story ever wilder than the last or an escapade even more zany. He loved this wild reckless lifestyle, it was a crazy, abandoned beautiful way to live. The mountains would stand forever, rock and roll would never die.

It would be very unfair to the memory of Al to portray him with single unconnected instances. He was a nice fun-loving guy with a wild streak. I do, however, always savour the time Al took a cooked chicken from a rosteria outside a Deli in Chamonix. Dan Boone was reputed to have done the trick first when he tipped the chicken into his rucksack. The challenge was there, Al met it but even the best laid plans come unstuck. He walked up to the rotating rosteria, lifted the spit and slid the cooked bird into his hand. Big mistake. He hadn't allowed for the heat of the cooked chicken and had to make a hasty retreat to the road tossing the sizzling prize up and down like a rugby ball.

The rights or wrongs of our behaviour were never really analysed and the main motivation was simply the crack. Things seemed a good idea and no-one got hurt except ourselves. A pie fight at Mo's house in Wales was an example. Mo had a great party laid out with a whole spread of meringues, cakes etc. I came in from the pub with Al and Minks and just knew what was going to happen — it did. Eric Jones got the first pie over his shiny head and then all hell let loose with pies, cakes, custards etc., flying left, right and centre. No-one got anything to eat but there was food on the ceiling, on the floor, the walls and all over everybody. Al looked like a dervish next morning with his long unruly hair stiff and straight with sugar, cream and fruit.

Our vagabond existence, combined with push, good fortune or both, drew us further afield to the Himalayas and even

Patagonia. I was in Buenos Aires with Leo Dickinson, Don Whillans, Eric Jones and party en-route to Torre Egger when Al came through with his team bound for Fitzroy. He was with Carrington, Minks, Geddes, Barker and Donini. A good-time crew by any man's imagination. They had travelled overland from Columbia on public transport and as expected provided a font of stories and information. BA is a great town for partying and Al as leader of his team had his work cut out as they boogied and boozed the hot days and nights away. Two of his team lost their passports, two lost all their money, one lost his trousers on a night out and this was finally capped by one of the lads being brought home naked by the law. On this latter occasion the law thought we were a bunch of revolutionaries as we lay in a disorganized mass on the floor of Hector Vieytes's place. They were finally convinced that we were all 'sportsmen' and departed having failed to spot the stash of grass on our mattress — much to our relief.

We finally managed to clear B.A. and head to the far south where we were joined eight weeks later by Al and Co., now called 'The Dirty Dozen'. Due to various reasons neither team managed to climb their main objective but we did manage to reduce the local sheep population. Along with one or two others Al and I became quite adept at skinning and gutting sheep.

It was inevitable that eventually the group would begin to fragment as people went their separate ways and the get togethers became less frequent but no less rowdy. Rather ironically, the last time I saw Al was at the funeral of Al Harris. Eileen and I came over from Ireland and drove to the crematorium with Joe Tasker and Maria, along with Al; skinned up all the way there and back to the Padarn with youthful zest. The Harris record collection had been set up in the Padarn and we all partied with a vengeance throughout the day and far into the night. I laughed, joked and kidded with Al, Minks and the Vagabond crew, the crack was as good as ever.

Next morning we straightened out with mushroom tea made by Alex MacIntyre. Things hadn't changed. Al and I kept in contact with the odd letter and he advised us on our trips to Nepal and the proposed one to Bhutan. We were sure to meet again, but it was not to be.

9

A Storm

GEOFF BIRTLES

WHEN I VISITED the Alps in the summer of 1970 I arrived in advance of my companion and so fell in with a group of slightly villainous climbers who I knew quite well. Some, such as Leo Dickinson, I had climbed with previously and I pitched my tent in their corner of Snell's Field at La Praz beneath those most fabulous of Alpine peaks which surround Mont Blanc, a mere walking distance from Chamonix, its bright lights, bars and some colourful company. Amongst the complement were the rest of Leo's team who would climb and film the North Face of the Eiger a few weeks later; Eric Jones, Cliff Phillips and Pete Minks. There was also a social support group with the likes of Big Dan, Mick Coffey and a few more besides. And, up on the hill when I arrived there was another climber, Alan Rouse who I had not met but of whom I had heard so much. I had been impressed by reports of his rock-climbing ability and his audacious ascent of The Boldest on Cloggy; a hard and serious climb held in the highest regard. The news which so surprised me was that this hitherto unknown 18 year old had *soloed* the climb, which caused more than a few eyebrows to raise.

I would have to wait to meet him. The first day in Chamonix ended with a severe indulgence of drink, continued at the campsite with duty free liquor and a middle of night rumba using dustbin lids for rhythm and beat. Eric Jones, dear, kind boy, insisted I have a drink and holding the back of my hair poured whisky down my throat. The result was that I spent the next day incarcerated in my tent, occasionally putting my head out to be sick and, on one occasion, to say hello for the first time to Al Rouse. He, with Geoff Tabner, had just retreated from the West Face of the Petite Dru. Anticipating a semblance of health to return to me at any moment we immediately made plans to climb the following day.

I was wrong and it was a sick man who took the last telepherique to the Plan de l'Aiguille late the following afternoon. I was ignorant then of the debilitating effect of dehydration which a sustained bout of vomiting brings on. Added to this was the effect of altitude and a lack of fitness suitable to Alpine climbing. Our objective was the Brown/Whillans route on the West Face of the Blaitiere. The weather forecast was good until the following evening by which time we should be safely up and down.

For the night we settled on a wide boulder-strewn ledge one pitch below the renowned Fissure Brown. Wrapped in a duvet with my legs in my rucksack I sat, slightly chilled, enviously watching the lights of Chamonix far below, struggling to get to sleep if only to take away the discomfort. Huge sonic cracks split the night as a piece of hanging glacier fell away to our left. It prompted the thought that the boulders on the ledge must have fallen from above. I put on my helmet.

As dawn crept upon us, slowly as it does when it's cold and you want it to hurry up, we shared a tin of corned beef which was my introduction to solid food. Al led the first pitch, a nice Mild VS corner, to a comfortable belay. From there the wide crack which Joe Brown first climbed in 1954 brought my already exhausted body to a halt. I tried but could not lead it. Anybody with an ounce of common sense would have gone down to the valley right away but had I been so gifted then I would not have been there in the first place. Without complaint, Al took over the lead and progressed steadily for some 20ft to where the off-width technique is needed. The crack here is almost identical to the crux of Right Eliminate on Curbar Edge, technically 5c but instead of two moves there was a whole pitch of it. Al tried, he knew no better, but after a few scrabbling feet parted companywith the crack, fell some distance and ended up hanging from the rope directly in front of my belay.

There was a brief, polite conversation. 'I thought you were supposed to be a genius at climbing,' I queried.

To which he replied: 'I've only climbed one crack before.'

Climbing in Peru. Photo: Rab Carrington.

I thought this was a fine time to tell me and told him so, noting that he accepted the 'genius' tag without the slightest flicker of abashment. He went back up and being a quick learner thrashed his way up the pitch. An early bath was out of the question now and I had to follow, besides which this pitch is the only really difficult part of the whole route. Above, we had a choice of grooves and chose the wrong one. The solution was to make a tension traverse to gain the route proper, by which time another British party, John Yates and Richard Johnson, had caught and passed us. We pressed on with Al leading all the difficult pitches. Throughout the day he had taken the responsibility and taken care of me though we were both glad to reach the Fontaines ledges which provided the option of escape to our left instead of a couple more awkward pitches to the summit.

We opted for the traverse, a decision which in consequence may have saved our lives. The climbing was simple and led to a ridge and relatively easy climbing down. At around 6pm, a time when many climbers were still high all over the Mont Blanc massif, the storm broke. It came from the south and gave us no warning. What had one minute been a clear sky now glowered with thunder cloud. I was traversing an ice couloir in the lead trying to gain the Nantillons Glacier, chopping footholds and handholds the old fashioned way. Then I was deluged with hail pouring down the ice accumulating all over me. I had to do something before I fell off down the crevasse below. As I was by now only about 15ft above the soft snow of the Nantillons I jumped for it, cleared the crevasse and rolled over in the snow. Al followed the same way and we walked quickly down the easy ground. By this time the cloud base had sunk below us and thunder shook our every bone. The hair on our skin stood up in the charged atmosphere and the ice-axe head tingled in my palm. Never have I heard thunder so loud.

The combination of a lower altitude and adrenalin brought me round from a sleepy day. Spark plugs in my energy banks began to fire though I had by now another problem in the form of a pair of jeans which were wet through, awkward and cold. The possibility of a bivouac crept into my mind which I didn't relish in my soaked and drained state. I kept my dry duvet in the sack just in case.

Alan had descended the Nantillons before which was fortunate in fading light and dense cloud. We descended a snow-slope, me in front. At the bottom my feet went through a hole. I was in a crevasse up to my waist, my arms splayed out on the surface. I recall waving my legs around, finding something to push on and steadily eased my way out and subsequently jumped across what I hoped to be its full width.

We were still together but something was about to go wrong. I was moving more strongly all the time while Al was slowing down, though this kind of observation is not so consciously obvious at the time. Moving carefully down easy-angled hard ice, without crampons I reached the top of a rock cliff which I took to be the rognon we had to descend. I looked round, Al was some 20 yards behind just visible in swirling clag. I scoured the edge of the cliff and though unable to see to the bottom chose a shallow chimney and set off down. I don't think it was the normal line as the difficulty of climbing was too great for a descent from a popular glacier and eventually, facing out, I became stuck. My only way on was to turn round and face into the chimney in order to use a chockstone as a handhold. But, I couldn't turn wearing my old leather bottomed Joe Brown rucksack inside which was my camera and more importantly my duvet. I would need neither if I didn't do something quick. I unclipped one shoulder strap as you could with that model, slid it off and dropped it into the mist with no idea of how far it would fall or on to what it would land. I then made the turn, used the chockstone and made good my descent, a mere 30ft to soft snow as it turned out, where I recovered my sack. I could see now that I was in an ice valley below leaning seracs.

I had made a mistake setting off down the rognon without Al and was about to make a second one, doubly so. Firstly my confidence all day had been in Al as the stronger member and hence I didn't see him needing my attention. I do not know exactly what went wrong for him but he told me afterwards that the driving snow on his glasses had blinded him and instead of climbing down the rognon he had opted for a series of time consuming short abseils which took him into darkness.

My second mistake was not knowing the descent. I should have gone straight up the other side of the ice valley which would have led me to an easy snow slope which ran down to safe screes. Instead I went straight down into a steepening chaos of ice and soft snow beside huge gaping bergschrunds. My crampons were in the sack when they should have been on my boots and inevitably I fell and for the first time used an ice-axe brake to arrest myself. For some time I had been chanting a coarse but fateful saying inside my head and felt calm about my predicament. I slipped again, stopped, looked down a black hole between the ice and rock and knew I was off route. One more mistake would have been my last. Facing in I kicked across to the left and finding a steep snow arete straddled it and shimmied down to a point where one more awkward move led round to an easier slope and what would be safety.

But where was Al? Was he now in front of me or behind? The simple answer was that I didn't know and unlike earlier where two decisions had been mistakes I now took the only choice I could and kept moving down.

Eventually I crossed the scree shaken by the ferocity of lightning which, striking the summit of the Midi, danced furiously down thousands of feet of cable to the telepherique station where it exploded. Odd sheltering heads peered from odd boulders, all of us frightened. Unbeknown to me there were some climbers sheltering inside the station quite safe by some odd scientific phenomena.

At last came the trees and still miles of descent to the valley. I afforded myself the luxury of the duvet and stumbled into the blackness of the trees which was futile as my head torch had been broken when the sack was dropped. Two foreigners, or were they French, passed by and I tagged on. Unable to keep their pace and past caring I stumbled on and lay where I fell stream or no stream. But when the spirit is willing enough the journey can be made and hours later I emerged into Chamonix at 11pm.

My friends? Al's keepers were in the Bar Nash and bedraggled I went in hoping to see Al but he was not there. I asked if had they seen him. They hadn't. The enormity of it all sank upon me. They stared at me. That was the moment I realized the mistakes, not earlier on top of or below the rognon, but there, stood dripping in a Chamonix bar.

He turned up next morning. It had taken him an age to descend the rognon and had only made the tree line by 1am where he bivouacked. Thankful for his safe delivery I went into Chamonix and recuperated in the sun with wonderful French coffee.

A few days later I read that fifteen climbers had been killed by lightning that night on Mont Blanc, recorded as one of the worst disasters in the mountain's history. Of those, two were British, Arthur de Kuzel and Richard Caine; happy young men drinking with us all a few nights before. They had been caught in the storm on the last pitch of the East Face of the Grand Capucin. On the summit, two more Brits, Ron Prior and Steve Suthorn survived being struck though they were temporarily paralysed in one hit, one totally and one from the waist down. Both survived thanks to the one giving the other mouth to mouth resuscitation.

By contrast Al and I had been lucky.

10

Cambridge

NIGEL LYLE

WHEN ALAN WENT to Emmanuel College, Cambridge in autumn 1970 to read mathematics, he left his climbing gear at home with the intention of pursuing an undisturbed academic career, at least during term time. This resolution lasted out a few days for the Societies Fair found him at the mountaineering stand, making a serious attempt at the club's bullshitting record. Inevitably climbing and its associated 'socializing' continued to be his main interests.

The Cambridge Mountaineering Club (CUMC) had at that time several contributors to climbing developments in various areas. Most significant, for Al, was the presence of Mike Geddes (Jimmie) whose longer course overlapped completely with his. Mike had recently become the 100th Munroist (tops included as well), the youngest ever, and so was the ideal companion to introduce Al to the delights of Scottish winter climbing. With a combination of his experience, persistence and good fortune they were able, despite a 400 mile disadvantage, to be in the forefront of the developments precipitated by the new techniques of curved picks and front points. Mike's tragic early death from cancer has prevented him from covering this period but his account of the second ascent of the Direct route on the Orion Face of Ben Nevis (reprinted later in this book), captures the essence of these ascents.

Throughout this period Alan continued climbing with established partners, particularly during vacations. At college, he enhanced the club's standards by climbing with a wide variety of members, giving some a dramatic introduction into the

Extreme grade. My own was at Gogarth, a first visit for me, during a wild winter. The crag was deserted. Alan pointed out the line of his recently completed new route, Positron. My innocent enquiry as to the grade (Extremely Severe 5c,5c,5c, and one of the hardest routes at the time), had me dismissed up the first pitch of Rat Race. After that, I was content to follow all but the obviously easy pitches.

We were both in Emmanuel and as Al's digs were distant, my room proved a convenient festering spot. The following year the situation should have been reversed as only Second Years lived out. However, due to an accident, the college had to find me a room at short notice. Simultaneously, Alan who had got a *special* (Cambridge euphemism for nearly failing) in his second year exams, had a letter to the effect that the college would have to leave some Third Years in digs and that because of his 'unique academic qualifications' he was the natural choice. In the event Alan too was on crutches after rebreaking his ankle in Yosemite and so was found temporary accommodation in the guest room which was not much bigger than the bed. In the end he had the better deal because my room was totally taken over by the club.

Alan relished this sort of scenario, feeling that the inconveniences of the circumstances were far outweighed by their potential for a good tale in the pub. Appropriate distortion of the facts to enhance the effect was quite legitimate though the right degree of exaggeration had to be applied to suit the audience. Inevitably this exaggeration rapidy went off the top of the scale. In this context he was a strong supporter of the theory that stories are best retold by someone divorced from the incident who wouldn't be constrained by the truth.

As we raced one another about on crutches, Al realized that my physiotherapy consisted of swimming with the nurses. With a sex ratio of one to eight the wrong way at the university, he immediately had his GP refer him for some therapy. Unfortunately the doctor's writing lived up to its reputation for illegibility and Al ended up at occupational therapy, sorting out coloured beads and sawing up small blocks of wood. Instead of resolving the misunderstanding, he preferred to complete the course for the story value claiming it to be ideal mental relaxation from pure mathematics. (The exercises were, in fact, designed

Al Rouse and Nigel Lyle at Cambridge.

to manipulate his ankle as they had to be done with the toes.)

It was while in plaster, and a little plastered, that we did our only night climbing of sorts. This was only a short traverse, required to get into a locked room. Unfortunately we were observed, but the Don took little convincing that he had the wrong room when confronted with two sets of crutches.

Night climbing was no longer sufficiently demanding to enable the Cambridge mountaineers of the '60s to practise locally the skills required to meet the increasing rock-climbing standards of the distant crags. Dramatic improvements had already been made by the development of disused railway bridges; an idea imported by Geddes from the Wa's of his native Edinburgh. Al arrived as the lines were becoming worked out; he donned his exploding T-shirt, green velvet flares and fur coat and added a few 6a climbs which remained the ultimate challenges. The routes required a little maintenance by thwarting BR's own maintenance attempts by 'contaminating' the ominous piles of repointing materials, so that after use these could be easily re-chipped out.

The majority of official club meets were early Sunday morning starts, crowded semi-conscious into an uncomfortable, smelly van up the A1, breakfast at Tony's cafe, the boredom of the last leg relieved by searching the papers for the most unbelievable story and finally the relief of straightening cramped joints at the foot of some crag. Al's exploits often involved early ascents of such Derbyshire classics as Our Father, Wee Doris, Adjudicator Wall, Darius... On other occasions it was the elimination of aid used by first ascentionists as on Southern Rib, Central Wall and Left-hand Route on Ravens Tor, Dovedale. These last three, plus another two would still be a good day's climbing, even with chalk and sticky rubber. Al had a very strict interpretation of the use of aid, presumably from soloing, in that any resting, exploring, retreating after an attempt etc., counted as use, even if the moves were subsequently completed 'free'. By this definition, aid was used on one of these ascents, due to a vicious Vindaloo the previous evening. Seconding, I did not even pause to contemplate its elimination.

On grit, Al did more soloing, often with transistor blaring. At Stanage he must still hold the routes-per-meet record. On this occasion, after soloing Easter Rib and flying from Quietus, he amused onlookers when forced to admit defeat on Verandah Buttress, one of grit's 5b Diffs.

After these days, the return journey's discomfort was made tolerable by drink and raucous, tuneless singing, finally ending in an attempt to minimize costs by coasting in with a near empty tank, the inevitable miscalculation resulting in one midnight marathon push.

Weekend meets and vac trips to Wales produced more in the way of new routes for Al, from his comprehensive list of possible lines complete with estimated grades. Direct starts to Sheaf on Cloggy and Big Groove on Gogarth were completed with CUMC partners and these were complemented by Gemini and Positron on the corresponding crags with Dickinson and Minks.

Further afield in Scotland, a trip to the infamous Jacksonville, the black rat-like hut that squats beneath the Buchaille at the head of Glen Coe and home from home for Glasgow hard-men, saw our club's representatives uncharacteristically subdued as the Creag Dhu related wild tales of recent events. One CUMC member even deflated his lilo after persistent barracking from the floor-ridden locals. Honour was partly regained with ascents of Carnivore and Shibboleth, the former starting with an exploratory solo which resulted in gear being donned while hanging from a sky-hook.

Completing the spectrum of British climbing leads back to Scotland in winter. The club meet in March 1971 saw the introduction of the annual 'Standing Outside in the Nude in a Blizzard Competition' at the CIC hut, Ben Nevis, and less importantly, the return of the club to the realm of grade V, Mike Geddes leading .5 Gully and later the second ascent of Gardyloo Buttress and a direct line on Hadrian's Wall. Alan was part of the four-man team on the first of these.

This experience, with clear skies and good conditions, hardened the resolve to make the most of the following winter. Supervisions were arranged for mid-week to allow for numerous long weekend dashes north. Course topics were selected with no lectures before 11am to enable catching up on sleep. Al's tutor never did work out the connection between the odd combination of topics which ensued. Energy reserves were built up in the college dining hall by finishing up other peoples' left-over food. It transpired that one unfortunate, who appeared to have left, had only gone to collect a spoon for his desert. One last detail was required to finalize preparations, a source of pseudonyms for staying unbooked in SMC huts; Private Eye's Barry MacKenzie and the Neasden Hippie Commune obliged.

The journeys to and fro required more stamina than, and had almost as much danger as the routes themselves. I vividly recall waking to find us twisting down Loch Lomond side round blind bends on the wrong side of the road. Al, driving, assured us that he'd had a clear view from several miles back of the whole section. We only accepted this deception as, earlier that morning his psychic claim that 'it sounds warm outside' had subsequently proven correct. Having survived these severe bends, we later spun the car on the only bend left on the A1 within half an hour of home. Fortunately a gap appeared in the stream of oncoming traffic through which we shot (sideways), ending up neatly parked facing the wrong way in a layby; no one hurt but the car undrivable. The hire company seemed reluctant to oblige on the next occasion; perhaps as well in view of the expense which was prohibitive despite Al persuading anyone with a driving licence that they had nothing better to do than squeeze into a small car for 24 hours. Even longer thumbs were the only answer.

Perseverence paid off and the weather was kind more often than not. The resulting crop of routes included the second ascent of '59 Face route on Craig Meaghaidh for Jimmie and 'an unknown English climber' (Mountain). This quote upset John Robinson not Al (credit at last). It was Jimmie and Alan, however, who scooped the prize of Smith and Marshall's Orion Face Direct, described elsewhere by Mick Geddes.

Subsequent to their success, their arrival back in Cambridge after the hitch caused quite a stir. It was past closing time and so they burst, dripping, upon the crowded St.John's late bar (Al was partial to an 'esoteric' pint). They were still bedecked with sacks, ropes, axes, cagoules, gaiters and boots. Not remarkable in Fort William but in Cambridge, without so much as a hill for miles, an incongruous sight and a stark contrast with a group of smooth trendies. Celebratory rounds were provided by M.Mouse, (Bar Account No.53), J.Smith (No.176), and A.N.Other (No.97), bills being settled, or not, at the end of term.

It was inevitable that work would suffer, or rather it was incredible how well Alan managed to do despite these trips. In other ways too, he had a very relaxed approach to academic study. He had a theory that he did better in exams by answering questions on topics about which he had not attended any lectures, as his thinking would be less constrained. This was borne out by a double Alpha in his third year. He meticulously prepared detailed revision schedules with great resolve, which would be promptly rendered out-of-date by the omission of an allowance for being tempted out for a pint or his difficulty in getting up. Action lists became a tool he always used, though he was never able to make due allowance for his weaknesses. One day he claimed to have been walking into lectures, trying to puzzle out what seemed wrong, at last realizing that the sun was setting not rising. When corresponding with some solicitors about the final account for the club dinner, he suggested they 'phone him, requesting that this be in the afternoon as he was 'not prone to rise till noon'.

During the power cuts of the 1971-1972 winter, the conscientious studied by moving from one lighted sector of

Cambridge to another, others preferred to perfect festering techniques. The decision as to who would make the brew was usually resolved by the kettle boiling dry or a neighbour, unable to stand the whistling any longer, bringing it in for us. The brew itself we learned to like without sugar, milk and even tea as each ran out, due to idleness not impecunity. Pure festering was relieved by interminable games of cards. Alan showed us his ultimate sang-froid when he continued a trivial game of three handed bridge so far past the start of an exam that the porters arrived, expecting oversleep or an oversight. They were somewhat taken aback when thanked politely, but informed that he thought there was time for 'just one more hand', as the doors were not locked until half an hour after the exam start.

Mention must be made of the CUMC dinners. Or, on second thoughts, must it? After sanitization and the removal of libellous material there seems little to say other than a good time was had by all. Perhaps it should be recorded that Noel Odell, of Everest fame, had donated a pair of ancient boots 'for the use of a worthy beginner'. These were far too unique and so took pride of place at dinners, instead of a gavel to call for 'a sense of decorum' from the assembled gentlemen. The resulting tricouni scratches were not appreciated by the authorities. Any other sordid details involving beer, boots, bottles and bar billiards at the Bun Shop are best left to the imagination. The morning after one dinner Alan came round to find a letter from an American Foundation, a potential sponsor for the Fitzroy Expedition, saying that their secretary was in town and could meet Mike and Alan that day. His metamorphosis to respectability and sobriety was chameleon-like, though Mike was clearly going to be incommunicado for several hours. Realizing the lack of a second member would be a drawback, one of the guests was sobered up, briefed, dressed in a suit and told to leave most of the talking to Al. Fortunately the visitor did not materialize and it was with relief that they adjourned to the pub.

After the Alps in 1972, Alan and Rab also went to Yosemite (USA) where about a dozen routes were completed. While on the Half Dome with another partner he took a short fall (a rurp again) very badly re-breaking his ankle, not fully recovered from the Fou the previous year. The experience of self-rescue gained then helped now, because his partner freaked out and it was Al who had to help *him* abseil down five pitches to the foot of the face where the rescue services met them. Rab took part and benefitted from Al's insurance in the form of the rescue fee and so was able to stay out longer than planned.

One tends to forget when looking back on the achievements of this period that Al's output was curtailed due to significant parts of the time being spent nursing his broken ankle back to strength; the second break was particularly complicated. There is no doubt that he made a substantial contribution to the standard and character of the CUMC. In return it helped to change him from a self-confessed, slightly biased, parochial rock star, a reputation he liked to exaggerate, provocatively 'only divvies climb in the Lakes', to a broadminded, all-round mountaineer. 'The only decent sea cliff is Gogarth, because it's a mountain crag.' (ie Holyhead Mountain). However, most important of all were the friendships made, which despite long distances and infrequent meetings, he could pick up immediately.

11
Orion Direct

MICK GEDDES

THE NORTH FACE of Ben Nevis hangs there all winter long, pale with snow, green with ice, blue with moon, shadowed with sun. And the biggest hang of all is the Orion Face, dribbling down from near the summit to the steep bowl below Zero Gully. Summertime has seen dribbles of scree and jumbles of ribs, through which rambles the summer route, Long Climb, while wintertime sees a central spidery snowfield, with its Fly trapped above and that glistening spidery stuff linking top, Fly, Spider, and bottom.

Legend has it that the master of determination, Robin Smith, and Dick Holt spent 12 hours together on the Long Climb to make the first winter ascent in 1959.

In 1960 Smith and Marshall spent a week together on the mountain and one day followed the line of the glistening stuff to make the Direct Route. Twelve years later saw both routes unrepeated, and the Direct well plastered with reputation; the typical reference ranging from 'probably the most formidable route of its kind' (Patey, 1961), to 'the highest water mark of Scottish ice climbing' (Marshall, 1971). Its second ascent had therefore become somewhat of a prize, aspired to by several teams and fortunately a very elusive prize. One pair would seem to have foregone their local crags most weekends for a whole winter to travel across Scotland to the SMC staging post at the foot of the crag, the CIC hut, while the Glencoe Steam Team were twice defeated on the route by bad weather.

Well, ice-climbing's easier now, so Rouse and I went up the Allt a'Mhuillin one Sunday in February, with the dawn and three others, hoping that the Steam Team hadn't been up that week, as reliable information only extended to the previous weekend. It was all for nothing but mopping snow and mopping climbers because ice-climbing was off for the thaw, so naturally we all festered till the three went home. We two stayed, sleeping and optimizing on blue specks in the sky. In the afternoon, Dundee climbers came back from Minus Three Gully with wild enthusiasm for conditions but shady looks for us, as they knew we were banned from the hut. Still the drips dripped and the clouds clouded the sky, so we slept some more till we could see some blue hope and gossip with newly arrived English friends. Later in the evening it started to freeze, so we went to bed all wound up. The alarm unwound us falsely at two, so Al fixed it while I couldn't sleep for the sound of a strange calm sitting around the hut, and sure enough there outside the clouds were gone with the wind.

We unwound from those great new blankets once and for all at five o'clock. We ate quite a lot, kept the others awake, read a war story, and screeched out of the door amidst encouraging comments and a warning that we weren't to be expected back. And there was the beady eye of the Spider frowning down from on high, bringing back worries about that 80° chimney and vertical corner fabricated by the Steam Team. But we stumbled on through the lights of our miner's lamps into the shadowed pit between North East Buttress and Observatory Ridge, all excited and thinking about the aura of the route. Then we were lost in the Alps for a while on the steep snow beneath the north face, lamps bobbing in the clear cold dark, us gazing at the route, gazing at the stars, the hut going down, the dawn coming up.

The lamps faded into the morning snow just when we'd tied on, which was fine, so Al climbed the first pitch on something between good snow and dodgy ice at grade three. The belay search was taking a while so I started, only I forgot about some big balls of snow hiding my crampons, so the first time I went shooting down about 6ft worrying about reaching the end of the loop in the rope. Next time I woke up, and bundled the loop up as I went. We found a manky peg and I set off up the second pitch, the 80° chimney, which proved to be a mainly slabby groove with a few bulges.

Alan Rouse in Scotland whilst at Cambridge.

The stuff we were climbing on was funny. It wasn't snow and it wasn't ice, but there was a wee bit of ice underneath, about an inch lying in manks on the rock. But it seemed to be good for climbing on, especially for the feet, so I was soon searching for the scene of the peculiar belay described by Marshall as an ostrich act. I thought I'd found the curtain of icicles so smashed them away but it might have been the wrong stage, for the peg crack wasn't there. So I dithered and doddled sideways and upways and got very annoyed with myself till I found where

I was and Alan was coming up. He walked off round the 'vertical corner', spent a while on a steeper bit, and announced 'Hey Jimmie, the way's clear to the Basin' (that's the Spider), which sounded like a quote and I told him so. I charged on up to his belay and on through soft snow to a stance in the very eye of the Spider, all very happily on a steep snow field with the drop growing below, the clouds growing above, and hopes growing all the time. Rouse was soon above, belay searching before the exit from the Spider with me gathering the coils again over some easy ice and then surprising him with self plus rope as he shrieked down at the depths.

Various ways looked possible, but we took a hint from the 1960 team and looked round the corner on the right. They'd found a steep wall shining green in the evening light, all we found was a steep wall of this funny stuff hanging in the gloomy morning mist. But the gloom lay in bulges so you balanced from one to the next with useless hands for a superb diagonal pitch, unprotected and way above the ground. Then the gloom came down in hissing spindrifts to curse Rouse's glasses, but through he came over the last bulge, the pick of his axe woefully mangled, if not right angled. He battered away at some deceptive grooves like a woodpecker with a bent beak till he couldn't find a belay and I bobbed up and down and whipped my peg in and out while he said it wasn't easy and eventually belayed to half an ice screw. Now we were thick in the clouds, lost even from Observatory Ridge, and I was climbing the grooves past the grotty belay into the Fly.

The final tower of the face sat above in a dim menacing hump. The previous visitors felt their way up the tower in the dark and might have felt the wrong way. I thought they'd climbed this stupid steep groove above, so after Alan and bent beak arrived looking tired I set off towards some ice-climbing on the left. I rushed up this steep slab of ice looking for somewhere to piss, and found a litle niche, and later on, a peg runner at the back, for an overhang lay above. After a warning to the dim figure a hundred feet below, I set off to avoid the icicles and found myself not tending the points as usual, but thinking of Marshall's article — 'a trouser-filling traverse was made on to the right wall, along a short ledge, then a frightening move, leaning out on an undercut ice-hold to cut holds round on to the slab wall of a parallel groove'. And sure enough it all fitted superbly. So I informed Rouse with enthusiasm that we weren't cheating and thanks to Mr Chouinard teetered off round the rib on to one inch ice. There wasn't enough rope to continue up this groove, so a few moves had me hanging from a good old jug handle higher up on the rib and swinging back left on to the top of the overhang to finish a great pitch. We found no belay in 10 minutes, so we moved up for a while to a mass of blocks. Rouse climbed to the icicles and, intending to emulate Weech's series of frozen jumps, announced that because of his mangled pick he'd climb the rope. I sighed as people do and hauled for ages and ages of groaning and panting and despairing from the depths, till eventually he emerged through the streams of spindrift pouring out the clouds and down the slopes.

And that was it, bar the snow, and a seat on the plateau, lost in disbelief.

This article first appeared in the Cambridge University Mountaineering Club Journal of 1972.

12

Scottish Ice and Alpine Winters

RAB CARRINGTON

CHAPTER 1 — WHEREIN is explained our circumstances and reasons for a visit to Chamonix in December 1974.

From his many successful seasons to the Alps in summer Al had developed a great love for the region, its mountains and its life style. Winter climbing in these mountains came to him through accounts of drama on the Grandes Jorasses with Desmaison and newspaper cuttings from the Eiger North Face with Haston and the Germans. Combining the Alps with winter should produce the purest of climbing pleasure for him. Though reports of winter climbing seemed to rely heavily on planning, back-up groups and helicopters with journalists in close attendance, this is not how Al saw it. He wanted to see if it was possible to turn it into a cross between a Scottish day on the Ben and an Alpine summer route.

Throughout that summer Al had been living in North Wales, climbing a lot and even working, so they tell me. Brian Hall had been there as well, at college writing a paper on the flora and fauna of a certain forest in the region which had the misfortune of being burnt down a year or so later. John Whittle was also in Bangor. Between them they plotted this jaunt. I was in far off Argentina sewing and stuffing sleeping bags for the military with Hector Vieytes when a scrawled message reached me that I was to be a participant in this activity and, therefore, could I please return to England by the middle of December.

Left to right: Brian Hall, Al Rouse and Mick Geddes (dancing to keep warm) and Grant Davies below Craig Meaghaidh, Scotland, winter 1970/71.

Al, by some devious means, secured us an extremely posh apartment in Argentière for the entire winter season. The cost of it was to be borne by the four of us though, visitors would be invited to contribute to the expenses incurred.

Duly I returned from BA in November, and within a few weeks was crammed in the back of a heavily laden Ford Anglia chugging out to Chamonix. Brian Hall and John Whittle hitched out a day or so later.

Chapter 2 — Wherein is explained some of the problems encountered in climbing.

Looking back on it now, 12 years later, it is hard to imagine the difficulties we encountered. The equipment that we so readily take for granted now was not then available and all gear had to be modified for the job. Full gaiters for our double boots had to be hand sewn and then glued and stapled in Snell's workshops. Cotton over-trousers and bivvy bags all had to be adapted for use. Also, the problem of trudging through deep powdery snow had to be overcome. Without skills in skiing we were forced to use the rather inelegant 'raquettes'. What a sight we must have presented to the flash skiers as we laboriously plodded our way up from the La Flegere to the Brevent in order to test out our equipment for use in the depths of Alpine winter.

Chapter 3 — In which the climbing is explained.

There was a kind of religious sanctity surrounding the whole affair of the Alps and Winter. And those who were already activists in it took on an almost God-like status. So it was a severe shock to our system when, while we were still pussyfooting round the edges with our sole successes being a bivouac at the Brevent and an insignificant two-day ascent of the Col de Jardine (subsequently skied down in 30 minutes no doubt) that two unknown dwellers in our flat had the audacity, the cheek to go and climb the Cornuau-Davaille on the Droites. We were outraged — but kept our mouths shut — after all we were supposed to be Britain's best. However, the good that came out of it was that taboos were broken and we were forced into action.

Al's immediate and predictable reaction was to go and climb a new route — The Super Couloir on Mt.Blanc du Tacul. Typically the first couple of pitches required aid and our artificial skills were nil. After a fruitless couple of hours trying to free-climb the wall we decided to alter our plans and climb the adjacent Gervasutti Pillar.

On that climb we learned the most important lesson about Alpine winter climbing; its majesty, its solitude and remoteness. For three days we struggled on that climb, snowed-up cracks, verglassed slabs and icy chimneys all added up to that wonderful experience of winter climbing.

After that we got out of phase with the weather and spent two weeks chasing our tails, a broken ice axe caused a retreat from one route, bad weather at the Trident. Finally Al looking from the balcony of the apartment said: 'Let's go and climb that.' I couldn't see what he was pointing at but readily agreed and the next day we were stood at the foot of the N.Face of the Pèlerins. It is not surprising that the route has now become a winter classic Pitches of perfect snow-ice lead up and up to a final steepening of the rock. Here, laybacks failed and pegging proved once more to be an embarrassment. We embarked on a tenuous traverse down and leftwards on thin, thin ice to reach a secondary chimney system leading to the top, a few quick rappels down the other side, Telepherique to Chamonix and straight into the Bar National — wonderful.

Chapter 4 — In which some of the social activities are revealed and the problems which ensued.

When Al first saw the posh apartment in Argentière his eyes sparked like a kid's at Christmas. He was in his element, a life of luxury at last. Lunches were of Parma ham, exotic cheeses and fruit washed down with a crisp white wine; a far cry from the chip butties and mugs of tea in Sheffield. The ski slopes glistened five minutes from the door and Al threw himself at them, determined to ski properly in two days flat. The fact that he was returning wet-bottomed from the nursery slopes didn't deter Al; he was becoming Chamoniard and this was the price he had to pay.

And then the friends started to turn up, only a trickle at first, then, as word got around, more and more. Some came to ski, some to climb and some just for a good time. And the good time was had by all, especially Al who was in his element. Skiing by day, bullshitting in the pub every evening, and partying all night long. The apartment rocked to the strains of 'Band on the Run' and 'Jessica' while our neighbours wondered what was going on. At one stage the entire Everest SW Face Expedition turned up on our doorstep, the inevitable party ensued and irate neighbours were mollified with glasses of brandy.

So, all in all that social winter in Argentiere left many lasting memories. Al met Gwendoline and they had many happy times together, great times were had with the Canadian Ice Hockey players, Pete Minks didn't make friends with the nightclub bouncer and received a black eye and severed ear for his trouble; and several people made friends with the local doctor for social diseases. It is a wonder that any climbing was done at all. Needless to say our deposit wasn't returned.

Chapter 5 — In which we look at the consequences of that visit.

That season spoiled Al and myself for summer Alpine seasons. Thereafter everything seemed so common, so noisy and dirty. The winter became the Alpine season. A year or so later Al and I had a couple of weeks' school holiday spent in Chamonix. The first day we warmed up on a route on the Peigne and then set out for the North-East Spur of the Droites.

We felt detached from the jostling multi-coloured horde as the last telepherique of the day swept us 4,000ft up the mountainside to the Grande Montets station. At the top station the feeling of distance was accentuated as the skiers departed. Alone, the immensity of the climb we were about to tackle almost became overpowering and we busied ourselves preparing for the morrow. Ropes, pitons and slings were sorted again, food repackaged and sleeping gear organized. Finally, we ate and drank.

The first morning sunrays projected fingers of light between the Aiguille de Triolet and the Domino to find us stumbling through the thick winter snows of the Argentière glacier. Heavy rucksacks and snow-shoes made progress slow but eventually the snowslope steepened and we had to stop. Off came the snow-shoes and on went the crampons. Out of the sack came the rope, slings and pegs, each item being checked before being slung round the body, last of all the ice-axes.

The first day passed quickly as we alternated leads up the snow couloir. Occasionally an icy bulge or rock step covered in verglas slowed us down. By the day's end we reached the brêche — a gap between a detached pinnacle and the main face — overlooking the broad sweep of the north face proper, and an icy ledge provided respite for the night. Rehydration was the main task as the dryness of the air and the exertion of the day combine to make thirst the demon of the climber. The snow and ice slide tantalizingly slowly down the sides of the pan to join a tiny puddle which never seems to grow, then follows another interminable wait until the water is hot enough to brew the tea. After three hours, three brews and a dehydrated curry the gas cylinder had to be replaced. Screwing it in I realized the cylinder was not fitting properly as bubbling liquid gas hissed out of the stove. That left only one more cylinder. Al started to fit it carefully but once again it started hissing. This time Al was ready for it and managed to screw it tight before all was lost, but with barely half a cylinder we were on short shrift for three more days' climbing.

Throughout the night the wind rose and set the bivouac bag slapping over our sleeping bags. Morning brought no release from this terrible wind. With gas so short we did without breakfast and slid straight from our sleeping bags to start climbing. The white snow we had climbed the day before was replaced by black, hard ice polished to a sheen by the ever-present wind. Particles of wind-driven ice whipped into our faces as we made progress diagonally across the face, sometimes committed to the ice, at other times picking a twisting route from rock to rock.

Whilst climbing concentration was total — trying to pick the least problematic line, always making sure the two front points of the crampons were biting securely, selecting the best placements for ice-axe and hammer and trying to ignore the pain in the calf muscles as the full body weight was taken on the toes hour after hour. But at the end of each pitch there was time for the mind to wander its own course and for the eyes to take in the scene.

Halfway through the day Al's ice-axe succumbed to the hardness of the ice as the last two inches of the pick dropped off. It meant that I must lead.

The light started to fade, but still we carried on up the ice looking vainly for a ledge, anywhere where we might sit without sliding off. On a tiny snow ridge in the gloom we cut a niche to pass the long night. We settled down with sleeping bags and bivvy bags pulled over our heads as protection against the spindrift which the wind persisted in lashing across the face. The stove produced a meagre half pint of water before running out of gas. Freeze-dried strawberries and prawn curry lay useless in the rucksacks. We sucked on boiled sweets trying to get moisture into our mouths.

Morning came too quickly — the climbing and the constant cold drained away all strength and our bodies needed food and sleep for recovery. The climbing became steeper and more difficult as we tried to regain the ridge. The ice thinned and verglas covered all the holds on bared rock. Thick outer gloves had to be stripped off to silk inners so that some small crease in the rock could be used to provide purchase. Eventually the ridge was reached; this is usually a happy moment, but we had at least a day's climbing still in front of us. It proved more difficult than expected; wind and snow had combined to form an elaborate wave along its edge, overhanging sometimes one side of the mountain and sometimes the other; progress was precarious. Our thoughts were fixed on thirst and the realization that we had come too far to retreat.

The day was passing quickly. I had led a last pitch looking for a bivouac site but no ledge appeared and there was no belay. As I searched frantically it became completely dark. It was too dangerous to return to Al so we spent the night separately.

The fourth day dawned, still with good weather though clouds in the west looked ominous. I continued up the ridge but it proved impossible. Only by descending into a gully on the left did there seem a way of escape which we hoped would lead to the top. Two pitches later the way was clear to the boring, energy-sapping slog to the top; every eight steps there was a rest and a lump of ice to ease parched lips. One rope length, two, three, then on the fourth I was blinded by the sun as my head poked over the summit.

Quickly, rejoicing in the warmth of the sun, we abseiled down the ropes to the glacier. We reached the main ski run and Al's girl-friend, Gwen, swooped down the slope. From her sack came bottles of lemonade and sandwiches. Other friends arrived, and the hardships of the climb were in retreat. Soon they would disappear except for a distorted memory which would rise like cream to entice us into action again.

The following day I returned to teaching in Chester. Al, who also should have resumed work at the same time, decided to extend his holiday by one week on the pretext of frostbite to the toe. On his return to school a week later he reminded himself of the injury to his toe by ramming a handkerchief to the end of his shoe, thereby giving him a pronounced limp. To support this story in the eyes of the Education Authority he requested weekly trips to London for special treatment for the frost-bitten toe. Ah, such was the mettle of Al.

13

A Tale Of Two Cities

BRIAN HALL

I SHARED A room in Leeds with fellow geography student, Nick Parry. He was Al's climbing partner at school, seconding him on many of his early routes in Snowdonia. Nick was excellent on rock and equally good at climbing bullshit. Slowly the trips to crags got less and the bullshitting got greater and Nick stopped climbing. Al had stayed on at school to do his Cambridge entrance exams, so the obvious attraction of weekends at Leeds University were too good to resist. He visited Leeds frequently and I started climbing with him. It was a lively time at Leeds, with characters like John Syrett, Roger Baxter-Jones, John Stainforth, Bernard Newman, John Porter, and Alex MacIntyre, to name a few. There was little transport available, apart from John Stainforth's yellow mini, so most of the time we hitched, often arriving at the crag just in time to turn round and come back.

Great plans were made for each weekend, but generally we drank too much, and stayed up listening to music till late, then didn't get up till the afternoon. The gritstone cliffs north of Leeds were the popular venue and John Syrett was becoming their master. A friendly rivalry between Al Rouse and John was fought on the walls of Almscliff or on the boulders of Brimham. John fared better on the cracks, the wider the better. Al's forte were the walls which reminded him of his native sandstone on The Breck or Helsby. Longer excursions were made into the limestone dales when time was available. Malham and Gordale were particularly attractive but because the university term was autumn, winter and spring and the summer was out of the question because of exams, a lot of the climbing was in appalling conditions.

Al moved to Cambridge University and soon became bored with the social and academic life, though he was intelligent enough to do just enough work and remain at Cambridge for the duration and get a degree. He was more attracted to Leeds and the weekend would start when Al arrived late on Friday afternoon after hitching from Cambridge. Drinking would start almost immediately in the Fenton, Royal Park or University Bar and carry on till closing time. This was followed by gatecrashing a party in a seedy terrace house. The male to female ratio was invariably 50 to one, so there was little alternative but to get drunk. The following day started with a liquid lunch. If the weather was good a trip to the local gritstone, if bad, as usual, and with the accompanying hangover, the climbing wall was visited, or more often the afternoon was idled away bullshitting and listening to music. Saturday night we often went to see a group and the early 70's in Leeds was an excellent place to see live music, such as Led Zeppelin, the Stones and Pink Floyd and after the group another party or late drinking round at someone's flat. On one memorable occasion we all ended up at Did's flat. Chouinard axes and hammers had just come into the country and their use was a revelation. Al had just bought a pair at Tiso's and demonstrated the technique by donning crampons and front pointing round Did's flat, driving the new curved axes and hammers into the decaying plaster walls of the old room.

Sunday morning arrived too soon and so did John Stainforth with the old mini. He didn't drink and so was incredibly keen while the rest of us were invariably suffering from hangovers and it took a while before we could wake up, dragging ourselves out into the Leeds drizzle and only really waking up over a greasy breakfast at the Skipton tranny. Heads might have cleared by the time we arrived at Malham but the body generally felt like lead. We climbed most of the routes on the Right Wing at the time, some days bathed in glorious Malham winter sunshine, other times it was a struggle against the elements and I remember one particular occasion following Al up Wombat in a snowstorm and having to clear snow off the final crux holds.

We were all very keen, although a little misguided and were

easily diverted by drink and debauchery. Al would stay Sunday night and hitch back to Cambridge on Monday morning. I doubt whether Al's tutor approved of his four-day weekend.

In midwinter, we would organize mini buses to Scotland, in particular Creagh Meaghaidh. There was always room for Al and his flat mate and winter climbing companion, Mick Geddes. They usually arrived just in time to catch the bus after hitching up from Cambridge separately. Al was usually dressed in moth-eaten half-length fur coat, flared trousers, tie-dyed vest, with matching long hair, the uniform of the well-dressed climber in the flower-power era of the late 60's and early 70's. Mick was obviously dressed by the same tailor and sported a full-length navy greatcoat and matching hair. Climbing gear was packed into ageing rucksacks which were reluctantly carried. A cassette player was obligatory when hitching and also when climbing, even in depths of winter. The Stones LP 'Let it bleed' being a particular favourite, it was guaranteed to spur Al into action, either dancing wildly at a party or surmounting the crux of hard climbs. It was the job of the second to make sure that the volume was loud enough for the leader to be inspired, and to change the tape at suitable moments. (Al Harris was the master of musically accompanied climbing.) On one crazy occasion John Porter, Alex MacIntyre, Alan and I were all at the bottom of an obscure gully in the middle of Scotland. The race was on. We set the cassette and started the LP and we all started dancing, climbing, racing our way up the gully like some primitive ritualistic procession, the idea being to finish the climb before the LP had finished. (We later found out, by the way, that it was a new route). Alex was making a name for himself in Scotland by then, and there was definitely a competitive air, particularly between Al and Alex.

The journeys in the mini bus up to Scotland were painful affairs, too much gear and too many people in under-powered Transit vans. This made it a long and tedious journey. Without beer and music it would have been torture. By the time the Scottish border was passed everybody was in good humour and by the time we left the tranny at Perth it was usually well after midnight. The camp site by the road below Meaghaidh was reached in confusion as a rabble of drunken noisy climbers tried to pitch tents in the most unsuitable places. It was a sorry state of affairs next morning and often the faint-hearted preferred to ignore the alarm clock and turn over and go back to sleep.

Lots of routes were climbed, particularly by Al and Mick who climbed the hardest routes on the crag: 1959 Face route, North Post, Pumpkin, and the Wand. At the time these were the test pieces of the crag. One Sunday they had their eyes on sterner stuff. Between Smmth's Gully and 59 Face Route was an imposing face, steep and only thinly smeared with ice. By all accounts the climb was extremely difficult, probably a grade harder than anything attempted in Scotland at the time, with little protection and poor belays. They got to within 100ft of the obvious ledge system when darkness arrived. This would normally have been an advantage for Mick, who specialized in climbing in the dark, but unfortunately the ice ran out and they could not make further progress. Meanwhile the rest of the Leeds team had finished their various climbs and were waiting back at the mini bus, impatient to leave for home. The descent from Al and Mick's high point was precarious with poor anchors in turf or tied-off knife blades. Needless too say it took hours and it was not until after midnight that the dishevelled pair arrived back at the mini bus, to be greeted by a rather emotional group of climbers.

Leeds was a happy time, when there never seemed to be enough hours in a day to climb, enjoy oneself and study. Studying came off worse and it was a wonder that any of us got degrees. It was only when the exams came that panic struck. Al would not be seen for a couple of months and even though the weather was invariably good over that period, it wasn't until the holidays and the Alps that climbing started again.

The year at Chester was an alcoholic haze. By a series of strange and obscure circumstances, Al, Rab and Sue Carrington, the Burgess twins and myself, followed later by John Whittle, all ended up staying at Davvy's spot in Chester. The motive was plain enough, to earn sufficient money to go away to South America for nine months. Why we chose Chester is harder to explain. In short it was found that large comprehensive schools in Ellesmere Port were short of teachers. We all had assorted degrees and were out of work and with confident bravado rang up the various headmasters of the schools and asked them if there were any supply teaching jobs. Our initial contact was Davvy who was a full-time teacher at a large comprehensive called The Grange. Once one person got a job, they passed the message on that there were other jobs available and within a month, we were all teachers. Al managed to get a job at the old Grammar School, though now a comprehensive school, which was regarded as posh compared with The Grange where Davvy, the twins and I worked, or Sutton where Rab worked.

Our living conditions would have shocked fellow teachers, pupils and parents alike. Al slept in the corridor and I slept on the floor of the living room. Evenings were spent in the Count House drinking and mornings were chaos as yet again we had little transport; in fact only Davvy's beetle, which could certainly not fit all of us in. We sometimes caught the bus, but often missed it and had to hitch. It was amazing how few times we were late. As we were supply teachers, the actual teaching at first was rather varied and often was more child-minding than academic. As we became more experienced and settled into our temporary jobs, teaching became more rewarding. Al, in particular, fitted well into teaching maths.

Every weekend we would hitch out of Chester, either to Snowdonia or to Derbyshire. The Padarn and Harris's were at their height, as was The Moon in Stoney Middleton. Around this time a loose group of climbing drunkards formed The Piranha Club, whose motto was a variation of 'more than enough was not sufficient'. Anybody could be a member as long as they didn't ask and they could drink vast quantities of alcohol. John Sheard's transit was the preferred transport which was often accompanied by Tim Lewis's moggy thousand van. Each weekend would see this amorphous group plaguing some unsuspecting pub. Tim Lewis, Paul Nunn, Rab, Al, the twins, John Sheard, Bob Toogood, Davvy, and Al Harris were the main culprits. They led many a person astray on the various potholing and climbing meets in Yorkshire, Derbyshire or Wales.

The results of the darts in The Moon, or the antics and various wild competitions and dancing at Harris's were often more important than the rock. Climbing was a bonus. Generally everybody was too hung-over for the odd occasion on which we climbed. There was a constant battle between trying to get fit and climb and the temptations of the good life. Al started training again, particularly on the Chester racecourse walls, and became very fit. He had the potential and knowledge to do many new routes but in general was led astray by the excesses of his friends. Drunken punk stomps with the Eldon Pothole Club or Tideswell Well Dressing were all mixed with a hard day's rock climbing on Cloggy or Stoney.

Drugs such as hash and grass were all part of the climbing scene, but were only taken by a minority and often on an experimental basis. The equally strong drug, alcohol, was usually sufficient for most climbers though climbing in Asia and America widened their outlook.

However, whilst at Chester we had our first taste of the Drugs Squad. One fine evening after work, Al, the twins and I had just returned from a run round the city walls and were doing sets of pull-ups under the outside wooden steps of Davvy's flat. There was a loud commotion and three sinister looking blokes and a large Alsatian dog ran up the steps, almost squashing Al's fingers as he did his pull-ups. 'What the hell's going on?' We all rushed upstairs ready for a punch-up, as our uninvited guests were now inside. Two had rushed upstairs and the twins were virtually on top of the remaining guy downstairs, casually disregarding Fido the Alsatian. Little did he know how near death he was, but luckily his reactions were fast and he shouted 'Police' and held out his warrant card in front of the imminent onslaught of Burgess's fists. He was obviously a little taken aback and not used to such a welcome. He explained or rather ordered us in the usual police monosyllabic language that we all had to sit down in the front room and not talk. It was a drug raid.

More police arrived, some in uniform, and started to search the flat. The crackle of the walkie-talkie occasionally interrupted this intense job. Each of us was interviewed and then strip searched, though the whole proceedings started to become comic when visitors started to arrive. First, Bob Shaw and his girlfriend Kath popped in to be greeted by: 'In there and take all your clothes off.' Bob did not grasp the situation fully and rather abusively told them so. This only made matters worse. Second to arrive was the respectable housewife from downstairs who often came round to find out 'what we were doing' under the pretext of borrowing sugar. This time she got an unwelcome surprise as she was stripped and given the third degree. She was still there half-an-hour later when her disgruntled husband, Pierre, came in complaining that the dinner was burnt and he was hungry. He was strip-searched and interviewed. Meanwhile his small Scottie dog, (named after Rab much to his disgust) which had followed him upstairs, took a fancy to Fido.

By now the front room was crowded and all attempts by the police to keep silence were abandoned. Davvy started arguing and the whole situation became confused. An hour later we were all at the Police HQ, but by now it had become a farce and the police knew it. Apparently they had been following Davvy and his girlfriend (who was a doctor's daughter) for some time as there were rumours in the area of dealings in morphine. The police had got their wires crossed. They had been watching our flat with interest for over a month and our peculiar lifestyle and habits had warranted further investigation.

Whilst in Chester, Al and I tried to earn valuable extra money by acting as tutors in the evening. We had the brains but not the venue, so when the lady from the agency came to interview us we borrowed the flat below which was smart and clean. The prim and proper lady was impressed and next day Al and I had one very nervous 17-year old girl each, one for maths and one for biology. We used our flat for the tutorial. I am sure the girls were more than shocked by the appearance of the place and more so when Davvy came home swearing and cursing and proceeded to cook dinner. Davvy could not cook but tried on many occasions with disastrous results. His main problem was that he did not know what all the different utensils were for. For example he would often be seen heating up soup in the electric kettle, or making custard in the frying pan. These tutorials allowed us to earn that little extra bit of money but in fact very little was saved and as the summer drew to an end and the autumn came we were all worried about how we were going to raise the money to go to South America. But then, worse than this, Al received a real set-back. His shoulder started to dislocate, which was not only very painful but dangerous when climbing. Al had not had much luck with his body. He had had two previous bad ankle breaks, the first on the Fou whilst soloing, and the second on Half Dome in Yosemite, which had left him with a partially deformed ankle.It was amazing that he could walk, let alone climb. But Al's shoulder was a different matter and it was very urgent now that the problem be solved. Al had been involved in the organization and planning of the South American trip and I had a feeling that if he could not go the trip would be called off. He consulted specialists and was recommended to have an operation, partially experimental, which involved putting a bolt through his shoulder joint. The operation was a total success, but left him very weak. Disasterously Al's health was again a problem when he got appendicitis and had to be operated on just a month before leaving.

Al's drive and keenness for the mountains won through. We left Chester. It had served its purpose. The money had been scraped together and we set off for South America.

Al Rouse rock-climbing on
Great Gable in 1984.
Photo: Chris Bonington.

Galibier

Above: The successful Kongur summit party in 1981.
Left to right: Joe Tasker, Chris Bonington, Pete Boardman and Al Rouse.
Photo: Bonington collection.

Right: Alan walking out from Kongur. Photo: Jim Curran.

Left: Al on Ogre 2 in 1982.
Photo: Paul Nunn.

Al Rouse and porters during the walk-in to Jannu during the monsoon.
Photo: Brian Hall.

Above: Al on Karun Koh.
Photo: Chris Bonington.

Left: Al retreating from Fitzroy West Face in 1978.
Photo: Rab Carrington.

Right: Al emerging from an ice-cave in Peru.
Photo: Rab Carrington.

Climbing in Peru. Photo: Rab Carrington.

14

South America

RAB CARRINGTON

IN 1976, AL organized a super-trip to South America. The basic idea was that three pairs of climbers accompanied by girlfriends, wives etc, should travel for a year through S.America starting at the south in Patagonia and heading northwards as the seasons altered. Each pair of climbers were to operate independently and have their own objectives. So it was in early December we all found ourselves in Parque Nacional de los Glaciares.

Me, Al and Patagonia had a common bond — the mighty West Face of Fitzroy. We first broached its flanks in 1974 on our first disastrous trip to Patagonia. On that expedition we had spent three months and all our money in Buenos Aires as we tried to extricate our climbing gear from the Customs. And eventually, after a million hassles, six derelict climbers had turned up at Parque Nacional late in the season and fed up with the whole affair. A dismal joint attempt on the East Buttress of Fitzroy fizzled out before we even touched rock. This left Al and me plenty of opportunity to explore.

A very minor success on Mojon Rojo gave us a bit of confidence and so with three days' hill food we set off for Fitzroy. As we walked up the Torre Glacier the enormity of what we had embarked upon never really struck me. The mighty tower of Cerro Torre, Torre Egger, Stanhardt flitted by unnoticed. A 10,000ft unclimbed face being attempted by two completely unfit climbers with only three days' food — we must have been mad. So it was, in the crisp grey light of the morning we shouldered our gear and started soloing up the lower slopes. Al was the better soloer — always had been — and was in the lead. Things went easily until middayish when it steepened a bit, and a little rocky nose slowed Al up. I asked him to wait for me at the top; I struggled and at mid-height straddled a nose of rock groping desperately for the crucial 'out-of-reach' hold. Al realizing my plight, hugged a spike and lowered his foot down for me to grab. At that moment, 1,500ft above the glacier as we hung together I realized that this was serious.

We roped up after that and continued to the ridge which led into the centre of the West Face. Here we bivvied. Luckily the weather turned bad during the night, or maybe we just realized the silliness of the situation. Whatever the reason, we retreated the next day and scurried back to Base Camp where faces, looking up from reading or letter writing, enquired if we had been anywhere interesting. We kept quiet.

Our next involvement with the mountain was in 1976. Organization was better this time; no hold-ups in BA and money in our pockets. Similar to 1974 we had arrived in the area unfit. This was especially true in Al's case as he had just had an operation to a dislocated shoulder (the result of climbing) quickly followed by an appendectomy (the result of Bruce Forsyth's Generation Game — Al had been watching it at the time).

A month climbing in the Marconi range of Patagonia had got us fit again and it was time to tackle Fitzroy once more. We were slightly better equipped this time, and even had an altimeter — Al's pride and joy — to tell us when good weather was due. Accordingly we set off for the West Face. This time we dispensed with the boot-hanging sketch and quickly moved past the old bivvy site. This year's bivouac was a beautiful flat slot just where the ridge joined the face.

That night Al sat and planned the route. Just to hear him speak of major obstacles with a 'we'll just Jimmy up that corner, then slide into the diagonal then it's a dawdle'. He dismissed the route in three sentences and I felt better.

The next day reality set in. His first sentence took all day; a nightmare rising traverse across steep unstable rock. Luckily the weather held good and the third day found us in the corner trying to 'Jimmy' our way up it using fair means and foul but all very slowly. That's when, glancing over my shoulder, I saw bad weather clouds lacing through the fingers of the Torres. It was time to leave.

Al fixed the first abseil and all went well but the second got caught on a flake of rock which left us with one rope. It was going dark as we crossed the snow patch to the start of the traversing section. The third abseil wouldn't pull and I lost the toss and had to go back up to free it. By the time I got back, Al already had his head torch out. Mine was discovered smashed at the bottom of my rucksack. The next eight abseils were appalling. Al leading the way, fixing the anchors; me following, fumbling in the dark, sending loose blocks crashing into the black void below; all the time terrified lest we dropped too low and missed the crest of the ridge. Luckily the abseils worked and at midnight we dropped back into our bivvy slot, which brought to an end the second attempt.

After that try, the weather turned bad and we were stuck around Base Camp a lot. Much of the time was spent reading whatever books were available: Solzhenitsyn and 'Zen and the Art of Motorcycle Maintenance' were read, though not always understood. However, one afternoon, Al decided to turn his logical mathematical brain to things philosophic and picked up one of John Whittle's books 'Philosophy' by Wittgenstein. After an hour of studious reading, Al put the book down, saying to John that it was all right but a bit too terse for him. At this point John decided to let Al know that he had spent the entire time reading the contents headings. Such is the problem of having a mathematical brain.

Eventually the weather did turn good and we went back on to the hill. This third time we made faster time up the initial slopes to the first bivvy just below the snow patch and the second day into the corner and up past the dangling tattered abseil rope. At the same point as last time the weather started to look ominous; this time we carried on. The wind howled and tugged at our clothes, the ropes arced under the pull of the wind. Still we climbed, out of the top of the corner and round on to a snow slope. Here we carved a niche for the night. Cooking was impossible; we huddled in sleeping bags and cowered. The wind rushed at us like an express train. Spindrift was alternately poured down from above then up from below as the wind buffetted us about. Al developed a technique for rolling, lighting and smoking cigarettes, all without emerging from the bowels of his sleeping bag and thus he passed the night. I sat in silence alongside.

Finally the night passed but not so the weather. In the morning we peered out on glistening rocks. Not wet from rain but covered in a substantial layer of verglas. Once more time to go home. One last look at the route above us 'the diagonal — a dawdle'. I wonder if it really would be as easy as that.

By the time we had got back to Base Camp we had decided to give up the West Face direct and go for a softer option. Al decided the alternative route to be the West Face of Poincenot and that was done. But it's that big face on Fitzroy that sticks in my mind.

Soon after Sue, Al and myself left the Parque Nacional, back to Rio Gallegos. A short trip over the border to Chile and the Paine region was the plan. But it rained non-stop for eight days and we were glad to leave — in fact I think Al and Sue were lobbing food into the river at night so that we could leave earlier.

From here we moved on to the bright lights of BA. Setting up camp in Hector Vieytes's back garden we spent some time enjoying the sights and pleasures of urban life. Such was the lure of sights and pleasure that I left Al and fellow bachelor Aid Burgess to their quest, while Al Burgess and myself continued north to climb the West Ridge of Huayna Potosi in Bolivia. We all met up again in La Paz and jointly continued our journey to Lima, Peru.

Al must have been in chastened mood when he filed our application for an MEF grant. In the section designated 'Objective' he merely put Rondoy West Face. Under normal circumstances he would have made a list of all the mountains in South America and called that his objective. However, Rondoy West Face in the Cordillera Huayhuash definitely had the Rouse Hallmark. Joe Brown and Mo had refused to set foot on it, Bonatti had turned back from it, and only an LSE expedition had climbed it — using fixed ropes — and that was to be our descent.

A cold July night found us — Al, girlfriend Gwendoline, Sue and me— in a ramshackle Peruvian bus en route for Chiquian. Above us on sagging luggage racks lay our four rucksacks. Next to them our recent acquisition — a Peruvian Primus stove which insisted on dripping paraffin on the couple in front and their baby. The bus ground to a halt, but it was still dark outside and we could see nothing. We waited and still nothing happened; the bus had reached its destination but its passengers were not for moving. We snuggled deeper into our pits and stayed put till sunlight came through the bus windows and people started leaving. Breakfast was to be had in the market place with a choice between chicken soup with a leg floating in it (the bit we usually throw away — claws and all) or last night's spaghetti fried up in a puddle of grease. Ideal for 5am.

Two days later we were in Base Camp — three tiny tents pitched on the banks of the Jahuakocha with the summit of Rondoy and Yerupaja rearing up in front of us. The camp site was idyllic, with permanent blue skies and sunshine from 6am till 6pm. Then we were plunged into blackest night and hoariest frost till the sun popped up again 12 hours later.

We were lucky to have a guidebook to the area with us; unluckily it was all in Italian. Al studied the book till his head spun, until near the end of the book he read: 'Nevado Rasac Principal (6,040m) — ... il suo fianco sud, il piu bello della montagna...una stupenda parete ripidissima...verticali muri di ghiaccio...un grosso e logico problema alpinistico...'

Al shut the book, homework finished. He had found our warm-up route. That warm-up route took us three days but was an absolute delight of ice-climbing and as we came out on the top we looked across at Rondoy, the route we had really come to do.

Back in Base Camp we lay in the sun or fished for trout with more than occasional glances at the West Face trying to locate a safe passage through its vastness. One afternoon a distant roar drew our attention and looking up we could see cumulus clouds of snow billowing up from the base of Rondoy; the whole central section of the face had just been swept by a huge avalanche. By that evening our route had been decided for us: the left flank of the West Face leading up to the col between the North and South summits.

The next afternoon we set off intending to bivouac at the foot of the face and so get an early start. Typically it drizzled during the night and we hummed and hawed a bit before setting off.

Eventually we set out on our route. The bottom section was steep and difficult mixed climbing: thinly iced grooves, and rocky walls in crampons and gloves led us up and leftwards in our bid to reach our desired icy couloir. By evening light we tumbled into an icy cave overhung on all sides. Bivouac site number two was most luxurious. The yellow evening light played along the fringe of icicles and we were inspired to take the odd snapshot whilst dinner was cooking. Buying hill food in Peru had proved to be a bit of a joke and meals revolved round tins of fish (mostly bone and water), tins of corned beef (mostly fat and gristle), and packets of frankfurter sausages (mostly horrible). The petrol stove throbbed away on its third brew as we settled down for the compulsory 12-hour kip. Those 12 hours gave each of us plenty of time to assess our situation. Typically we were travelling very light; only five ice pegs and six nuts. On the terrain we had already crossed, retreat would have been very difficult if not impossible.

Morning arrived and we had the immediate problem of negotiating our way out of our doss for the night. Al struggled into the recesses of the cave and making full use of potholing skills soon had a hole sufficiently enlarged to squeeze through and emerge above the slopes of the couloir proper. Pitch followed pitch of hard water ice, occasional steps cut to ease aching calves. Two ice pegs for the belayer then a peg every 50ft and one to bring the second up on. As the day progressed so the pitches got shorter. Mid-afternoon and a steely grey drizzle set in; time to find a doss for the night. Unfortunately the angle of the slope was steepening as the couloir reached up to the final head wall. I headed up rightwards to what looked like a rocky ledge in the gathering gloom but it proved too sloping and without belays. I was forced leftwards as the headwall pressed in from the right. By now the sudden night was upon us, I groped along blindly till the rope went taut at my waist. But still no sign of a belay or ledge or anything. Al removed the belay and started climbing. I continued crabbing across the face, first on the crest of a wave of snow, then down into an icy trough then back up to the next crest. I could hear Al cold and miserable below scratching away in the dark a tiny pinprick of light from his headtorch. He reached the rocky ledge, the scene of my last runner. There we were, three-quarters of the way up Rondoy, in the dark with 150ft of rope looped between us, with not a runner or belay in sight.

We had just set off again when my hand pushed a hole in the snow, I pushed again and the hole grew. Peering inside I could discern a horizontal slot in the ice not two foot high. I squirmed in on my belly and shouted with relief to Al that we had a doss for the night. Al was not as relieved as myself. He still had the 150ft of traverse between him and the haven. Eventually like a seal Al landed in the slot beside me. Thus we spent the night, head to head as the two foot slot wasn't wide enough to allow us the comfort of sleeping side by side.

The next morning was again clear, so we could have a good look at the problems ahead. What we saw was not too good; two or three pitches of steep unconsolidated snow lay between us and the col. Retreat was totally out of the question so we had to push on. A further traverse left took us to the easiest line up the wall. The snow was atrocious and each hand and foot hold had to be packed down to bear bodyweight; every move was made gingerly, lest the whole lot fell down. At 100ft I fell into a hole and took the opportunity of bringing Al up to have a closer look at the predicament. A final nerve-racking pitch brought us on to the col and with it the blinding brightness of the sun. We luxuriated in its warmth. Al looked at the higher South summit then at me. I shook my head and we set off for the North Peak and the way home.

Climbing up to the North summit was not too difficult or unnerving but the subsequent snow ridge proved to be a nightmare. The wind and sun had whipped the snow into souffle-like consistency then blobbed it along the ridge with complete disregard to symmetry or form. We were roped together purely for mutual reassurance. Any idea of safety was dispensed with the moment we stepped on to the ridge. Occasionally as we crabbed along the ridge our ice-axes would break through the crust of the cornice and we found ourselves peering 4,000ft down into the valley below. From time to time snow mushrooms or steps in the ridge forced us to traverse lower on to the steeper face below the ridge. These we negotiated with the loss of our two ice stakes and a lot of nervous energy.

The ridge finally gave out into a broad fan-shaped face which was the obvious line of ascent of the LSE boys. We commenced the down climb still roped together which meant that at least one climber was protected. The stressful climbing of the previous days and the horror of the ridge stretched our concentration to the utmost and we had to be particularly careful on this comparatively safe section not to relax too much. Night caught up with us before we reached the foot of the face. Our fourth bivouac was taken on a rock outcrop in the centre of the face. Food reserves were low and we were reduced to a drink of soup and tea.

The next day dawned clear and we quickly dispensed with the face only to find ourselves at the head of a chaotic glacier spilling into the valley below. We followed the line of least resistence to lose height quickly but that promptly led us into a cul-de-sac jammed in between a rotten rock ridge on one side and tottering seracs on the other. Vague memories of the LSE expedition book prompted me to suggest the ridge, Al's route was to traverse horizontally under all the seracs and get on to green grass as soon as possible. Al won the day and with me tagging on reluctantly behind, dropped into the icy depths. With ice creaking and groaning above our heads we threaded our way across the glacier till eventually we landed on a grassy knoll. We lay in the grass, closed our eyes and the tension of the climbing soaked away and gave way to warmth and a certain smugness.

But resting was not for long — we still had to get back to Base Camp and seeing that we had dropped down on the opposite side of the hill, that was going to entail a long walk round. By following a high grassy valley we gained access to a col which led towards Base Camp. Sometimes we walked together, sometimes separately, rarely speaking, each with his own thoughts. I can't remember having said anything to Al for those four days. We thought as one, we climbed as one, words would have been superfluous.

After climbing Rondoy we had a long rest, a visit to Chiquian then one final climb to the South Face of Yerupaja. When that was completed we were free to go home. Al travelled north with Gwendoline to the USA and some guiding work in the Palisades.

15

A Walk On The Wild Side

ALAN ROUSE

MY SCHOOL REPORT gravely chronicled the advent of a new side to my character. The previously quiet worker had become anti-authoritarian with the possibility of expulsion looming over the horizon. It is hardly coincidence that my first climb, Monolith Crack, had been made in the February of that year.

Having purchased Don Roscoe's Llanberis North guidebook, complete with its lurid epistles on the Exceptionally Severe routes of Brown and Whillans, I proceeded to list the climbs to which I aspired. I had no hesitation in selecting such routes as The Thing and the Cromlech Girdle, modesty being a rapidly retreating virtue at this stage.

My fourth weekend in Wales I spent in the company of a school friend, Nick Parry, of similiar inexperience to myself. We climbed the Nose Direct on Dinas Mot before ascending to the Cromlech to view the legendary routes of the Rock and Ice Club. I imagined myself 'bombing up the Gates' as Rusty Baillie was doing in John Cleare's fine photographs in the book 'Rock Climbers in Action in Snowdonia'. Nick declared himself free from any such illusions.

One party had just terminated their efforts with a fine and fashionable peel from just below the stance. I scrambled up to them to enquire if I might join them for a further attempt.

'Have you got a rope?' the second queried.

'Yes,' I replied, producing rather proudly my 100ft of No.4 hawser.

'That's not long enough, and anyway you're not going to climb in those, are you?' He pointed to the conspicuous holes in my overlarge kletts, while I shuffled around uncomfortably.

After some bargaining, I was permitted to join them on the unexpected condition that I was to lead. Though my protection techniques were hopelessly inadequate and I needed assistance to tie on with a bowline, I was encouraged by a series of in-situ runners remaining from the last attempt. I reached the ledge of the girdle traverse before the full aura of the route really hit me. I had trained on Merseyside sandstone and the actual climbing was of a familiar nature, but the exposed situation of the stance certainly was not.

I had tied on to the belay pegs rather loosely, and when my second fell off I was plucked from the ledge to hang uncomfortably from my waist.

The final crack is technically a much simpler proposition than the first pitch, but I climbed it in absolute runnerless terror. After this experience I reduced my standard back to VS, much to Nick's relief.

1970: Solo Convert

The week before I had cautiously added my first new route in Wales, Gemini on Cloggy — but to my untrained eye, new lines were hard to find.

For the last few years many leading climbers had been content to repeat existing routes and it was left to a few, perhaps most noticeably Drummond and the Holliwells, to continue the development of such crags as Gogarth and Llech Ddu. However, even those crags were drying up (neither of them literally!) and the direction of future climbing seemed uncertain. A small yet significant minority of climbers had turned to soloing.

My own introduction to unroped climbing came when I hitched to Tremadog and got picked up by Eric Jones, whom I did not know at the time. Since he was obviously a climber and alone, I suggested doing a few routes together. He said fine, but he didn't want to use a rope! After starting with Grim Wall we moved across to The Fang, and by the end of the afternoon we had completed a dozen routes and I was hooked.

Al Rouse making first ascent of Tax Exile E5, Le Pinacle, Jersey.

I had decided before the weekend that I was going to solo The Boldest. A degree of anxious excitement dissolved in the Padarn on Friday night but revived next morning, as did the night's beer. Leo Dickinson wished to enact some filming fantasies on Idwal Slabs and, as he was the only friend with transport, Cloggy was postponed until Sunday.

Bored, I looked for interesting pieces of rock or females to spend time with. My quest eventually led me to Holly Tree Wall, where I received a telling off from a traditionally clad leader. Amazingly this was not the first or last time that I received an earful about the danger I was causing to other climbers. Sometime later a reader of Rocksport wrote to complain of 'soloing yobbos'. Anyway, the criticism spurred me on to descend, and solo Suicide Wall. The route went smoothly, apart from little hesitation on leaving the halfway ledge. Pete Minks then showed more confidence in me than I felt was justified by following me up a rather damp Suicide Groove, staying just a few feet behind me.

By 10 o'clock on Sunday morning we had arrived at the Halfway House en route for Cloggy. It was a beautiful day, and obviously a lot of people had designs on the Black Cliff. The atmosphere was hazy, and the features of the cliff only became discernible when the screes were reached. I walked over to the Boulder, a huge slab of nearly featureless rock separated from the main section of the West Buttress by the Black Cleft. I drank in the sombre atmosphere; this was the one place where I didn't bring my tape recorder and climb to the accompaniment of the Rolling Stones.

Hesitantly I tried the first groove of The Boldest, but came down from a tricky move at 40ft. Needing a warm-up, I took in nearby Longland's Climb. I looked at Vember and Great Wall, neither of which I had done before. The second pitch of Vember looked too imposing, so I finished up Curving Crack.

I climbed the classic VSs on the East, then spent a couple of hours wandering from pitch to pitch on the West, up some and then down others. I had never climbed on the West Buttress before, and I shall always remember the sheer joy of freedom to climb where I wished. I was filled with a rare confidence, and inevitably I was drawn back towards The Boldest.

Tut Braithwaite had just led the route and Paul Nunn was busy seconding the first section. I hovered around until Paul was well up the first pitch before launching out on the initial groove. This time I didn't hesitate. I quickly gained the small roof which caps the groove and marks the start of the real difficulties.

I enjoyed the awkward traverse left, but a little higher I had a nasty moment. I questioned momentarily the solidity of a hold that I was using, and almost immediately I felt my control disappearing. I had to fight to regain it before completing the half-finished move. I arrived at the resting place a little shaken.

I completed the final section past the bolt with mixed emotions, each powerful and claiming attention. Intense elation was tempered with an undercurrent of fear. I relaxed on reaching the traverse of the Boulder, with only the final section into Black Cleft remaining.

1971: Steptoe and Son

One weekend in April 1971 the inclement Welsh weather had condemned me to visit Gogarth, a place for which I have always held an unfashionable dislike. In order to avoid the appallingRed Wall, I had taken the precaution of extolling the virtues of the Main Cliff while we were commuting from Llanberis.

After consuming a pot of tea at the desolate cafe, Pete Minks and I walked across to inspect a new line between Rat Race and Dinosaur. The prominent arete seemed devoid of protection so I started over to the right, where a series of holds led temptingly up and left before petering out in to steeper rock. I was soon wondering why the hell I had started, as I swung across the impending rock wall with only a poor Moac separating me from the briny below.

I gained the arete, where I was able to have a precarious rest before launching out across a rounded bulge. Over on Rat Race, the identical twins Alan and Adrian Burgess were trying to cross the difficult traverse. Our routes were converging, and I shouted to Alan to ask if he could see any holds above the bulge. He replied that there weren't any. Upon trying to descend, I realized that the moves were irreversible, so I made a few panicky moves to reach the good ledge.

The second pitch started with a hand traverse around a large roof to gain a bottomless groove. The entry to this groove proved very hard. Hanging strenuously from the overhang, I had to pull on to the slab with only one small pocket, on to which I had manoeuvred one hand and one foot. A precarious move brought good jams within reach, and the stance was gained more easily. I looked around the corner, but the wall looked awful and we decided to call it a day.

During the next week, I gained confidence to the extent that I was prepared to have a go at the top wall. It is surprising how frightening enterprises become attractive prospects after a suitable break. Thus it was that I arrived next weekend at the still desolate cafe at South Stack.

The mood of the team was distinctly festive, despite a

prolonged session the previous evening. Minks had brought his radio/cassette recorder for a long spell on the stance. The initial problem was how to get back on to the route. Pete had conceived the rather frightening scheme of soloing across from Gogarth to reach the stance of Rat Race. Since no actual route took this line, it would certainly be interesting.

Listening to Pink Floyd's 'Set the Controls for the Heart of the Sun' we wandered up, down and around — much to the amazement of one leader on Gogarth when we appeared unroped round an arete and then disappeared down an overhanging groove. We arrived below the chimney pitch of Rat Race fully psyched up for some more exciting climbing.

Pete took the radio off his waist harness and hung it from a convenient nut in the crack above the stance. I swung round the corner using a huge spike and tried not to look at what was above. Curiously, an old piton was in place which, I suspected, had originated from Drummond's explorations. Climbing quickly I gained 20ft but I needed a rest from a nut.

After resting I tentatively moved higher only to find myself unable to climb down or up, or even place a nut. There was a perfect nut placement right in front of me but I couldn't take a hand off the rock. I shouted to Pete: 'I'm going to jump off.'

A voice from around the corner replied: 'Hang on a minute. there's a good bit on the radio. It's Steptoe and Son.'

'I can't hang on — my fingers are opening out', I shouted back. ''OK, you can jump now'.

The minute I let go, I regretted it. I tried to snatch the hold as I toppled backwards but to no avail, of course — the will to survive is a strong one. I went down head first, facing out to sea. Twenty feet lower I stopped, out of reach of rock and gently spinning.

I climbed hand over hand back to the last runner, where I took a long rest. On the next attempt I carried a Moac between my teeth, pirate fashion. The nut went in well and I rested again, though I was careful not to gain any height by it. The final section into the top of Dinosaur was great climbing. Further and further away from the last runner, but getting easier all the time, I got a tremendous kick from solving the moves quickly and efficiently as each hold slotted into place.

It is not often that I have climbed to that standard or enjoyed myself so much. We declined to take on the obvious but loose top crack, which seemed rather unnecessary to the route, and we soloed off down Cordon Bleu.

The route was named Positron.

1974: Mountain Man

I had just returned to Britain from Buenos Aires via most of South America. When I had flown into Miami from Colombia the immigration official had given me a meagre five days to quit the States, scotching my plans to hitch-hike over to sunny California. Thus the summer of '74 saw me ensconced in a cottage near Bangor.

During my absence, Alec Sharp had established himself as king of the Welsh climbing scene. He seemed a very honest and staightforward type: fun to be with despite his whiter-than-white appearance.

One Sunday I ended up down Easter Island Gully at Craig Gogarth in company with Brian Hall, Alec, Leo Dickinson, Brian Molyneux and Steve Humphries. Brian Hall, then a relative unknown, was later to become famous with his legendary puke at an ACG (Alpine Climbing Group) dinner,where he walked up to some people playing darts, asked if he could have a 'throw', and proceeded to hit double top with his first puke.

Alec had come to climb the crack opposite Wonderwall. Brian Hall and I were suffering from appalling hangovers, and we looked a sorry team compared to Alec and Steve. Brian was wearing his Top Hat, so he lent me a knotted handkerchief to keep my hair out of my eyes.

Alec was soon powering up his Supercrack while the rest of us felt sick with the smell of seaweed and swell of the sea. Alec had recently free-climbed Wonderwall, but I had no such honourable intentions towards it.

The first section was much easier than it looked and I was soon hanging from the aid point. My push had dwindled to nothing, and the strength I had once had seemed irretrievable. Obviously I had become a mountaineer at last.

Note: This article first appeared in issue 11 of Crags Magazine, December 1977

16

Jannu

BRIAN HALL

OUR SOUTH AMERICAN trip had been a total success and Al, Rab and I were now keen to climb in the Himalayas. It was the autumn of 1977 so we had to move fast to get permission to climb a peak and organize a trip for next year. Looking back it is hard to believe that we knew so little about the Himalayas; the positions and characteristics of the peaks, the complex procedures involved in applying for permission to climb and the involved nature of organizing food, gear and transport for an expedition. Up to then we had been naive, we had been used to the immediacy of the Alps and South America, where you climbed what and where you wanted, whenever you liked. The Himalayan bureaucracy acted like a filter ensuring that only the keen, knowledgeable, organized and rich succeeded in climbing. All we had was a cocky, self-assured keenness and like every generation, a belief that we could climb better than our predecessors. We spent the next nine months trying to become knowledgeable, organized and rich.

Al was our research expert and he immediately started ploughing through the masses of literature to come up with a 'good' mountain. His memory was one of his greatest assets and he used it throughout his climbing career to pick out plum routes in Britain,the Alps, South America and now the Himalayas. His memory was also used to great effect in argument, much to the annoyance of the 'opposition' who were often confounded by obscure facts and theories of the universe, economics and maths. Al's suggestions for an objective were as wide-ranging as the Himalayas themselves. We talked about the then unclimbed

Paul "Tut" Braithwaite's wedding. Left to right (men only): Al Rouse, Doug Scott, Tut Braithwaite, Chris Bonington and Tony Howard.

Saser group in India, the Gasherbrums of Pakistan and Jannu in Nepal.

Applications were sent to the Indian and Nepalese governments, but not to Pakistan as you had to send part of the peak fee with the initial application and at that time we had no money and had not worked out how we were going to pay for the trip. I'm not sure whether we actually got a reply from India but it soon became obvious that the Saser group was out of bounds due to political and military reasons; the Himalayas encompass many delicate and disputed national boundaries and it has been the curse of mountaineers throughout history that vast areas of mountains are out of bounds to climbers.

It wasn't until the beginning of April that we finally got confirmation that we had permission to climb Jannu in the post-monsoon period of 1978. The practical side of organizing the expedition could now start as we had an objective to build the expedition around.

Whilst searching for a suitable objective it was considered that a team of four was the ideal. The choice of the fourth member was really quite difficult. He not only had to be an extremely good climber, but had to have a strong personality to fit in with the rest of the team. We all felt that expeditions should be groups of existing friends, as the stresses on relationships on an expedition can cause many problems and you stood a better chance of success if you knew the other members well. Many people think there are numerous people who would be keen to go on a Himalayan trip. There might be, but when you limit it by the necessary criteria you are left with very few. Roger Baxter-Jones was an obvious choice as we all knew him well and I had climbed with him many times in Britain and the Alps.

With the team together, we discussed a method of climbing. None of us had used fixed ropes or oxygen and we didn't fancy learning half-way up a mountain. We were all used to climbing in pairs in the Alps and so we settled on the way we knew best; Alpine-style. In the expedition report we wrote the following: 'Many leading climbers from all countries of the world feel that the future progress of mountaineering lies not in climbing harder and harder faces with more and more equipment, but in climbing with less equipment and not using fixed camps. Climbing Alpine-style has several advantages:
1. No time is wasted in tedious load carrying on fixed ropes.
2. Hazardous sections of the mountain need only be traversed once or twice instead of numerously as on a fixed rope expedition.
3. The level of personal satisfaction is increased greatly as everyone on the expedition is very likely to climb all the route and reach the summit.
4. With modern techniques and a large fixed rope expedition, virtually every face in the Himalayas can be climbed. If the challenge changes to a question of style rather than the conquest of the mountain by every means available the mountaineering world will be left with major challenges for many years to come.

There are, of course, some disadvantages particularly in case of an accident but we feel that accidents are much less likely. The tremendous difficulty of getting high on the mountain ensures that only the fittest and most competent mountaineers are found high on the mountain.'

It is interesting to reflect on this philosophy and Al's other major expeditions, particularly K2. This was written at a time when the 'big' expedition was the norm and only a very few big Himalayan mountains had been climbed in Alpine-style. Many peaks have now been climbed in Alpine-style, though often anything goes as Himalayan climbing becomes more of a sport, sheer success, efficiency and speed of ascent becoming, for some, more important than style.

Alpine style climbing has one major advantage over larger fixed rope trips: it's a lot simpler to organize. You need less equipment, food and porters and hence less money. This was a blessing as even the £1,000 per person was a real problem for all of us to raise. We lived a nomadic lifestyle out of a rucksack, sleeping on friends' floors or, if you were lucky, someone's bed. Any spare cash from the various temporary jobs we had should have been saved, but instead was drunk away at the Moon dartboard or at the do's which we hitched around the country for under the transparent excuse of going climbing. Rab had settled down with Sue, bought a house and was by far the most organized out of the four of us. Whereas Rab worked hard and saved money and mysteriously always drank his fair share of pints, Al neither worked nor saved and equally mysteriously always drank his fair share of pints. Al always had the most outrageous schemes to build financial empires in Geneva or London and continually wrote down lists of figures to justify continual extravagance without working. Work, he felt, was beneath him. He was the thinker. On the other hand, Roger was the mystery. He was the type of person who was never around at the normal do's, but turned up at the most unexpected times or places and then left to go and see some obscure friend, not be seen again for weeks. When you tried to pin him down, he just grinned like a Cheshire cat. Needless to say, when the time came to pay money into the trip, there was a fair amount of panic as banks and friends were persuaded to lend money.

Because Rab had a base, was organized, reliable and made the mistake of volunteering, he became leader. I always felt that Al resented this, especially after the expedition when we were successful and he decided to make a 'career' out of climbing. Power over other people is at the best of times difficult to handle but in climbing situations with friends it can be virtually impossible. Leadership of a small Alpine-style expedition such as ours may seem a formality, but in retrospect it was important to Al (and probably to Rab at that time) and I think this was one of the reasons why Al and Rab parted company, later, on Kantega, after years of successful climbing together. Many people thought that Al was the brains and Rab the muscle, but they were alike in many ways, both highly intelligent maths graduates, though Al was more a dreamer and aspired to higher refined things (or so he thought) and Rab was more practical and would often camouflage his true feelings with a rough Glaswegian veneer. Al was aiming to become a second Bonington, but could not handle power over other people and especially his friends. He was an individualist and loner rather than a leader which contributed to unfortunate and tragic outcomes on both the large expeditions he led, Everest in Winter and K2. Both Roger and I were more interested in the climbing than the consequences and were happy at the time for Rab to be leader, though later we all crossed swords.

Al's research had drawn a magical 'picture' of our mountain. Jannu (25,294ft or 7,710m) lies in the beautiful north-east corner of Nepal close to the borders of Tibet and Sikkim and next to Kangchenjunga (the third highest mountain in the world). Frank Smythe, one of the first Europeans to see it, called it 'one of the most appalling rock peaks in the world'. From the Yalung Glacier a tormented mass of rock walls, ice slopes and hanging glaciers rises 4,000m to the distinct shoulders which give the mountain its Hindu name 'Kimbukama' the shoulders of Kama (who was a mighty warrior). Above this rises the final problem, a 600m high head of icy granite.

'Of all the bastions nature has thrown up against man's courage and will to win, Jannu must surely be one whose resistance is hardest to overcome'. Lionel Terray, the great French mountaineer wrote this after retreating from near the summit in 1958. Three years later he was to succeed at the head of a team of 10 of the best French mountaineers. Supported by high-altitude Sherpas and using oxygen, they only won through after a six-week struggle by climbing an extremely long and difficult route on the south-west side of the mountain from the Yamatari Glacier. In 1974 a Japanese expedition repeated the French route,

Bass Charrington presenting the sponsorship cheque for the Jannu expedition. Left to right: Al Rouse, Roger Baxter-Jones, Rab Carrington and Brian Hall.

and then in 1976 another Japanese party climbed the extremely difficult North Face from the Jannu Glacier. All ascents used oxygen, sherpas, fixed ropes and camps. Our aim was to make a lightweight ascent of the mountain, preferably by the enormous East Face from the Yalung Glacier.

The last few days before departure on any expedition is totally chaotic. Roger and I had been dealing with equipment and food and we'd had an impossible itinerary, travelling round a dozen companies in as many counties. We visited Berghaus, who were our major gear sponsors (and for whom Al and I subsequently worked as consultants) to pick up rucksacks, boots and shell clothing; Mountain Equipment, for down gear and numerous other small companies whose help was vital to expeditions like ours. Rab and Al were trying to sort out the travel and money side and just to confuse the whole issue a continual stream of well-wishing friends insisted on buying us beer, or the poorer ones (the majority) coming to drink the many cans of beer supplied by another major sponsor, Bass Charrington.

We were leaving on Tuesday August 15 and by the Saturday we still had not started packing. The Saturday was Tut Braithwaite's wedding, which certainly lived up to all expectations. Next day was a blurr of aspirins and lists, cups of tea and weighing scales. Al was very sick and it was only after several large helpings of his anti-sickness potion — pea and ham soup, that he managed to start packing. He was the worst packer in the world, crampons were mixed with cameras and ice-axes with down gear. Whereas Rab got all his gear into one neat sack by lunchtime (Rab never seemed to get hangovers). Al was still trying to pack his second sack, swearing and jumping up and down on it late into the night with a floor still knee-deep in gear and his first packed sack looking like a bulbous Henry Moore sculpture about to explode at the seams.

Air India were very helpful at Heathrow but the problems started at Delhi, where they insisted that we go through customs, even though we were in transit. This was okay for the individuals but the 300kg of gear would all have to be declared with all the delays, unpacking and re-packing, and expense that this entails in India. Their system is modelled on the British but it seems to involve much more bureaucracy and occurs at all stages of the expedition, from customs to permission to climb. It is like office 'snakes and ladders', with numerous visits to small dirty rooms with paper-filled desks and revolving-fan ceilings, to meet extremely polite, white-cotton robed officials who ask you to fill in forms in triplicate with totally irrelevant information, in sauna-temperatures and humidities designed to make the blood boil and temper explode. Rab as leader soon regretted the post as we had nominated him our chief negotiator and from then on the petty officials would listen to no one else. We left him to it and went to look round an old fort near the airport that turned out to be a disgustingly dirty and poor squatter settlement. We were deeply shocked. When we arrived back, Rab had a big grin on his face, he had turned officialdom into a game and settled the problem for a paltry amount.

Kathmandu airport has a very similar bureacracy and they were particularly keen to look into our bags for walkie-talkies, radios and film. Quick as a flash, Al noticed that all bags that had passed customs inspection were marked with coloured chalk. We soon 'borrowed' some chalk from the desk, marked our bags and walked through the inspection gate with all our bags intact, without being challenged. We were starting to get the idea of how things worked out here. The 'proper' way, which cost time and money and the majority of the westerners followed, and the 'quick' way which involved a few short cuts, was considerably cheaper, and the majority of Asians followed.

The next few days in Kathmandu were amazing. The medieval atmosphere of the old parts were unreal and the people were so friendly. Nevertheless we had a lot of work to do. Mike Cheney of Sherpa Co-operative was our agent and guide through the system and he supplied us with a cook called Kusang and a Sirdar to look after the porters and help at Base Camp, called Padaam. They helped us buy food, and kitchen gear then pack everything into 31 watertight loads. Meanwhile Rab and Al negotiated with the Ministry of Tourism and organized a Liaison Officer. The week passed very quickly and looking at my diary for August 22nd brings back many memories. 'Sorted out food, all is bought apart from oats and stuff to be bought in Dharan. Get poly containers to transfer everything from glass eg pickles. Finally get permission for Jannu from Yalung and Yamatari. Al and Rab meet Liaison Officer, he's a policeman and stroppy cunt. Eat too much Chinese food. Beer very expensive but find a place that sells chang Rs2 a bottle, and Nepalese spirit (Rackshee) at Rs3 a large glass. Rab and I get very drunk, Al and Roger get really stoned. Go to British Embassy and watch Peter Sellers in Pink Panther. Make fools of ourselves. Hilarious.'

Due to severe shortage of cash and a life, over the last few years, based on climbing and travelling, it seemed only second nature to adopt the lifestyle of the locals. So when the time came to travel to Dharan Bazaar in the east of Nepal, it was only natural that we arrived at the local bus station with all our expedition gear; over a ton in many bags. Needless to say the bus driver was not amused and it was only after a certain amount of obstinance on our part that we managed to persuade him that there was room on the roof of the bus. The bus was packed to capacity, with people standing in the aisle and a dozen on the roof. The obligatory tinny wail blared from the radio, a sound which must be specially recorded for all buses in Asia and South America. Regardless of the gross overloading, the brightly painted bus took the first corner at the usual high speed, tyres squealed and we almost toppled over. Inside the bus was mayhem. In fact it was a standard bus journey in Nepal, where death by bus is one of the commonest forms of mortality. Our Liaison Officer, Mr.Ghale, a Nepalese police officer, was not impressed. He had heard of the rich western expeditions and the fantastic gear and food, the life of luxury and the kudos that a Liaison Officer was to expect. Instead he got us. From that point on his attitude turned against us and we had nothing but trouble from him.

The journey should have taken a day, but after six hours the back axle broke and the bus had to be unloaded whilst some 'remarkable' repair work was undertaken amidst rapid shouting and a host of novel suggestions. Whilst we were held up Al started bouldering on a roadside outcrop and after an hour his athletic antics attracted a larger crowd than the 'mechanics'. A day late, the bus limped into the steamy heat of Dharan.

We were not used to the heat. In fact, a body thermometer we bought was already reading 99 degrees by nine o'clock in the morning, and all our chores were done at a snail's pace. To save money we anticipated sleeping rough, but when we observed that a lot of the houses were on stilts, and were told this was due to the danger from the King Cobra, we changed our minds and hired a room in a cheap hotel. Meanwhile Padaam hired 31 porters, each of whom were to carry loads of 30 kilos. Due to our natural distrust of locals, instilled in us from our travels in South America, we carried most of the vital gear ourselves. This resulted in us carrying ridiculous loads of similar weights to the porter-loads. On 27 August we started on the 18-day approach march which would take us to the far north-east corner of Nepal.

The first long hill out of Dharan was a killer as we laboured under the hot sun. In fact it was not until the day after, when we had gained some height on the ridge above Dhankuta, that the temperature dropped and, despite the monsoon, we were blessed with pleasant walking conditions. Unfortunately our problems started soon after, when Roger virtually collapsed due to sun/heat stroke, which must have been contracted on the first two days. Roger rested in semi-delirium for a day with Al and I whilst Rab carried on with the porters. It was the first time we had been employers of this number of people and it was a strange time and place to learn how to solve all the many problems. This was made worse as we found it very difficult to trust Padaam, our Sirdar, not because he wasn't trustworthy, but because we were so used to doing everything ourselves.

The party reunited at Dhobhan, from where we ascended the hill to Taplejung. Here we changed porters for local hill-people and had a rest day. We soon found the local chang house and consumed far more than was good for us. Ghale thought we were irresponsible and was hardly speaking to us, a matter made far worse by Rab. That night Ghale was sleeping on the balcony of the 'guest house' under the window of our room. During the night Rab awoke from his drunken sleep and with no lights or toilet he pissed out of the window. Ghale was sprayed from head to foot, a gross insult in any culture, even though it was an accident. Next day he was livid and wanted to stop the expedition under the pretext that we did not have a walkie-talkie for him to communicate. He had never been into the mountains before and was petrified at the thought. Al fuelled his doubts with horrific tales and several days further along the walk he turned back (due to 'altitude sickness' which we diagnosed), to stay at the police station at Taplejung.

During the four day walk to Yamphodin we encountered many problems. The monsoon came with a vengeance soaking us to the skin from dawn till dusk. With the rain came the leeches and despite soaking our socks in salt and dettol we suffered from their blood-letting. Roger suffered particularly badly; on some days he would accumulate perhaps thirty or forty leeches on each foot. If you did not pick them all off before sleep these worm-like vampires would find their way to the most intimate parts of the body to gorge themselves. Roger again became the centre of attention when he stumbled on the wet, slippery mud and badly twisted his ankle. He walked painfully slowly and on one particularly long day, when we lost our way on the often confused and small paths, he did not arrive into camp till after midnight.

From Yamphodin onwards there is no habitation and the paths became steeper and more rugged. There were few places for the porters to shelter at night and as we wanted to be fair to them, we lived like them and did not use our tents. One night was spent in a small leaking barn full of cows, we were packed in like sardines with mud and hay as our bed; another night was spent under a large dripping boulder. As we gained height the leeches disappeared, but it became colder and none too pleasant for us, or our porters. The rain was incessant.

Ramshey was the last 'place' before the glacier and luckily the weather improved giving us our first spectacular views for days. The porters fared better than expected on the giant moraines of the Yalung Glacier and that evening we set up camp on a grassy terrace on the true left bank. During the night it started to snow heavily, so we unpacked the five tents for the first time and tried to fit 37 people into them. We failed but most got some form of shelter. In the middle of the night there was an almighty commotion and the smell of burning. We rapidly jumped out of our pits and went out into the blizzard. The scene was sordid. The stronger porters had got into the tents leaving the weaker ones to stand in the snow-covered misery outside. To keep warm the porters were lighting fires inside our Vango tents, whilst Padaam and Kusang tried to stop them. Altitude was affecting many of the porters and us and next morning we had little option but to pay most of them off and retain a few volunteers to ferry loads a day's walk up the glacier, to Base Camp. This was situated on a beautiful small grassy terrace, 100m above the glacier and opposite the enormous East Face of Jannu. The giant mass of Kangchenjunga lay at the head of the glacier, while behind lay Kabru. The height of Base Camp was 4,800m, so the first week was spent acclimatizing, walking and bouldering around camp and organizing gear. The weather in general was poor and we got few views of our objective.

During the brief glimpses of the East Face, we ascertained that the key to access on to the face was via a hanging glacier. Entry on to the glacier was guarded by seracs which cascaded steep rock walls. In an attempt to gain access to the bottom of the face we climbed the rock walls to the left. We had two days of appalling climbing reminiscent of the worst in Scottish summer climbing; wet rock, rain, scree-covered ledges and great wet grass sods. This was not what we had travelled thousands of miles for, so we retreated and returned to Base. Immediately an almighty row broke out.

It was becoming obvious that any route on the East side was going to be extremely difficult, long, and above all, dangerous. The views in the short periods of fine weather when the clouds cleared, emphasized this, but Rab, backed by Al insisted that we make a concerted effort to climb the face. Roger, backed by me, argued that when the good weather came, if indeed it did, time would be short so we would only have time for one major attempt and if this was on the East Face it looked as if it would fail. Instead, insisted Roger, we should walk all the way round the mountain to the south-west side and repeat the French route. At least on this route we would have a greater chance of success. The argument carried on well into the night and it only finished when Roger lost his voice.

Next morning the atmosphere could have been cut with a knife. The argument erupted again and we split into two teams, one to attempt the East face, the other to climb the French route. Roger and I left that day for a reconnaissance walk round the south side of Jannu. This entailed a week-long walk and crossing a 17,500ft pass, the Lapsong La. Al and Rab made a more detailed study of the East Face and came to the conclusion that the best chance of success was by climbing the line to the col between Jannu and Kangbachen and from there climb the long ridge to the summit. Having decided on this plan they established an Advanced Base below the route and climbed the lower slabby rocks to get a closer look.

At the beginning of October we all returned back to Base where the atmosphere had changed dramatically. It was as though a great weight had been lifted from our shoulders. I think the pressures of organization and then the travel and walk-in had all got on top of us. We had all gone for a 'walk-about' and come back refreshed. The task in front of us was daunting and if we were to succeed we had to stick together, though both teams were still keen on their own plan . Sense prevailed and we worked out a compromise which, in retrospect, resulted in the ideal formula to climbing the mountain Alpine-style. The plan was to go for the route on the East side of the mountain that Al and Rab had reconnoitered; if this failed on the first attempt, we would hopefully have just enough time to go round the mountain and attempt the French route. Time was not on our side as we were running out of money and food, and the further we moved into the autumn, the higher the winds and the colder the temperatures.

We started packing our gear. On the first recce by Al and Rab, their sacks were too heavy and they found it almost impossible to climb and so we started to prune the gear to a bare minimum. Bivouac sacks were substituted for lightweight tents, gas stoves for paraffin stoves and the food was reduced to a seven-day supply. Rab even went so far as to cut the labels off his clothing, including his underpants.

On 7 October there was a distinct improvement in the weather. In fact it was the long-awaited end of the monsoon and we headed up the glacier to our Advanced Base Camp. Next day we started climbing up. We had left Britain seven weeks ago and it seemed rather strange to start climbing. Over the next four days we climbed granite slabs, unstable snow flutings, a long couloir and finally steep unstable snow slopes to reach the col at approximately 21,500ft. As the climb faced east, the snow conditions rapidly deteriorated during the day, and combined with heavy sacks and the altitudes it was exhausting climbing. We established a method and rhythm to our climbing; ascending as totally separate pairs and alternating leads as the situation dictated. Bivvy sites were small but good enough to sleep and our gas-tower stoves worked well so we could cook adequate meals. We all enjoyed those four days; the challenging climbing, the companionship and the fantastic atmosphere of being in such a remote and beautiful place without another expedition anywhere near. It was a pity it had to end.

At midday on the fourth day we were standing on the col, the view down the huge vertical North Face was impressive and in the distance we could identify Makalu, Lhotse and Everest. The weather was perfect and we all felt well, though a little tired from the altitude, but we had used over half our stock of food and fuel. We estimated that the route ahead would need at least another week of sustained effort. It seemed pointless to carry on as the chances of success were so small. With a great deal of sadness we decided to retreat and after a long series of abseils we reached the glacier and then base in two days.

The following day was a rest day and we discussed the various possibilities and eventually decided to walk round the mountain and attempt the French route. It would have been preferable to spend a few days recovering from the previous attempt but because of the pressure of time, we had to pack our bags and leave the next day.

We had monstrous sacks and needed Padaam to help carry them to Ranshey. From there we recruited two nomadic Tibetan yak-herders to help carry some gear over the Lapsang La, and the next day walked up the Yamatari glacier to bivvy at 16,000ft below the start of the climb. This south-west side of the mountain was altogether different from the East Face; it was generally not as steep, though very complicated with precipitous glaciers and ice-falls twisting between long contorted snow ridges, all culminating in a steep summit dome of pink granite. Our challenge was not only to climb the 9,500ft to the summit but to find the complicated line of the French route over a distance of six to seven miles horizontally.

We set off before dawn on the 17th and loaded with heavy sacks we picked our way through an ice-fall, on to a glacier which we followed to its head, then on to a rocky ridge, with bleached remnants of fixed rope, to a good bivvy site at just over 19,000ft. Our climbing plan was simple, efficient and worked well, though a little crazy as we operated as two completely self-sufficient pairs. Even the most difficult pitches were done separately, though the pair that led was alternated as trail-breaking was an arduous task. Usually one pair led in the morning, we then stopped to have a brew, drinking a lot at midday as the warmer temperatures made it more efficient to melt snows. Then the second pair would take over at the front. However, we only had one 9mm rope for each pair, so abseiling would have to be a joint affair.

Above the bivvy the real problems started and over the next two days we climbed the most difficult and dangerous snow climbing that any of us had ever encountered. It is difficult to grade this type of climbing, but it was near our limit, though in retrospect the difficulty was enhanced by the weight of our sacks; something which is impossible to reduce on a difficult Alpine-style ascent. Al once summed it up by philosophizing about grading systems in general: 'The criterion of difficulty is how many people can do it, not some vague quality that's supposed to exist independent of people. How can the rock or snow itself have this quality of difficulty? It's purely subjective difficulty. I mean if you think it's hard either because of technical difficulty or because you think you'll get the chop, it's a hard route.'

A long, complicated snow-ridge led to the Tête du Butoir — a giant snow gendarme. The climbing was in, under, and around giant unstable snow mushrooms, with no belays. The snow was deep and bottomless and prone to give way at any time. A second bivvy at 21,000ft on relatively safe ground gave some mental relief before another harrowing day.

The next day started badly when on the first pitch, snow gave way and I fell, landing in a crevasse. Luckily Roger was able to arrest the fall and with the help of Rab and Al, pulled me out. Whilst I recovered Al and Rab led on, up a ridiculously steep snow-flute, whose side walls eventually closed around you and then all you could do was squirm until it became so constricted that a hole was battered out and an extremely precarious exit was made from the hole on to a vertical snow-wall. Even this pitch was climbed separately by both teams. Higher, the slopes became avalanche prone so we followed the edge of a bergschrund hoping to minimize the danger. As we climbed the snow got deeper till we were virtually swimming in waist-deep snow — making progress was ridiculously slow and tiring. Whenever the ground got steep, in an effort to gain purchase for the feet, the snow was kicked away from underneath, undercutting the body and increasing the angle, the difficulty and the effort required considerably. Progress was only then made by liberal use of the ice-stake we each carried. We were all becoming increasingly frustrated by this awful climbing and a big question started to occupy our thoughts — how the hell were we going to get down? It was hard, dangerous work with no enjoyment. We were on the point of retreating.

The turning point came in mid-afternoon, directly below the Tête de la Dentelle. Rab was leading a particularly horrible pitch and had not managed to make any progress for 15 minutes, despite exerting enough energy to light Glasgow for a week. Over the last few pitches he had become ominously silent, but on this pitch all hell was suddenly let loose with a string of expletives that would have made a docker blush. He slithered back down and confronted us, sweat dripping from his nose. 'Fucking hell! I wouldn't climb on Ben Nevis in conditions like these let alone pay £1,000 to come out here to climb.' A heated discussion followed where the odds on going down were fairly high. Were we putting a noose around our necks by climbing on, as it was becoming increasingly difficult climbing that could be impossible to descend? We were travelling very light and only had two ice-stakes and a minimum of technical gear, so descent was going to be a real problem, as we would have to down climb most of the route. If the weather turned bad we could be stranded and even when we set off we only had 12lbs of food and three gas cylinders (two of which had leaked empty) per pair and only sleeping bags for bivouacking. If the visibility became poor we could easily lose the route and stray into suicidal ground. When you considered all these points, our situation wasn't all that rosy.

The tactical discussion on the climb was resolved in a rather undemocratic, though effective way, when we noticed that the rope was snaking off round the corner and Roger wasn't there. He had found some 'better' snow in some avalanche runnels round the corner which enabled us to reach our third bivvy at 21,650ft. To describe it as a bivvy site was an overstatement. We were at the start of relatively easy ground that led on to the Throne. For once there was plenty of flat ground but no shelter from the bitter wind. We constructed windbreaks out of blocks of snow with what remaining energy we had left and settled down on the snow with just our sleeping bags to protect us from the wind and cold. There was spindrift everywhere and it made life a misery, particularly cooking which had to be done by precariously balancing the tower stove on one's lap, whilst the snow slowly melted into a few cupfuls of lukewarm tea. We had a poor meal and too little to drink.

Crossing the plateau of the Throne next day was a slog. The

snow was deep with a crust that broke through with every step and although it looked no distance at all it took a whole day of hard graft. It felt very strange to be on easy ground after the past few days of difficult climbing and yet in such a serious position, vulnerable to the slightest change in the weather or the most trivial of accidents.

We were grateful to find a sheltered bivvy site in the bergschrund below the summit as the wind had increased as we got higher and the cold was intense. We slept little and just after midnight started to cook breakfast, a tedious process which took three hours to produce a mug of tea each and liquid for cereal. The gas stoves were very inefficient in the extreme cold of around -30°c. Whilst we were waiting for the snow to melt we put on our boots, a difficult task with cold hands and one that had to be punctuated continuously to warm the fingers. At this altitude the body works very inefficiently and frostbite is a continual threat.

Today was the culmination of all our plans, the day that mattered. We would have to climb from about 23,000ft to the summit 2,300ft higher and return to our bivvy in the day. It was going to be a long hard day and a gamble that could easily fail. To maximize our chances we abandoned all unnecessary gear and climbed without a sack; just a headtorch and a couple of bars of fudge stuffed into the pockets of our down suits. The only way to cover such a distance at this altitude is to travel light.

At 3.30am we crossed the bergschrund, each person's world was the pool of light from their headtorch and the private hopes and fears of the day ahead. The wind and cold were extreme, yet the snow condition good and the climbing conditions steep but fairly straightforward, at about Alpine T.D. I remember being totally 'spaced out' with slight double vision and stars in front of my eyes. I was confused and thought I should go down. Roger persuaded me to carry on for a little longer, so we followed laboriously in Rab and Al's tracks. We hoped it would get warmer as the sun rose; instead the wind increased and conditions deteriorated. We passed a tricky mixed section of climbing which looked far harder than it was but was difficult enough to prompt another wave of self-doubt and the subsequent mental debate. By now Rab was forging ahead brilliantly, all his reservations about the climb behind him now. His enthusiasm was infectious and by the time we reached the summit ridge we were all climbing strongly. At 11.30am we reached the summit ridge within a few minutes of each other. There was no time to reflect on our success and so after a few photos and a cursory glance at the stupendous view, we set off down to try and reach the safe haven of our bivouac before nightfall. At about four o'clock we arrived back and crawled into our sleeping bags exhausted.

The descent to the glacier over the next two days was made unexpectedly easier by our ascent footsteps being partially consolidated. Nevertheless there were many difficult and dangerous down-climbing pitches and a few abseils off dubious powder-snow bollards. Food and fuel ran out and our energy levels rapidly deteriorated as we reached the safety of the Yamatari Glacier and our adrenalin levels came down to normal for the first time in seven days. It took two more days of hard walking to reach base with our bodies virtually refusing to work without food. At Base Camp we ate and ate before sinking into a deep sleep.

17

Nuptse

DOUG SCOTT

AL ROUSE, BRIAN Hall, Georges Bettembourg and myself climbed the North Face of Nuptse during October 1979. The actual climbing from the Western Cwm went so well it only required six days up and down; there were no epics, struggles in storms, no illnesses, no incidents or accidents of any kind on the climb. We seemed to enjoy each other's company enough to be supportive of each other from start to finish. To this day, no one made more of this excursion than was felt by all concerned at the time. I do not want to spoil this unblemished record now — we climbed our route and returned as friends, nothing can alter that. But I have to decide to find out why we were successful on all levels in this further account of our climb. I should warn the reader this is not an easy expedition to follow. Not many are that involve a variety of peaks and people as in the autumn of '79. It was not just Nuptse that we wished to climb, but also Everest by the West Ridge.

Georges and I had been on Kangchenjunga, in the spring of the same year, with Peter Boardman and Joe Tasker. Our success there certainly influenced my plans for Everest and Nuptse. Primarily I knew first hand that big mountains could be climbed safely without oxygen. What a wonderful feeling to be climbing high without the weight of two oxygen bottles and all the fittings on my back. It turned out to be an act of liberation opening up the possibilities of Alpine-style climbing of all kinds and within our own financial resources without the need to rope in media sponsorship support.

Al and Brian had only ever climbed once in Alpine-style in the

Himalaya — or anywhere for that matter — and that was on Jannu during 12 days in 1978 with Rab Carrington and Roger Baxter-Jones. For them there was no other way but to set off from the base of the mountain as a self-contained unit and to keep on hiking until the summit was reached, or until impossible conditions put the operation into reverse.

Georges was of the same opinion, having all but climbed Broad Peak (26,400ft) with Yannik Seigneur in a four-day round trip.

As for myself, well I had climbed a number of Himalayan peaks in a variety of styles from pure Alpine, through to lightweight with some fixing of ropes, and to all out siege climbing as on Everest South West Face and the West Face of K2. It was on K2 that I decided I would not employ such methods again on any of my future climbs. Nick Escourt had been killed in an avalanche whilst humping loads between fixed camps. I narrowly escaped the same fate but survived to realize first-hand the inherent dangers of siege climbing tactics. To cross dangerous ground once may be a justifiable risk but to repeat the crossing many times is foolhardy.

Actually, siege climbing is inherently boring. Only on Alpine-style climbing or when I had gone beyond the fixed ropes did the climbing register as at all satisfying. In short, we just assumed that the only way to climb Nuptse North Face was in Alpine-style. There was never any discussion about alternative methods.

Al, Brian and Rab Carrington went for Kangtega. Georges, myself and Michael Covington went for Kussum Kanguru so there were originally six of us. (I said it would not be easy to follow this one.) The idea of six also sprang out of Kangchenjunga, where we had been four — two self-contained pairs working together trail breaking, digging out bivvy sites, fixing a 1,000m length of rope. It had worked out well enough to get us up. When Joe was ill on our first attempt, we became three as we were when Georges gave up on our third and final push. But it had been a very serious expedition without much humour, grimly grinding away at the mountain like a job of work. The old adage that two's company three's a crowd was born out as far as I was concerned on that final push.

To cover all eventualities — illness, work-load, team morale etc., it struck me that six was the right number for big mountains especially where there was the probability of debilitating trail breaking through deep powder-snow. So much for the climbers.

Wives, children, girfriends and other friends were all invited to Base Camp. I arrived with my wife and two daughters, Rab with his wife Sue and Mike Covington with fiancee Chumjee Sherpani of Namche Bazaar and their child. Various friends of Brian, Georges and Al trekked in to see us as well. For the visitors our expedition was a peg upon which to hang a trip into beautiful country, and for us their presence would help create a balance and reduce the seriousness, and maybe aggression, that can creep into the all-male expedition isolated for months at a time.

Georges, Mike and I climbed up the 1,000m rocky North-West Buttress of Kussum Kanguru. Unfortunately Mike was ill from severe intestinal infections. He remained just beyond the top of the buttress whilst Georges and I scurried up the final snow arete of the North summit of the mountain. We descended to Mike and down to Base Camp, all in a four-day round-trip.

Leaving family and friends in Khumjung, we set off along the trail to Everest Base Camp. It was now late September. I was, at this point, particularly subdued having been told too many home truths by my wife with whom I had got into various arguments, through my failure to understand just what a responsiblity she had undertaken and how worried she was on her first visit with children to high altitude.

Georges had talked at length about various conversations he had had with Pete and Joe on the walk out and after our Kangchenjunga expedition. They had let him know their true feelings about myself, there was a lot of truth in what I was hearing but nevertheless it was very painful and all I could do to alleviate that pain was to assume it to be the state of affairs that does occasionally occur between older and younger climbers. I felt that I had been in the way of their ambition, Joe's in particular. All this was good stuff if only to relieve me of the burden of my own self-importance.

Going up the ice-fall into the Western Cwm had, to some extent, taken me out of myself for the higher I got the higher I felt, but then I didn't get that high with my head still churning over recent events. (Lessons?). By the time we got to Camp 2, Mike was quite drained by his continuing stomach problems.

His heart was no longer in the climbing that autumn.

We went down to Base Camp to hear of the terrible accident, just below the summit of Everest, that had hit the German expedition on the South Col route. Ray Genet, the Alaskan guide had died of exhaustion and a few hours later, the leader's wife Hannelore Schmatz succumbed to exhaustion too. Ray, renowned for his strength and vast experience on Mount McKinley had failed to survive, probably because of being weakened by a flu virus picked up in Kathmandu right at the beginning of the expedition — severe enough for him to be hospitalized at the time. His American wife, Kathy, and their young child were in Base Camp. Mike, who knew Kathy and Ray from his time spent guiding in Alaska, elected to take Kathy down to the airstrip and see her and the baby off home. Mike would remain in Namche Bazaar to marry Chumjee, Sherpa-style.

Georges and I now decided to go up to the Lho La and inspect the West Ridge of Everest — the way we were hoping to climb the mountain. We reached the Lho La (6,600m) in six hours of desperate climbing, first finding a boot on the glacier from a climber killed years before. Climbing up a very solid looking buttress a lump of rock broke off, falling between Georges and myself. Then just after crossing a couloir a rock-avalanche screamed down, planing it smooth. After climbing 300ft of electron ladder left by the Yugoslavs in the spring, I reached the top rung only to discover that the retaining pegs were so loose in the crack I could pull them out with my hands. We were quite shattered by all this as we reached the Col and looked down into Tibet — the way was so much easier on that side. We left a gas cylinder and stove as a cache and returned to Base Camp without further incident. Perhaps, I thought, we were not meant to go that way again.

I left Georges at Base Camp to check out the family and also to locate Brian, Rab and Al after which I was to take part in Mike's wedding ceremony as unofficial 'best man'. On the way I met Al and Brian, both very solemn and Al somewhat shaken. Rab was not with them. He had decided to stay in Khumjung with Sue and my family. Al and Rab, after a brilliant climbing partnership over the years, inseparable companions, had had a violent argument. As so often happens, a fruitful partnership had broken up for each to move in a new direction. I thought then it was better for this to have happened on Kantega rather than high up on Everest. They had not managed to climb Kantega, but had given it their best, trying one route, then another, eventually ending their attempt on the North Face at 20,000ft in deep snow and threatening weather.

I ran on down, reaching Khumjung on the same day and found everyone well. Rab was cheerful enough and I reassured him that we wanted him up on Everest with us, but he had definitely lost the drive to climb any more that season.

A day or two later, with due pomp and ceremony, Mike was married. After much feasting and drinking, by midnight most of the hundred or so guests had passed out.

I returned alone to Base Camp meeting Dr.Schmatz en route. He asked me 'When are you British going to climb? All you do is walk up and down the valleys.' I told him we would climb when the time was right. He was talking strangely of the accident and of the Sherpa Sundare, who went to try and save his wife and whom I had seen badly frostbitten in Khunde hospital — one of the hospitals set up by Edmund Hillary for the Sherpas. I think the doctor was in a state of shock. Offering my condolences, inadequate as they were, I joined Brian, Al and Georges at Base Camp. Al and Brian had been up the ice-fall and into the Western Cwm to Camp 2 at 22,000ft. They were still recovering from their ordeal. They had gone from 18,000ft to 22,000ft in one very hot day. Al had vomited all night and developed other symptoms of altitude sickness. Brian was also quite shattered from this too rapid ascent into the rarefied air. Their retreat was a case of out of the frying pan heat of the Western Cwm, into the fire of fighting for their lives over yawning chasms of ice. The ice-fall had moved. Their only way down was to perform a 40ft Tyrolean traverse on a 7mm perlon rope at full stretch over a 40ft deep trench in the ice. They committed themselves to the rope, not knowing what it was anchored to on the other side. Al got over safely then Brian got into a tangle with his jumars and hung in space for an hour before extricating himself.

Georges had been up the Lhotse Face of Everest, solo, by using the German fixed ropes. All this had been going on whilst I'd been living it up in Khumjung. Georges was now far more highly motivated than he had been on Kangchenjunga. No one comes out of a Himalayan expedition as quite the same person who walked in and Georges had not made the summit on Kangchenjunga and was, at least on the surface, outwardly calm about that. Inwardly I felt he was nursing wounded pride and was now bent on restoring his own self-respect. As for me, well I had reached the top of Kangchenjunga and that should have satisfied me for the year, but I was keen to try out this new multi-peak approach. Yet as I've explained, I too was somewhat subdued as were Al and Brian.

So there is an outline of recent events affecting our motivation, and maybe our judgement, and attitude to the climb and to each other. It was the first time Georges and I had climbed with Al and Brian in the Himalaya, although, of course, I knew them well socially, as did Georges, from winter meetings in Chamonix. Brian and Al were not originally down on our permit for Nuptse but now after the various team changes and comings and goings, it seemed sensible that they should climb Nuptse with us. I made the arrangements with our Liaison Officer and put through a call on the radio in Namche Bazaar to Kathmandu, This took some doing and it was with some amusement that I thought that Jan, Martha and Rosie — Martha aged six and Rosie nine months — had permission to climb Nuptse whilst Brian and Al had not.

Anyway all this worked out well in the end and we set off through the ice-fall using ladders and equipment left by the Germans and also a Polish expedition that had just retreated from Lhotse. We had the whole place to ourselves now. We went from the Base Camp at 18,000ft up to Camp 1 at 20,000ft and then walked two miles steadily uphill to 22,000ft, there camping below our Ridge on Nuptse. The Germans had camped here and left all their tent stakes looking like anti-tank devices — bits of angle-iron sticking up out of the snow; there was also masses of food, probably more food here than we brought on our whole expedition. In fact the first thing we did was to start to open these tempting gold galvanised cans but invariably it turned out to be rotwurst or worse. Luckily we had enough food anyway.

The next day Georges, Al and myself set off to reconnoitre the broken ice and seracs at the base of our buttress, leaving Brian to nurse a slight headache and cook us all the evening meal.

Nuptse had only been climbed from the South by the British in 1961. Dennis Davis and Sherpa Tachei reached the summit first, then next day Pemba Sherpa accompanied Chris Bonington. The North side had never been climbed at all. Dougal Haston and myself had made plans after our South West Face climb; every day on the Face of Everest over three expeditions we'd looked out over the Western Cwm and there was the North Ridge of Nuptse.

We'd made plans to go there in 1976 but were thwarted by a Japanese expedition on the West Ridge who wanted the whole mountain to themselves. Tut Braithwaite and myself were going to go there in the autumn following our climb on the Ogre but he had a damaged thigh from a rock I'd dislodged on a preliminary attempt on the Ogre and I had broken both ankles so we thought that with only one good leg between us, we'd better give it a miss. Mike Covington and myself, with Joe Tasker, came in the autumn of 1978 but with huge falls of snow that year the Face was never in condition, and we had to retreat.

Now at last there was room for optimism. We were all full of enthusiasm for the line and it was in condition — we could tell that as soon as we got among the seracs. We wound our way up, Georges leading the way, climbing steep steps, jumping huge crevasses until we could exit on to steep slopes of snow. We came back to Camp 2 to eat a good meal, we slept well and took off next morning with enough food for four days. We re-traced our steps, climbing a couple of ropes we'd left hanging, retrieved them and continued up through the last of the seracs to the open slopes and into a wide open couloir. Early in the afternoon we reached a bergschrund and immediately started to fashion a comfortable sleeping place inside. The bergschrund gave us a good start and it didn't involve too much labour before we were flat out snoozing and brewing, eating a big meal then sleeping through until dawn. Brian and Al, if not Georges and myself, were still not fully acclimatized and ready to go for it.

As we were carrying two 250ft 7mm ropes we decided to have a leisurely day stringing out the ropes before returning to our commodious bivouac. We spent the afternoon brewing and listening to Al's stories. He and Georges really hit it off well, Al speaking French and liking the French from all the months he had spent over a Chamonix winter and summer. In fact Al had met his girlfriend Gwen Rawiso in Chamonix so there was much to chat about and reminisce over late into the second night on our route that was even better than the first. We slept soundly and woke up and went full steam ahead jumaring up the fixed ropes still in shadow. After pulling up the ropes the sun came slanting through the South Col of Everest and all day we would benefit from its warmth. It was a perfect day. There was just enough snow lying on the ice to make adequate footholds without too much strain on the ankles. At every belay we left ice-screws with strips of orange markers so we could locate them on our descent, thus ensuring a rapid retreat if we were hit by storm or illness — also saving us having to carry them up the mountain. We shared the lead which was a relief from the tedium of jumaring up behind the leader; but this was the fastest way, the most economical way to climb this route of nearly 4,000ft of steep ice and snow. We were taking a subsidiary ridge, as the main North Ridge ended up as a truncated spur where the Western Cwm glacier in earlier times had chopped off the base of the spur. Just below where our subsidiary spur met the main North Ridge we ran into rocks when Al was in the lead. After 1,500ft of climbing we stopped the night 500m above our first ice-cave. Al and I dug into the slope whilst Brian and Georges fixed the ropes for the following morning.

We had taken advantage of a natural break in the ice but even so it still required a lot of effort for two men to dig out a cave for four. When Brian and Georges returned, the job was done, the stove was on and we were all sitting round clutching pots of sweet milky tea. We had just over 1,000ft to go now for the summit; the weather was good and so was the view from our cave, looking across to the West shoulder of Everest to shapely Pumori and to peaks in Tibet beyond.

Next morning we warmed our frozen boots over the stove, stored gear in the cave and set off light, heading for the summit. The weather was changing and we knew we had to go fast, clouds were racing across our mountain from the south. What if we had massive falls of snow, how much could this face take before it avalanched? Would we be able to locate the markers and the pegs which we would need to abseil down rapidly? The lower part of the face would become extremely dangerous. I had seen avalanches streaming down it after snowfall many a time during my various Everest campaigns.

We were off just after dawn. Brian and Georges had done a good job in fixing the ropes, definitely helping us to move at a good pace. Brian and Al went into the lead and Georges and I followed behind in their steps. Some 400ft from the top we changed leads, with Georges and I now heading for the summit in freezing cold. The sun above was shining through a yellow halo with rainbow colours radiating out. Mist and cloud were racing over the summit, north into Tibet. The weather was definitely getting worse, for now on the 20 October, the winter winds were beginning to set in. Just below the summit the snow was deep and the summit cornice took me half-an-hour to hack through. I stood on the Ridge top and Georges walked a few paces west towards the summit only 20ft away. But he stopped, realizing that the whole thing was a cornice, that at any time could head downhill — a huge 'whipped cream-roll' as Kurt Diemberger once called these mushroom cornices. I had seen these cornices break off particularly at this time of year in 1975. One of them from further along the ridge had fallen down to the Western Cwm and demolished our Advance Base Camp. So we were quite happy to stop just short of the summit. We could see over the top and round to Makalu, catching sight of the tremendous granite West Ridge — the Walker Spur of the Himalaya, first climbed by the French in 1970. South, we looked down on Ama Dablam, Kantega, Kussum Kanguru and all the others between Nuptse and Gaurisankar, where I knew Pete Boardman was leading a team attempting the first ascent of the South Summit. Way behind that we could see Shishapangma and so many other mountains. But above them all were these Whale-back lenticular clouds heralding the onset of strong winds and cold threatening weather. We didn't stay long before reversing our route of descent, down to the top cave. The next day, finding each of our abseil screws, we roped down to Camp 2 in the Western Cwm. Next morning we sauntered down to the valley, the weather clear, the sun bringing life and sparkle to the frosty snow of the Cwm. We were so looking forward to Base Camp. I'd been up and down the ice-fall many times, perhaps 50, I knew that it was possible to reach Base Camp from Camp 2 in under two hours.

After leaving Camp 1 we were in for a shock, for there had been a tremendous upheaval in the Ice-fall — the whole mass of ice had lurched down many yards, huge blocks of ice and snow had turned over on themselves. At first there was no sign of any equipment, but as we moved into the icy chaos, we spotted ladders at crazy angles sticking out sometimes hundreds of feet above us. Creaks and groans came from the ice where it had not settled. We were very worried men. We went down several false vales in the ice and finally had to resort to pegging up one 30ft hanging wall. Having got myself a reputation for artificial climbing it was strongly suggested that I dealt with this problem — at least I would have something to do to keep my mind away from worrying about the other two-thirds of this descent. I used snow stakes and all went well until nearing the top I realized that I was actually pegging up a thin sliver/slab of frozen snow, quite detached from the main block. When I reached the top I could look down the gap and see the end of my snow stake jutting through. I suddenly realized that this whole thing could easily peel off. I panicked and it showed in my voice. Al and Brian had ferried gear to the bottom and hurried out of the way. Poor old Georges was sitting there belaying — if the snow peeled away from the block he would have been crushed under hundreds of tons. I suppose I would have been catapulted out of the way, although probably pretty broken up. Anyway I reached the top, scrambled over, hammered in a couple of good ice pegs, tied the rope off and untied myself. I lay down in the snow absolutely exhausted whilst Georges jumared his way up.

I pulled myself together to haul the sacks and then from there we traversed round into what seemed to be the centre of disturbance, or the epicentre as we called it, for there before us was a huge crater perhaps 100ft deep, right down to the polished bed-rock of the Khumba Ice-fall. I had never seen anything like this before — none of us had. It was a weird and wonderful place but we didn't stay long before we were scampering and scrambling over more loose blocks, falling into crevasses, pulling each other out until finally we were in the area known as 'the eggshell' — a more gentle slope but deceptively dangerous. It was here that Brian made a fantastic leap providing the key to our successful retreat. We strung a rope across to Brian. Although it was tied from one slender ice-needle to another, we three were glad of the apparent security it offered.

We strode on down into the moraine and safety. Georges was on his knees holding bits of moraine up in the air with both hands, mumbling Hail Mary's as our friends from Base Camp came towards us, helped us across the moraine, down into Camp and the climb was over for us.

I don't think any of us had ever been as scared for so long. For the nine hours it took us to get through the Ice-fall, we had written ourselves off. All the way through just when we thought we were safe, we came across a worse situation. We had been through the worst day of our lives.

Maybe we had had scary moments before, isolated incidents but never a whole day of them like that. We soon put that to one side and basked in our success and the overall pleasure that this climb had given us. For we had got on well together, worked up a good energy between ourselves — more than any one of us could produce on his own, so much so that the climb had gone like clockwork and Brian and Al, despite being inadequately acclimatized, had contributed to the climb as much as had Georges and I. Because of all this it was a very, very successful climb. Looking back, perhaps the reason for that was a unity of effort demanded by the situation — four men, out on a climb so far from home, on unknown ground, dwarfed by the highest mountain in the world. No wonder we had come there more humble than usual, not out to prove anything, not to be the hard man, not to score points and put the other fellow down. It was a better climb for that.

Everest Base Camp by now was resembling Butlin's Holiday Camp, with Jan and the children scampering around up there with Ariane Giobellino, as well as Peter Hillary's girfriend Nena, camping with us whilst Peter was climbing Ama Dablam's North Face. Al sat there chatting to six year-old Martha, turning her on to theories of relativity which she seemed to understand. A group of Texans arrived, caricature versions with stetsons and checked shirts, six foot five some of them with long strides as they walked into camp. But they had come up too fast and soon retired behind various tents and rocks to be ill.

Martha emerged from the kitchen with a tray full of mugs of tea, much to the surprise and consternation of the Texans. They really couldn't believe they were seeing a six-year-old girl fit and well at 18,000ft and handing them mugs of tea. Martha invited them into the kitchen tent where nine-month-old Rosie was crawling around on the groundsheet. That really set them back — 'Gee, what is this, some kind of nursery school?' was one comment.

After a few days rest our attentions turned to the main objective — the West Ridge which we had booked and paid for. We now had to make the big decision. Brian unfortunately had frostbitten finger-ends so he knew he wasn't going to go on Everest in that condition. Georges had just received mail from home and was subdued after reading his letters. Al said he would have a go if anyone else would, but he wasn't that keen, anyway he had got Everest booked for the following winter and I think thoughts of that were beginning to fill his head. As for me, well I felt reasonably fit but Nuptse had been such a satisfying climb and to get me motivated for Everest it needed all the others to be really keen.

The morning came when we had to make the decision. I had awoken with the distinct feeling that I shouldn't go. The various incidents we had experienced going to the Lho La came back to me vividly as had the image of Ang Phu's mother. Ang Phu had died in tragic circumstances on the West flank of Everest that spring.

After Everest in '75 he had spent a week with us in Nottingham. He was a lovely man, one of the best. Coming down from his second ascent of Everest, this time with the Yugoslavs, they had to spend the night standing up the whole time in the Hornbein Couloir. One of the Yugoslav lads asked Ang Phu why he wasn't bothering to keep himself warm. He replied he was going to die anyway so what was the use, there was no need for him to bother keeping himself warm. He got down to their camp on the sloping shoulder. As one of the Yugoslavs in that camp came forward to greet him, Ang Phu stumbled, fell down on his back and just slid away without trying to turn over and arrest his fall with his ice-axe. He slid down over 1,000ft cliffs to the Rongbuk Glacier, where he perished.

In Khumbu on our way up, his mother had come across to us, knowing that her son had stayed at our home in England. All afternoon she had wept and hugged us close, not wanting to leave go, as if by doing so she retained a link with her dead son. So all of this was in my mind that morning when I decided not to bother. We packed up and walked out the next day.

Four years went by before I was to climb with Al again in the Himalaya and in that relatively short space of time, three fairly traumatic blows had struck at Al's self-esteem: on Everest the following winter, on Kongur in 1981 and another concerning Everest in 1982. By 1983, at K2 Base Camp, it was a different Al to the one I had known on Nuptse.

18

Everest In Winter

PAUL NUNN

LATE IN 1979, Al Rouse obtained permission to attempt the West Ridge of Everest in winter. Two things were immediately clear in a plethora of uncertainties. It was going to be very windy and extremely cold. By climbing standards in the past it was also going to be impossible. But that is what mountaineering is all about, for Chris Bonington as recently as 1972 had himself come to the conclusion that the South West Face could not be climbed in the post-monsoon period. The West Ridge had only been climbed in its entirety in 1979 by a party of 60 Yugoslavs, with Sherpa help, using oxygen after two expeditions. Planning through the spring of 1980 Al and I decided upon eight climbers.

The winter is different. The most reliable and up-to-date information on the conditions to be encountered came from the Poles who had more winter Himalayan experience than any other group beginning with an ascent of Noshaq (7,492m) in the Hindu Kush in 1972. Since then they had attempted Lhotse, losing one climber. They finally startled the climbing world by their success on the South Col route of Everest in February 1980. They completed the climb in mid-February, on the last day of their permission. It was a close-run thing, with 16 climbers, Sherpa support and oxygen. Their veteran leader Andrezej Zawada nearly died, when he missed the way in a storm near the South Col, and the summit pair suffered frostbite.

We had hoped for the first ascent of Everest in winter as well as the West Ridge, but we had the compensation that the latter is the longest and possibly the most technical route to the summit on the Nepalese side of the mountain. It is also terribly exposed to the jetstream winds of winter. There was little illusion about that after the Polish account. 'From the very beginning things looked hopelessly bleak. Wild winds started to blow from the north. The temperature decreased rapidly... The north winds continued and there were no windless days at all. Short periods when the intensity of the winds abated were sandwiched between long cycles of hurricanes, when wind speed rose above 100mph. In the Western Cwm the temperature averaged about minus 25 degrees centigrade and on higher stretches minus 45 degrees was recorded. These extremely severe conditions paralysed the climbing activities. Even the simple existence at Base Camp was unbearable at times.'

Despite support from the Mount Everest Foundation, the Nick Estcourt Memorial Award, a grant from the British Mountaineering Council and welcome cash sponsorship from 3M Limited, Bass Charrington, New Era Laboratories, Observer Newspapers and ITN, the Winter Expedition was planned as inexpensively as was feasible. In every respect, quality rather than quantity was the criterion. Al worked like a demon on the preparations, living at my house for several months at this time.

The membership all came from the Alpine Climbing Group, a subsection of the Alpine Club dedicated to Alpinism at the highest standards. Every member had scores of Alpine climbs to his credit. None had fewer than four past Himalayan expeditions. The list is a catalogue of the world's great peaks and faces, with successes on Kangchenjunga, Nuptse, Jannu, Changabang, Mount McKinley and Fitzroy and near misses on Nanga-Parbat, K2, Annapurna and Latok. Substitutes with the experience, competence and patience, had anyone dropped out late, would have been few. All were lead climbers, believed potentially capable of reaching the summit of Everest. They were considered to be compatible, a key-point when conditions were likely to be so trying. There were to be neither second stringers nor potential scapegoats.

The likelihood of bad conditions forced the party back on to conservative-looking climbing tactics. It is almost 12,000ft from Base Camp on the Khumbu Glacier to Everest's summit. Though most of the team's experience was of lightweight Alpine-style

Al Rouse emerging from snow hole on Everest in winter.

climbing on high peaks, of which Al Rouse was a leading exponent, this was manifestly impracticable on such a long high winter climb. There would have to be fixed camps and fixed ropes to have any chance of success. Unlike the Poles on the South Col the team eschewed oxygen and Sherpa porterage on the mountain. Oxygen requires porterage if it is to be of much help. Both are inordinately expensive while the risks to Sherpas in the unfamiliar winter conditions seemed unacceptable. A small number of medical back-up oxygen cylinders were taken to Base Camp but they had little chance of going on the mountain. Despite the problems of maintaining body-heat without oxygen, everyone agreed with this.

The advance group left England in early November 1980. Al, the Burgess twins, Dr.Pete Thexton and the film crew of Alan Jewhurst, Mike Shrimpton and Graham Robinson shepherded the equipment to Kathmandu and along the long walk-in to Kumjung in the Sherpa country above Namche Bazaar. John Porter, Brian Hall, Joe Tasker and I came later, flying into Lukla and reaching Kumjung a day or so ahead of the others. After rest and acclimatization we went up to Everest Base Camp between December 1 and 5. The mood was exhuberant as we set up the tents in good clear sunny weather.There was little awareness of the five degrees of frost (C) at midday. December was relatively kind.

Brian Hall, Joe Tasker and myself cut out an ice-cave for Camp One at Lho La (20,000ft) within a week of the establishment of Base Camp on 6 December. The Burgess twins had led the way in fixing rope to that point, climbing en route a granite wall of over 100m. The Yugoslav climbers had spent a whole expedition in summer 1979 on that section. In reasonable weather everybody carried loads and a steady flow of equipment and food reached the col. The cave expanded into two which could accommodate eight climbers and their gear. A precursor of things to come was a savage wind which shredded the door of the tent which had been the first Lho La shelter. Soon the ropes were being pushed up the 1,000m flank of the West Shoulder, at first by the Burgesses, Joe and myself. Watched avidly from Base Camp, Pete Thexton and Brian Hall led the rock band as the clouds swept in waves across the ice-slopes of the flank. Progress was steady until Christmas. At the time walk-in porter troubles, which had delayed progress to Base Camp by one week, seemed immaterial as the expedition had time and supplies to last until February. The mood continued energetic and optimistic, with ample gear and supplies going up the mountain and acclimatization allowing everyone to feel gradually stronger. Most people seemed seedy initially as jardiasis swept our establishment, but 'flagil' cleared it up. Al seemed to take longer to recover. He had managed the money and negotiations coming in and had been troubled by our Sirdar Dawa, who had misappropriated about 10 porter loads. It ill-suited Al's temperament to have to come heavy. Dawa was duly sacked, but the scale of the expedition and its style was more heavyweight than Al, or any of us, were used to and for a time it took its toll. Fortunately everybody had their jobs and got on with them — Brian with the gear, John Porter with food, the Burgesses always thinking forward, Joe and myself dealing with news reports and Pete doctoring all and sundry and the film team filming. For a time alternating duty on the hill just seemed to happen naturally and any individual's off-day seemed to matter little.

A violent North-Westerly struck on 23 December and brought a moderate snow fall at all altitudes. Temperatures dropped an average of seven to 10 degrees centigrade at Base Camp. The high quality downsuits reserved for climbing above the Lho La came into more frequent use in the carries to Camp One — people found it harder to get out of them, and further reserves of down-gear were brought out to survive at Base Camp. Conditions there became harsher as the last puddle of glacier-water solidified and all water had to be produced from ice.

Everyone came down to celebrate Christmas, with a big dinner on Christmas Eve. We shared brandy and whisky with those of the Japanese South Col Expedition who had remained below. But we were still keen to get on. Al, Joe and I set off for the Lho La late on Christmas Day despite worsening weather. Only Joe made it as Al was hit by a stone on the hand. Joe spent a lonely night before we joined him next day. Below, the mail runner meanwhile arrived with a huge bag of letters so we took up Joe's Christmas mail.

In the worsening weather before New Year the ropes were pushed further up the interminable West Flank, very securely fastened off one by one to ice-stakes and pitons. The experience tended to grow harsher, but eventually the ropes reached a potential site for Camp Two at 6,700m at the top of a shallow rib. Brian carried up a MacInnes box tent before retreating in the face of the weather.

Subsequently Al Burgess and I reached the site of Camp Two again. Al was very fast, or I was very slow, on the fixed ropes and he had already excavated a substantial platform when I arrived. In the last hour of light we struggled to erect the tent before the spectacular drop in temperature which inevitably follows darkness. Inside it was into sleeping bags immediately and tea brewing with the gas stove balanced between crouched bodies. The wind rattled the tent endlessly, but its aluminium tube frame construction stretched the fabric tight. Condensation formed ice over the whole interior and its occupants, even after a frost lining had been fitted, so that we couldn't move without a snow shower.

Next day Al Rouse and Joe arrived and set up a dome tent above, and Pete Thexton and Brian brought up loads. Pete arrived so late that it was already dark. We could hardly believe it but he seemed quite unperturbed at the prospect of over 2,000ft of descent in the dark at -30°C. We foisted a brew and an extra torch battery upon him, and he slid down into the night.

Life was so uncomfortable in the wind at the camp that we all envied him the eventual luxury of the Lho La ice-caves.

Persistent wind and debility from sleeplessness prevented us from fixing rope to the West Shoulder next day, and Al Burgess descended as he felt unwell. The persistent battering forced Al Rouse and myself to retreat the day after, leaving Joe trying to hold the fort as the dome began to disintegrate. He followed when the weather became even worse.

Attrition set in with a vengeance in extremely bad weather. In a good spell in mid-January the ropes were pushed out by Joe and Pete to the West Shoulder. They had the good fortune to discover an ideal site for Camp Three in a deep crevasse. At various times Adrian Burgess, Joe Tasker, Al Rouse, Pete Thexton, John Porter and I spent time at Camp Three and once the wind relented and allowed Joe and Adrian to traverse a section of the West Shoulder towards the summit pyramid and the proposed site of Camp Four. On other occasions Pete and John went to the Shoulder alone and the dome at Camp Two was destroyed in the night with John Porter inside, forcing him to descend in a blizzard. But the Shoulder proved more of a trap than was anticipated, a kilometre long ridge where fixed rope seemed essential if it was ever to be crossed in wind. A 'howler' came two out of every three days and made almost any progress impossible. Now and then the North-West wind ameliorated but as often as not a counter-gale developed from the great expanses of brown Tibetan plateau to the north. Inside the cave at Camp

Three it was around -20°C, but draughty as air rose from the yawning hole at the other end of the crevasse. Sometimes a thin 'Scots mist' filled the cave and provoked persistent altitude coughs, the ultimate of which left Pete alone in the cave with a cracked rib. The compensation at the Shoulder was the view. Everest North face loomed with the final pyramid giant and black, looking only a stone's throw away. The route beckoned, across the exposed ridge to the little gully of the Diagonal Ditch, then by wide exposed ice-slopes into the narrow slot of the Hornbein Gully, up to the last bare stratified rocks of the summit, where Mallory, Irvine, and more recently the great Sherpa Ang Phu, were lost. So near, and yet so far. The summit boasted a huge insanely tilted helmet of driven snow-cloud, Goliath emerging from flanking defendants.

The weather took its toll elsewhere. Of Naomi Uemura's six Japanese climbers on his 'solo' of the South Col route, one was out of the running early with frostbite. Worse was to follow. In attempts to reach the South Col one Japanese climber fell from a fixed rope and was killed. Soon afterwards four Sherpas suffered varying degrees of frostbite in their hands and feet. Painfully the survivors manhandled their dead companion down the crevasses of the Khumbu icefall with help from da Polenza's Italian group trying Lhotse. Afterwards, bad weather prevented their Sherpas from keeping the ice-fall open to the Western Cwm and both groups spent time cut off in a high altitude fridge.

Meanwhile, our film team, directed by Alan Jewhurst of Chameleon Films, laboured manfully in trying to produce ITN news reports and a TV film. They had to combat the cold, even at Base Camp, the tedium of camp life and the problems of shooting. Eventually film coverage of the ascent to the Lho La was achieved and Mike Shrimpton climbed to the Lho La with help from the climbers and stayed for a week filming on that high and wind-blasted col. He compared it favourably with the rigours of years of filming 'Whickers World'. Joe, Aid and I also shot film.

In the persistent bad weather and high wind of January, good days were so few that it was decided to keep some of the team at the Camp Three ice-cave to use any clearance when it came. In the last two weeks this was attempted but with unsatisfactory results. The discomfort of sitting through the bad days at over 23,000ft eroded the resolve and resistence of the climbers and after a day or two of inactivity they tended to come down if the weather remained bad or only improved slightly. Amoebic dysentery and jardiasis also continued to re-activate problems which had circulated since arrival at Base. Coughs and bronchitis grew worse. Most serious of all Wang Chup, the team cook, had a serious haemorrhage which at one time seemed to threaten his life, though he eventually recovered and went down to rest for a few days at Namche Bazaar. Bit by bit the party weakened physically. Al Rouse lost more than two stone in weight and had persistent coughs and everybody looked skeletal. One day late in January neither Al nor I managed to carry loads the 1,000m from Camp One to Camp Three as we had intended. Brian, Al Burgess and John Porter all weakened and Pete's injury put him out. Resistence to cold lessened. Two months beyond 17,500ft and below zero, takes an insidious toll despite good food amid ample medication.

The Nepalese Government had given extension of permission until mid-February and we felt that they and our staff were anxious that the attempt should succeed. But John and I had already overstayed by early February. Objectively Al Rouse and Brian tended to agree that the expedition had little chance of success, while Al Burgess and Pete both seemed practically to have reached the same conclusion. On February 2nd, Joe and Aid Burgess were still in Camp Three hoping for a clearance, but as there had not been one for more than two weeks and no progress had proved possible in establishing Camp Four, their vigil seemed unlikely to lead to success. That would have depended not upon further carries of food and equipment from the Lho La to Camp Three, but upon being able to get across the West Shoulder to below the summit cone and establish a cave or tent there. Camp Three was a secure crevasse ice-cave, well-stocked with food, fuel and equipment for higher on the peak. The problem was mobility upwards, not supply logistics.

On the day after John Porter and I departed, a radio debate between the supporting climbers at the Lho La, Aid and Joe in Camp Three and Base Camp, led to the decision to withdraw. Joe disagreed, regarding the few days remaining as still offering some possibilities. Aid would have liked to try again to go higher, though he admitted that the chances of climbing the mountain were small. Al Rouse thought them non-existent by that stage, and in my view was entirely correct.

Subsequently Joe had the job of writing an expedition book. As someone with a good jesuitical education I was not surprised when 'Everest the Cruel Way' was published, to find that it painted a picture of our expedition that particularly boosted Joe's role. It had been a good one, but no more so than that of several others, and arguably less than that of Aid Burgess when it came to hard work high. Moreover, everyone had worked extremely hard.

The film 'Everest in Winter' also followed Joe's script, and particularly highlighted 'leaderlessness' as an issue critical to the success or otherwise of the expedition. This annoyed me for its cavalier distortion of the narrative of the expedition in the cause of making Joe's case seem more authentic, but cut Al to the bone. He took such matters so seriously, as Joe did, in their attempt to make mountaineering at the highest standards into a profession. It was easier for those of us who were more hard-skinned, who knew it is rarely worth letting the truth get in the way of a good story. Yet on the surface Al and Joe, more or less equal in their high altitude abilities perhaps, hardly said an ill-word to each other at the time. Whatever scars there were remained meticulously concealed.

19
Changing Values

ALAN ROUSE

'IT'S NOT THE summit that is important but the act of getting to the summit.' So wrote Eric Shipton in the thirties. Shipton disliked the large scale expeditions designed to 'conquer' the mountain at all costs. By the fifties a military logistical pyramid had been perfected to climb the 8,000m peaks. This method involved large numbers of climbers, even larger numbers of Sherpas and large scale expenditure. The 1953 British Everest expedition was organized along these lines. The expedition was successful and thus it became a model for future trips.

Few people paused to question the worth of these large scale projects with one remarkable exception: Diemberger, Buhl, Schmuck and Wintersteller made the first ascent of Broad Peak (8,047m) as a lightweight party in 1957. By the end of the fifties all the 8000m peaks had been climbed. (With the exception of Shishapangma, out of bounds to westerners and climbed by the Chinese in 1964.) At the end of the sixties most of the major 7,000ers had been climbed. What to do next? Even bigger trips to climb technical routes on the highest mountains, or Alpine-style trips to the lower peaks of the Himalaya? Amazingly, most climbers at the beginning of the seventies regarded Alpine-style ascents of high peaks as a remote possibility.

If you wish to know exactly what Alpine-style climbing is, imagine that instead of being in a Himalayan base camp you are on a campsite in Chamonix. To reach Chamonix you would have travelled by car or train but to reach the Himalayan base camp you would have walked for perhaps two weeks using porters to help carry your food and equipment. Porters at this stage are of course essential as it is not possible for an individual himself to carry the two months' food he may need for the duration of the trip. Say you decide to climb the Walker Spur then with one or two friends you will set out from Chamonix with a few days' food and a selection of climbing gear. Next morning you will reach the foot of the route and the next day or two will be spent climbing to the summit and then descending the other side, eventually returning to the campsite in Chamonix. There would have been no prior preparation of the route unless you had made a previous attempt which had been foiled perhaps by bad weather. In this case the only preparation would have been a mental one, as no equipment would have been left behind from the earlier attempt.

For an Alpine-style attempt in the Himalaya you do essentially the same, although some practical modifications sometimes need to be added to the simple formula. The face to be climbed may be preceded by a long glacier and it may be advisable to carry a couple of loads each to a tent under the face itself. This is one example, but I will consider this question in more depth later.

The big fixed-rope expedition tactics have been exported worldwide from the Himalaya. Even the Alps, contrary to all established traditions, have seen the introduction of fixed ropes. The competition to make new winter climbs has led to such routes as the Eiger Direct and the Whymper Spur Direct being climbed by siege tactics. The climbers involved in these ascents are often the leading climbers of the day and thus consider themselves immune from the traditions operating at the time. They argue that no one else was capable of doing the route anyway. Why do they not leave these climbs alone until someone is capable of climbing them properly? Fortunately there are many fine examples of winter Alpine ascents and now the fixed rope brigade have either ceased their activities or moved elsewhere with them.

In Peru and Bolivia most of the mountains of interest to climbers are around 6,000m in height and are thus comparable to the minor peaks in the Himalaya. Although in the thirties Erwin Schneider and his companions made many first ascents in Peru without the use of fixed ropes or support teams, by the fifties we saw the widespread use of Himalayan tactics there.

Leigh Ortenberger and his American friends were the first to employ Alpine tactics to climb the more difficult faces in Peru. Their lead has been followed, particularly by French and English climbers in the seventies. Already the bulk of new routes are now achieved in Alpine-style and it is safe to say that big expedition climbing will soon die a natural death in the Andes.

In Patagonia the ferocious weather and the long very technical climbs have meant that the use of fixed ropes has become a tradition. The first major Alpine climb was the Supercouloir on Fitzroy, climbed in a single push by Jose Fonrouge, an Argentinian climber, but now even Cerro Torre has been climbed like this. I do not think that fixed ropes will die out as quickly here as in Peru, partly because of the extreme discomfort involved in spending a prolonged period on a big wall climb battered by appalling weather.

In Alaska all the best North American climbers have rejected fixed ropes and the only big expeditions are made up of Europeans whose achievements are not very significant. The Californian school of Alpinism as envisaged, and to a certain extent practised, by Chouinard and his friends is now having an impact on the big walls in Alaska and, to a much lesser extent, in Patagonia and the Himalaya.

The British expedition to the south face of Annapurna and the simultaneous French expedition to the West Pillar of Makalu in 1971 were heralded as ushering in a new era of Himalayan mountaineering. Certainly these two weighty expeditions completed technical climbs of a far higher standard than had been previously achieved at altitude. They really proved that anything was possible if everything was allowed. These expeditions were a step forward because they managed very hard climbs without using more climbers or equipment than on expeditions to climb the easiest routes up the 8,000m peaks.

The precedent set by these two ascents has been continued by climbers of all nations but at the same time a new exciting phase of Himalayan alpinism has been gaining in importance during the seventies. Messner and Habeler's two day ascent of Hidden Peak astounded the pundits — the first eight-thousander to be climbed in true Alpine-style. Now several major Himalayan peaks have been climbed this way and within the next few years so will all the rest. Simultaneously with these developments on the highest peaks, very high Alpine climbing standards have been brought to bear on impressive walls at lower altitudes, but it is still a minority of expeditions that dispense with fixed ropes. That minority is increasing as people learn by example just what is possible.

There are many reasons to prefer small expeditions to large ones. One of the most tangible from a climber's point of view concerns equipment. Big trips leave masses of fixed rope and other equipment in place on the mountain, which on many climbs lasts for a considerable time before disappearing. In 1978 on Jannu we encountered traces of rope, low down, that definitely dated from the French ascent in 1962. They did not of course affect our climb in any way but what if you arrived only the season after a climb had been made with fixed ropes? Even on a snow and ice route a lot of rope may remain and certainly on a rock climb there may even be enough gear left to just jumar straight up the route. This problem could be solved by the expedition members stripping the mountain after their ascent, but in practice that very rarely happens.

The debris on the mountain is just part of the dramatic effect on the environment produced by a big expedition. The ecological impact of a thousand porters walking over and living on a fragile Alpine meadow is obvious. The relatively vast influx of money and goods into the region completely changes the lifestyle of the locals which may not be a bad thing, but the real point is that the locals have no choice in the matter. Big expeditions tend to have disproportionately more gear than small expeditions and hence more porters per climber.

Most big trips, in Nepal at least, employ Sherpas above Base Camp for load carrying and sometimes lead climbing. The continual ferrying of such loads traversing the same dangerous terrain over and over again is usually the most likely way of getting the chop, and the Sherpas invariably bear the brunt of this danger. The Khumbu Ice-fall to reach the Western Cwm of Everest is a classic example. To climb Nuptse we each went twice each way through the ice-fall and carried all the gear we needed without external assistance. On a big trip for each member high on the mountain perhaps 10 trips each way through the ice-fall would be necessary. Most of these trips would probably be made by Sherpas and as the Khumbu Ice-fall is an extremely dangerous spot, the Sherpas are actually exposed to far more danger on the expedition than the climbers themselves. The majority of the people killed in this ice-fall are Sherpas who are being paid to carry so that the Sahibs will have a better chance of climbing the mountain.

Think of the expedition members who do not make it to the top even though some of their companions have done so and they themselves are quite capable of doing so. It is pretty nice getting to the top and important too. At least on an Alpine-style attempt everyone capable of making the summit stands an equal chance of getting there. They will have also done a lot of lead climbing instead of just a short section of leading and days of jumaring up fixed ropes. On some trips consisting of superstars plus various lackeys there are climbers who work every day knowing that they will never be given a shot at the summit. By its very nature everyone must contribute equally on an Alpine-style push, so the idea of a leader is rather absurd, except to satisfy the demands of bureaucracy.

The big expeditions are buying the impossible of today instead of leaving it to future generations. The large cost cannot be borne on a personal level so extensive publicity campaigns must be launched to ensure sufficient coverage for the sponsors. This can be resonable enough if there is a genuine public interest in the project but the real difficulty occurs when the team fails. The team members are doomed to writing a story out of what might have been a non-event and we, the public, are doomed to read about it. When the British K2 expedition was terminated because of Nick Estcourt's death I am sure the team members did not want to go out and write and talk about K2, but they needed to do so because of the cost of the trip and the commercial involvement. This team was a fairly light one as K2 trips go, but the Karakoram happens to be an expensive place to visit. It is difficult to mount even the smallest trip there purely from one's own pocket.

It might be thought that Alpine pushes are far more dangerous than fixed rope expeditions but statistics certainly disprove this at the moment, though the situation may well change. The repeated crossing of the same dangerous terrain I have mentioned earlier, but the other main cause of accidents is relatively incompetent people getting very high on the mountain, even to the summit. In many cases these people could never have got there under their own steam. A lot of accidents said to be purely bad luck are more in fact a case of this, allied with poor judgement or overriding ambition. On an Alpine push climbers unsuited to the project will never get high enough to get themselves into a serious situation. Nonetheless an ascent of a high Himalayan peak is always a fairly dangerous business no matter what style is chosen. In the future we are bound to see a competent Alpine-style party stuck somewhere above 8,000m because of bad weather. Its chances of survival for more than a few days will be slim.

In 1979 just before we arrived to climb Nuptse there was a German party doing the South Col route according to the well-tested formula. There were eight climbers and 22 Sherpas and amongst them were some very experienced people. Most of the expedition reached the summit without undue difficulity. The last party to go for the summit consisted of Ray Genet from Alaska and the leader's wife Mrs.Schmartz, both accompanied by competent Sherpas. They all reached the summit but on the descent a decision was made to bivouac. The Sherpas both thought that this was inadvisable and one of them carried on down to the camp at the South Col. The other Sherpa remained to bivouac because he felt obliged to stay. By the morning Ray had died and shortly after Mrs.Schmartz died of exhaustion while trying to descend. The Sherpa survived though he suffered severe frostbite. I do not think that these two climbers would have got into such a serious position if there had not been a line of fixed ropes to the South Col and Sherpas to assist with the carrying of equipment.

It is no use being completely dogmatic about the best way to tackle a mountain: different problems require different techniques to solve them. Often a pure Alpine-style ascent is neither a suitable nor a desirable method of climbing a particular mountain, but with suitable minor modifications the techniques can be widely applied. Take the South Col route on Everest as an example. It would be feasible to climb from Base Camp to the summit in four days without any prior preparation of the route. The problem in this would be to get sufficiently acclimatized to be able to make such a rapid ascent. A better way might be to make a couple of carries into the Western Cwm with say four climbers. After four or five days in the Cwm the climbers could nip up to the South Col and then descend again after which they would be in a position to climb to the summit in say three days from the Cwm. This seems to me to be the most practical approach.

If I wished to attempt a difficult route on a high Himalayan peak, then I would try to get permission to do the easy route on the same mountain beforehand so as to get acclimatized and also to become familiar with the descent route. Alternatively I would try for permission on some lower peak in the same region. Otherwise one is left with little choice other than to use the primary objective for acclimatization by climbing the lower sections several times, thus spoiling the chance of doing an Alpine-style ascent.

In the future I think we will see a general trend towards the lighter expeditions; some will be in pure Alpine-style, but many will involve practical compromises perhaps using 300m of fixed rope. The Anglo-French party on Kangchenjunga in 1979 provide a perfect example. Their trip was easily the lightest to climb a major new route on such a high peak. They used fixed ropes for the first very technical section but then climbed a push from there. The route was not really a practical proposition in pure Alpine-style. How would it be possible to become acclimatized when nothing else in the immediate region is permitted by the Nepalese authorities? The same problems of acclimatization become far less acute when the peak is below 7,500m. On a very hard technical climb, where progress is slow, it is even possible to get acclimatized while climbing the route itself. Thus we can expect to see many peaks below 7,500m being treated exactly as in the Alps with very hard climbs being done in a single push.

Note: This article first appeared in the 1985 Alpine Club Journal.

20

Ogre 2

PAUL NUNN

ON JUNE 6 1982, a Sunday morning, Alec Livesey and I drove into Fort William. We were cock-a-hoop after doing a long-spied new route in Foinaven. The *Sunday Times* told the story: Joe Tasker and Pete Boardman had disappeared on the NE Ridge of Everest. Only four weeks later, Al Rouse, Brian Hall, Andy Parkin and I met our Liaison Officer, Captain Liaquat Ali in Islamabad.

Everything went smoothly. Jean and David Corfield welcomed us into their home as they had in 1980 when Jean had nursed me through the worse stages of hepatitis after the RGS Karakoram Project. Their hospitality eased us into coping with the pre-monsoon furnace of early July, as did our welcome at the British Embassy Club. The Ministry of Tourism had streamlined its act, and we were little delayed. Nasir Sabir, conqueror of the West Ridge of K2, found us an inexpensive Ford Transit and driver for Skardu, and within a week of Al and Brian's earlier arrival we rattled overnight up the Karakoram Highway. Near the junction of the Gilgit to Skardu road the van ran out of petrol and its front suspension spring snapped. Ingenious welding allowed us to go on next day, after a stunning morning view of Nanga Parbat. Grossly overloaded, the van dipped and swayed along the endless bends, always seeming to prefer the option of tipping us towards the Indus a thousand or so feet below. Cups of tea, sweat and odd views of Minapin brought us to Skardu by evening.

At the K2 Motel Fadah Hussein and his son Nazir embraced me. Fadah Hussein had been with us in 1978 when Pat

Fearnehough died. Now he came again at the first hint, a guarantee of peace of mind as Sirdar of the porters. From Caphalu, he had taken part in the war over Kashmir and later struggles with India. With him was Ali Mohammad, the best expedition cook ever, who had just returned from Nanga Parbat with Yannick Seigneur. From the first day he kept us amused with jokes in English and French, and did the same with the porters throughout the walk-in.

Next morning Brian went round sagely testing the porters' lungs with a stethoscope while Fadah Hussein and I nodded or shook our heads wisely from behind mirror lenses. Al filmed and Andy looked on in sardonic amusement as we acquired 40 porters. We even had time to visit Skardu fort, and for me to take a peek at Bob Downes's grave that day, and at dawn next morning everything except us left for Dusso. We lingered a little over breakfast, then followed the gear in jeeps, to reach Dusso in the late afternoon.

Our walk-in was smooth. Fadah and Ali Mohammad had such respect from the porters for there to be little fuss. So we were free to walk on ahead or trail behind as we liked, to photograph, or in Andy's case sketch, or snooze at will. Only masochists like control. How much better when people just know what they are doing and do it competently.

One incident punctuated the walk up the Biafo Glacier. Al, Brian and Fadah Hussein were well out in front when the porter line faltered a mile or so behind. For a moment I feared the usual pre-Base Camp porter strike. It was not to be. Fadah Hussein and I walked back to find a young porter prostrate on the ice, with his fellows huddled concerned but superstitious all round. Fadah spoke gently to the others. We worked a piece of wood between his tightly clenched teeth in the hope that it would stop him seizing his tongue. I recalled an epileptic fit at work, and one of a friend after a bad head injury some years ago. He sees the faces of three women, he has lost the price of his bride, Sahib. We must blow in his ears,' volunteered Fadah.

So we did, and everyone joined in at intervals. In about half an hour his teeth relaxed, his muscles loosened and he soon took some tea. In an hour he picked up his load and continued in the line, pale and subdued but with only one more day to go.

These were strange times. May is often a season of bad news in Himalayan climbing, and we had not digested the impact of Joe and Pete's deaths. For Al it was complicated by the respect we all had for them and his past shared experience on Kongur in 1980 and 1981 and Everest, and the resentment of not being included on the NE Ridge team, which I think seemed to him incomprehensible. So it meant we approached our venture in a subdued frame of mind, not unlike that with Hamish MacInnes in The Caucasus soon after Ian Clough had died on Annapurna and Tom Patey with me on the Maiden Stack, in 1970.

After six day's walk Base Camp was welcome, at 15,500ft a green triangle amidst the crags and glaciers. Fadah Hussein took some of our film intended for BBC Newsnight and we paid off the porters and settled in. Ali Mohammad helped Captain Liaquat with his tent and kept him laughing. We slid plastic over the framework of walling left by John Sheard in 1978 for a cookhouse, and Brian arranged all the gear in a neat dump nearby. There were a few days to doodle, stroll and acclimatize, to contemplate and to feed one's soul with wonders of light and shade. Al and I worked on more filming and some interviews for the BBC. It was a good quiet time after the turmoil of travel.

Characteristically, Al was soon wanting to view peak 6,960, or Ogre 2, as the Japanese had labelled our objective. It had been tried twice, once very lightweight Alpine-style by a British party including Rowland Perriment and Chris Gilley, and once again, in 1981, by a big South Korean party who sieged up the North Ridge from Death Alley, the slot between it and the Ogre. They had got very high, but one climber fell to his death and the expedition was abandoned. So we strolled unladen towards the foot of the Ogre in cloudy indifferent weather, spying out a complex route on the north-west flanks of the mountain independent of the South Korean line. In truth we all wished to avoid Death Alley, as it is threatened on both sides by huge seracs which fall all too frequently, and we mistakenly thought it the place of the Korean accident.

Our next recce was to go up a steep little glacier towards the proposed route. It proved heavily crevassed, with some truly hairy snow-bridges, but eventually we made our way on to a fine upper snowfield, a sort of ice-shelf under the west face of the peak. That is impossibly steep and looming, an incredibly difficult bulging rock face of compact rock. Well satisfied that we could get to the route we steamed back down to pass the snow bridges before they softened and crossed the moraine to the idyll of Base Camp, in time for a late lunch.

So fine is this place that it was an intense pleasure just to be there. It is curious to think that it became a prison for Doug Scott and Chris Bonington, when Doug had crawled down from the first ascent of the Ogre in 1977. On a third visit I had not tired of it, unlike the insanitary moraines of the high base camps of Everest, K2 or the Gasherbrums. One evening I slipped off on my own to fix a commemoration plate on the cairn which Pat Fearnehough had built in memory of Don Morrison in 1977. The plate remembered them both.

Soon came the time to climb. With the initial big sacks of Alpine-style, we crossed the Uzzun Blakk to climb a subsidiary glacier under an unclimbed and unnamed aiguille. After a lunchtime start we reached the col in the early evening, and climbed a few mixed pitches on a narrow ridge to a convenient notch for a bivouac. Great walls plunged towards the Biafo and neighbouring mountains of Patagonian steepness. Next morning Al and Andy took turns to lead on up the ridge. After we had climbed a lot of good rock the ridge flattened but remained icy and narrow. After some delicate manoeuvres and climbing on rotten snow we at last came to a flat area below the final 600ft rock tower of the summit. Well content we settled into sleeping bags and brews with a view of peak upon peak to the west. We were coming together as a team. Andy was very fast and able and he and Al climbed well together. Brian and I were slower, but our pace was sufficient and my filming and the weight of equipment justified a slower pace. The gear was working well on the bivouacs. Everything boded well but a yellow and watery sunset. We slept soundly. I came awake with a sense of feeling that sounds were curiously muffled. Then it was awkward to turn over. Poking a head out I discovered a world of swirling snow. Without tents one could not sit this one out and we were forced to climb out of bed straight into the blowing snow.

The decision took little time. To retreat was necessary but which way. The tottering cornices of the ridge would be no fun in this and the ridge was exposed to the wind. A steep rock wall dropped from where we stood. Brian and I peered over, and saw ledges a rope length down, then plunging snow and icy slopes, a gully below. That should do we thought, and within the shortest time we were on our way. There were turns at going down first and fixing abseils and coming behind pulling down the ropes. Once down the head wall we were at least out of the wind, though it continued snowing. Sometimes anchors were hard to find, but we stuck to rock wherever possible, and kept on ridges and buttresses to avoid avalanches. Some long hoarded bits of rope and pitons were discarded systematically, but the last rocks led to a point quite low on the glacier from which descent to base was not too difficult.

It was disappointing not to have climbed the aiguille but now we had a team, acclimatization under our belts to over 18,000ft and great confidence.

In a few days the weather improved, so we rested on July 26th and 27th. On the 28th we set off at about 4am for 6,960m. The marker flags could just be picked out in torchlight on the glacier. In a hard frost the bridges seemed safe. The sun touched the high tops as we reached the upper plateau. Above, a steep snow and ice couloir promised access to a shoulder under the steep walls which surround the upper section of the mountain. We soloed the couloir for speed; carefully with the heavy sacks; in that, we beat the sun to reach the shoulder by 10.30am. Already it felt like a full day's climbing, and anyway the conditions dictated a stop. Brewing reverie took the rest of the day, and we excavated a small shallow snow-cave in the ridge.

Our initial chosen line looked too hard, above steep compact rock without a weakness for over 1,000ft. We had hoped for some hidden crack or chimney so that we could circumvent the enormous hanging seracs to our left by climbing the rocks and traversing above. Now it was a question of passing under the serac or retreat. It was a sombre day, but good weather. At first light I led across the traverse into the icy gutter, about 1,000ft below the serac barrier. The ice-cliff at its centre bulged like a glutton's belly, the base of the hanging glacier dividing the west and main summits of the mountain. In deep shadow we used the rope but climbed together for a few rope lengths until we could climb out of the line of fire. By 7.30am we had escaped annihilation. Above, a flattening ridge led towards the buttress east of the great serac. Towards 11am an ice-cave site materialized and we brewed tea. Andy and Al then went off to recce the buttress, and Brian and I made a comfortable and safe cave in a bergschrund. After the dangers of morning it was a welcome haven.

The rock buttress was split by a shallow chimney line which petered out at about 150ft above its base. Andy led some difficult rock pitches up very steep cracks to attain the start of this critical weakness. Then he and Al fixed a rope so that we could return next morning. The chimneys offered the possibility of climbing for several rope lengths up to a traverse which we hoped would allow us to gain the glacier lip above the serac barrier. From there the summit ridge of the mountain ought to be accessible.

When Al and Andy came back they were tired with their efforts, which beyond 20,000ft were formidable. I think we all had altitude headaches, in our case from a day's digging. There were high spirits nevertheless in the ice-cave, as we brewed and chewed into the night. Above all the weather still held.

Brewing began early next morning too, as much tea as possible and some fruit drinks, biscuits, chocolate, Alpen and Ready-brek mix. We did not know how long it would be before food preparation would be as easy again. Al and Andy were outside first, plodding up the snow slope towards the buttress. Tiredness there was, but a quiet confidence too, though they had said that their progress had been difficult to achieve. With all the gear the snow felt hard work, but I managed to film and do some stills across the last couloir.

The fixed rope hung free for more than 100 of the first 150ft. Carrying little it took the lead pair a long time to get up. I followed and while Al belayed Andy as he launched into the next section I hauled up all the sacks. The altitude made it hard work and my back was creased by the time all four were on the ledge. Even when Brian arrived Andy had not finished the next rope length. It was ferociously hard rock with ice on some of it, and little bits of loose stuff just to complicate matters. Classic Alpine V1+, it proved exhausting at 6,500m. Eventually Andy was safe and Al followed, and our relay was repeated with Brian doing the heaving, and so the day went on.

As long as the weather held all would be well. The buttress was going to be climbed, the hanging glacier reached, and in one, two or three more nights 6,960m (Ogre2) would be climbed. The terrain did yield fierce resistance, and eventually we all assembled on a narrow sloping ice-shelf. The difficulty was that the continuation line was steep and smooth, very icy but also running with water from the sun in its higher reaches. Perhaps it was too difficult and a traverse should be tried towards the ice earlier than previously thought. Al set out that way, but retreated in doubt as the snow and ice over smooth slabs was barely attached, and threatened to collapse taking him with it. We were just conferring on the idea of returning into the awesome direct line when it ejected a fusillade of ice missiles which smashed all around us and ricocheted on into space. Such a barrage caught us belayed in a most exposed position, but leading in the shallow groove above it would be lethal. Nor was there anywhere to dig in or get out of the way for a few hours until falling temperatures stabilized the situation. It overturned our confidence, leaving no alternative but complete retreat from the buttress, as there was nowhere reasonable to stop on it. Nor could we leave a complete fixed line to ease return, as we had only rope needed for climbing.

The day was spent when we regained the ice cave. There was some food for a day or two left but it was a grave setback. Three very energetic days must have taken a toll, and particularly the hard leads, steep jumars and hefty hauling on the buttress. The manifest objective dangers of the first two days perhaps played a part too and revived memories of past injuries in the mountains from the subconscious. Once down to the cave there did not seem to be enough energy to get back that way again, repeating so much very steep rock-climbing. Another problem was that none of us was anxious to reverse our route of ascent. We had saved that problem for later, thinking that we might abseil the North ridge previously tried by the Koreans. Such uncertainties are rarely good if they go on too long.

After a tired and dehydrated sleep we went down the rounded ridge below, and traversed a great hanging ice-shelf towards Death Alley's top. After an airy traverse on steep and brittle ice,

Brian fixed an ice screw rappel point, and we went down a few rope lengths of ice and rock. Below a steep snow-slope was soloable to the 'schrund, and the descent lay open but scary ahead.

Looking down Death Alley was an awe inspiring sight. To its north, buttress upon buttress of smooth granite swept up the South Face in one sweep to the central summit of the Ogre. Long bands of ice seracs hung from these in places, and their debris was scattered onto the narrow glacier below. On the other side a vast ice-cliff hung from the base of the shelf we had traversed that morning. From the top of Death Alley the great gaps behind the seracs perched on the edge of a vertical rock wall were obvious. We had no alternative but to run this gauntlet, and look out for the crevasses underfoot in the meantime. Fortunately, we thought, it was still only 8.30 and little sun was shining into this Bunyanesque canyon. Al and Andy were a little way behind, pulling down the last abseil ropes, and Brian and I set off. Though plugging the steps taken was awkward as deepish dry power-snow covered a litter of shattered ice blocks, there was little delay. Al and Andy followed even faster in our steps, and we virtually ran down about 500m of steep glacier descent. Nothing fell from above, to our immense relief, but as we crossed a safe lower glacier a rumble came from high on Ogre 2. Huge ice-lumps swept the ice-gutter of day two of our route of ascent, detaching themselves from the upper glacier. We would not be trying to be quite so creative on that face again. 6,960, had bared its claws.

All of us had distrusted the Death Alley route, and Al perhaps most of all. The South Koreans and Rowland Perriment's party had both gone that way, but the exposure to serac fall going up Death Alley seemed hard to justify, for one would be in danger for two or three hours rather than one. Yet they had suffered no accident there it seems, though at the time we had the mistaken belief that a Korean climber had been killed on that section. In fact he died in a fall high on the North Ridge, but the mistake influenced our preferences. So again we tried to exercise roaming ingenuity against a formidable adversary. Al was keen to see the South Face from the Latok Glacier, though I was sure we would not climb the peak that way from former visits. An ascent of the Latok Glacier satisfied that point, upon which Al and the others soon agreed.

However, Al was ingenious at finding a way out of the tightest corners. A couloir was spied coming down from a ridge SW of the West Summit, which promised to give access to that via a buttress route, with possibilities of traversing to the main summit from there. Our plans moved in that direction, rather than come to terms with the logic which had forced our predecessors up Death Alley.

Then disaster struck. We were all recovered and ready to go, to the point of enjoying boulder problems one afternoon near Base Camp. The weather had been good again for a time though less reliable than during our last attempt. On a boulder a few hundred yards from the camp Brian fell awkwardly and dislocated his shoulder. With relaxing drugs and correct positioning it went back into place, but was very painful. It put him out of action for the rest of the trip and disrupted our plans and our confidence a little more. Above all it sundered the team.

On August 7 Al, Andy and I retraced our steps up the little western glacier of Ogre 2. Beyond the crevasses we soloed a lot after a very early start and we were well up the ice-gully by 9am. Low down a few bits of fixed rope indicated an earlier recce, probably by the South Koreans. Eventually the sun touched the gully top, and Al out ahead tied on a rope. He went on to lead a large number of dodgy pitches of steep ice in ever-deteriorating conditions, as the Karakoram sun melted the upper sections into a state akin to that of the Bonatti Pillar couloir of the Petit Dru. It was four in the afternoon when we escaped, wet to the skin and tired from 12 hours of action. The drooping cornices above and hail of falling stones provided little relief throughout the day.

The bivvy site had a magnificent view of the West Summit above, and across past Conway's Ogre to the west. Unfortunately the crest was narrow, and the cornices cut right through it, so we had to be content to sleep on top of the undermined section of snow. The weather was good but it was not a picnic site. For all that, the brews came eventually and our gear dried out through its Goretex shell. By dawn I was warm, though wracked with old man's aches and pains.

In the dawn Al and Andy seemed in reasonable shape, and

we set off aiming for the buttress. I had hardly started when one crampon disintegrated, losing a central bolt. I tied it together, but cord would not suffice for a multi-day ascent. Mortally embarrassed, I shouted the others, expecting them to be annoyed at the disruption yet again of our campaign. It was too steep to solo down in all probability, though I would have considered it after about the three rope lengths protection that our available rope allowed.

It did not arise. Somehow instead it catalyzed other feelings no-one had admitted. Perhaps the buttress ahead again looked too hard, too indirect a way to the top we wished to reach, perhaps the physical and psychological exposure of the day before had been of greater impact all round than I thought. Perhaps the night on the cornice had effects too. If we were to avoid another such night we must go down, and the weather looked dubious, so go down we did. Apart from one big stone sweeping near Al and I as we untangled ropes low down whilst hanging from a bit of old fixing, nothing untoward occurred, but we had given up that route too. In searching for a way to avoid a potentially lethal three hour exposure in Death Alley our ingenuity exposed us instead to at least five or six such hours in the ascent. We wanted no more of that.

What then were we to do? It was go home or Death Alley. We had had enough adrenalin and little ease. We saw Brian, arm still in a sling, walk off towards Askole with Ali Mohammad. After a rest we bivouacked below Death Alley to get the earliest possible start. That we achieved and I led up the glacier as fast as my legs would carry me. Nearing the top of the crazy pile of fallen ice blocks at about 7.30 I was just beginning to think we had got away with something. Al and Andy followed roped, for there were big holes here and there. Nemesis began far away, as tons of ice detached themselves from the frill of seracs high on 6960m. The seracs fell more than a thousand vertical feet, house upon house. Then they pushed out a great white wave of powder snow before them. It swept across the whole width of the narrow glacier and set off down towards us. The noise seemed delayed, trailing behind the terrible visual reality. I looked round, to see Al's face anxious beneath his white helmet, as he, I and Andy ran sideways, seeking to get as far out of the fall line as possible. The rope caught on all the broken blocks around us, so we did not get far, crouching behind these fragments like dogs on leads as the white veil swept towards us. Then a wave swept over us. No pain, only cold powder everywhere. After some time, out from puny shelters, one by one we crept, pulling coils of rope out of the carelessly scattered snow. The seracs had come and gone, to me at least like a silent movie. It had missed, how I will never know. There were gouges everywhere to our right. In a trance, like toy clockwork men, we went up.

Upon reaching the steep slope leading to the North Ridge proper my rigidities dissolved. My legs went weak, I felt tears flow down my face. Reasonable fears and traumas and past pain mingled with a jumble of dead friends and a terrible sense of inadequacy. It came out as a sense of responsibility for us all being in line for that particular barrage. Oh, it had been a joint decision, but as Al had pushed the couloir, I had pushed this one. In their youth even so, they may have been up and out quicker without me, or so I thought.

I announced that I was off down, but begged them to go on, moving more quickly as two, as it was our last chance. Al would not hear of it. For fear of further accident to me, perhaps impressed enough himself in a bad year for excitement, we all went down.

In some ways, for success, this was the nadir of Al's expeditions. Exclusion on Everest left him bitter and shocked. After Gwen's death, the retreat from Chamonix, attrition on Everest in winter and some personal ill-health, failure to ascend a small though extremely difficult peak despite immense efforts of energy and will seemed too bad. Yet his reactions were positive in the extreme. He returned the following year with Andy, and climbed Broad Peak. Despite a sense of being beset by adversities he also recovered much of his old joy in rock-climbing, making a more than respectable comeback. A pity was that his fruitful new partnership with Andy Parkin ended with Andy's serious Alpine accident in 1984. It left Al highly ambitious, but alone, faced with the problems of personal objectives which he could not fully share as he had usually in the past. It placed him on a dangerous trajectory.

21

Broad Peak

GREG CHILD

HIMALAYAN EXPEDITIONS ARE strange, oddly business-like affairs they sometimes unite total strangers and plunge them into intense experiences, until, at the expedition's end, they drift away into their separate lives. In some ways on an expedition, one learns things about people whom one barely knows, that others who've known that individual for years may have never learned. We do not really 'get to know' our companions on expeditions, so much as 'experience' them. As such, expeditions are incomplete circles, but what we do learn about our companions is burnt into our memories forever.

I suppose I was first drawn to Alan's cynicism, that gift of his for extracting the macabre essence of a situation and embellishing the moment with his special sardonic signature.It was the spring of 1983, a busload of us — Doug Scott, Roger Baxter-Jones, Andy Parkin, Peter Thexton, Don Whillans, Jean Afanassieff, Stephen Sustad, Beth Acres, Michelle Stamos, Alan and I — were piled on the back of the clattering rattle-trap, rumbling along the Karakoram Highway to Skardu, on Pakistan's North-west Frontier. The hour was midnight and, as the junga weaved lost through the labyrinthine backstreets of Skardu, the junga's prow collided with a web of low-slung power lines and stretched them to snapping-point. Anticipating a flash of sparks and an untimely demise, we made ready to bail out, but Alan merely chuckled, saying: 'It looks as though the whole expedition is about to be electrocuted before we even see the bloody Karakoram.'

Those mountains — Lobsang Spire, Broad Peak, and K2 — lie 100km up the Braldu River Valley and the Baltoro Glacier. On

Lobsang's unclimbed 5,707m summit we planned a difficult rock-climb; on Broad Peak and K2 Alpine-style ascents.

The brim of Alan's straw hat unravelled as fast as walked along the arid approach to the Baltoro. With a few days of stubble on his chin, the pretty-boy I'd met in Sheffield resembled more a shaggy scarecrow. We entertained each other with the experiences from our life, and each night along the approach Alan related a different episode in the saga of his wild, drunken journey through South America. I lapped up his stories of vagabonding aimfully through life in the fruitful penury of climbing, a willing ear to his, at times, barely believable folkloric tales. The dedication to decadence that drove him through those experiences was of epic proportions.

But the pragmatic flip-side to Alan revealed itself from time to time, reminding us that we were penny-pinching our way into the mountains: 'Those books you're packing; do you really think you'll read them all? It costs a quid to porter a book to Base Camp so be certain you enjoy them.'

At the meadow called Urdukas the granite spires of the Lower Baltoro rose. Among those spires rose Lobsang, a shapely turret surrounded by steep walls, towering above the Biale Glacier. Lobsang's steep, smooth walls looked impregnable. No one had ever reached its summit. A 3,000ft high couloir divided Lobsang from her neighbour, the front-most peak of the Lobsang Group, an unnamed, unclimbed peak that we christened Biale One.

On May 23, Alan, Andy, Peter and I crossed the Baltoro to the Biale Glacier, punched steps up Lobsang's long approach couloir, and made for Biale One. The steep north-east face of the peak was buried under a thick hide of winter snow. The climbing was unpleasant — digging troughs of snow two feet deep to reach the rock — and the initiative to forge the route ahead soon became Alan's.

With the sun low in the sky and snow-clouds building around Masherbrum, we crested out on a jagged knife-edge that led almost horizontally to a bump some 30ft higher, yet 400ft away. We continued towards the logical fruition of the climb, despite the slim chance of reaching the summit before dark. As afternoon clouds scudded towards us and discharged their payloads of snow I began to contemplate a miserable bivouac on the ridge, wearing only the clothes on our backs.

'Two hours of light left, Al,' I said, as Al negotiated the crest.

No reply.

'We've got no bivvy gear, you know,' I added.

Still no reply.

'Is it really worth it, Al?' I finally asked aloud.

'Yes,' he said with unforgiving certainty.

But we turned about, without the summit, a few minutes later as snow and darkness set in, abseiled the wall, and dashed down the couloir to arrive at our tents at 10pm. Back on the Biale Glacier there was noticeable tension. Nothing was said, but there was the feeling that something up there hadn't clicked. Alan's intensity and my take-it-or-leave-it attitude had produced a rift.

'I don't get it, Pete. Al is pissed off at me for not wanting to go to the top, yet there was no hope of us getting there anyway,' I said.

'Al is on another wavelength,' Pete replied.

As I lay in my sleeping bag that night I thought about the day's events and our motives in these mountains. Alan, with his hunger for the summit, had appeared willing to suffer a miserable stormy night out on a tiny ledge in order to stand a few feet higher, accepting the tenet of climbing that states a mountain isn't climbed until the summit is reached. Alan's was an empirical logic, a function of his scientific mind, but Pete and I had shrugged it off, feeling that the ridge crest was good enough for us. Within each climber there are values that make one climb worth it and another not, in the same way that it might be worthwhile to carry home a hundred pound sack of gold, yet not a hundred pound sack of manure.

Were we a team I wondered? A collection of fiery, strong-willed individuals, yes, but not a cohesive group striving for a common goal. We probably couldn't have climbed 'as one' or 'for the good of the group' if we had tried. Alpine-style climbing is a sport of individualists rather than team players. Perhaps the biggest obstacle we faced was not the mountains, but the question of how we would come to terms with one another's very different attitudes about climbing and living.

Three weeks later, after Doug, Peter and I had climbed Lobsang by its South Face, and Alan and Andy had made an abortive attempt on its West Face, I sat back at K2 Base Camp, watching through a telescope as six tiny dots slowly rose towards the summit ridge of Broad Peak. Alan, Andy, Roger and Jean ploughed through knee-deep snow. One hundred metres behind, two Polish women climbers followed slowly. The angle of the sun highlighted their trail, and their slow, laborious movements showed the strain of climbing into 8,000m. A savage cracking sound rent the still air, and a piece of the serac below them peeled away, tumbling toward the Godwin-Austen Glacier. The two women turned around at 7,500m and staggered down, while the four rounded the col between the main and central summits and disappeared towards success. Peter and I packed our sacks and set off as twilight lit the summit rocks of K2.

Two days later, at 6,500m, we met Alan and Andy loping down the snows. We congratulated them on their success. Though their words were few I saw in Alan's face the fatigue and satisfaction, of having settled an ambition within himself. He warned us of the long summit ridge. The tensions between us dissolved. Up there they are meaningless. We moved on, they down.

Three days later I descended without Peter. He lay dead from pulmonary oedema, at 7650m. I moved down the mountain with Don, the Pakistani climber Gohar Shar, and a Swiss climber. Our hearts were heavy as we descended the final couloirs of Broad Peak. Standing on the glacier, watching our descent, were Alan, Roger, Andy and Jean. They'd heard the news of Pete's death from the Swiss, whom we'd met on the descent, and who'd sent a radio message to our Base Camp. Those on the ground watched as four figures descended, hoping that there'd been some mistake, that we were all descending safely.

As I sank through the final stretch of sun-softened snow to the pile of rocks where the others sat I looked into their faces. Alan stood and began to walk towards me. His lips were slightly opened. They moved as he searched for something to say. We stood silently, looking at each other for a long hard minute.

'Then you know...' I said.

'Yeah. Pete is dead,' he answered.

I couldn't contain my emotions any longer. Roger put his arm around me and supported me as my legs gave out. Alan kept looking up the mountain. We all knew the cost was too high, but we were held by inexplicable desires that drew us on and could not be ignored.

When I saw Alan again it was in 1986, in Islamabad. I was off to Gasherbrum 1V, he to K2. We bumped into each other outside the Ministry of Tourism. Our first reaction was to laugh at each other, like two rogues who'd caught each other in the act of some folly.

'Back again, eh Alan?' I said.

'Yes back again. Why do we do it?' he asked rhetorically.

'God, I can't work it out.'

'Well I've got to dash into the Ministry for our briefing. Let's try to cross paths and have a pint at the Embassy while we're in Islamabad,' he said.

'Let's do that.'

We turned and parted into the bright April day. We never had that pint.

22

Up The Kongur And Round The Karun Koh

CHRIS BONINGTON

AL WAS A great talker; it came in a bubbling, wide ranging flow, of climbing plans, schemes for the future and stories of past adventures. At times I switched off and let the torrent of words sweep round my own consciousness. I'd known him for some time, had even planned to go on an expedition with him and Rab Carrington to Kangtega in 1979, but it was with the chance of going to China in 1980 that I went on my first expedition with Al.

There were just three of us, Mike Ward, Al and me, with the task of making a recce of Kongur, an unclimbed peak of 5,719m in Sinkiang. We made an interesting mix with Mike, a veteran of the '53 Everest trip and pillar of the establishment, a recently retired president of the Mount Everest Foundation, myself, who'd started climbing in the immediate post-war period, and Al, product of the seventies, long hair, and flower power. He couldn't quite get over the fact that I was the same age as his mother.

But it was a rare and rather wonderful trip. We had none of the pressures of trying to scale a specific mountain. There was no competition between us. The age range precluded it and yet I didn't feel there was a vast difference in age with Al. I enjoyed his company and conversation and found that our approach to climbing was very similar.

The entire trip was pleasanty relaxed with sightseeing in

Urumchi and Kashgar, visits to the battered building of the former British consulate, where Eric Shipton had held sway in the early years of the war, the tomb of a former Chinese emperor's favourite concubine and just wandering through the bazaar, surrounded by throngs of curious locals, who, at that stage, had hardly seen any Europeans.

The drive to Kongur had all the excitement of any first visit to a new mountain area; this one especially so, as so little was known about our objective. At first glance, from the Karakol Lakes, our mountain appeared to offer few technical difficulties. The Kongur massif was like a huge stranded whale sprawled over the high and arid Pamir plateau. Our Liaison Officer, Liu Dayi knew the area. He had climbed Kongur Tiube, Kongur's sister peak some years earlier and assured us that Kongur was very difficult.

The summit itself was like one of the Kirghiz conical hats peering over the rounded shoulder of an intermediate summit. But how to get a viewpoint? We set out, a little cavalcade of the three of us, Liu, an interpreter, Peter Chen, a gentle, half Burmese who had been exiled to Urumchi, and our cook, three sheep, which eventually we'd eat, and a few yaks to carry our gear, driven by a couple of Kirghiz. Eric Shipton would have been proud of us.

Our first venture was to try to find a way round the end of the mountain range to get a glimpse of the summit mass, now hidden by the intermediate peak, from the south. We set out on 13 June, just the three of us carrying a week's food and tents, striding over the sparse desert, delighted by the small clumps of dwarf iris and primula hiding amongst the rocks as we gained height. It was a delightfully relaxed journey that took us to a snow-clad col, with a steep drop the other side, leading into a glacier that stretched down from the southern flank of Kongur. The route to the summit block was still concealed so we decide to climb the peak to the south, on the excuse of getting a better view, but, just as important, to bag an unclimbed peak.

The next morning Mike was feeling tired and so Al and I set out together; real climbing at last, crampons, biting into the hard smooth ice. The angle was easy. It was an unnamed peak of little more than 20,000ft, but that didn't matter — it had never been climbed. We called it 'Sarakyaguqi' after the nearest Kirghiz settlement. There was the thrill of discovering fresh views, not just of the summit mass of Kongur, but a myriad of other peaks to the east that were also awaiting their first ascents. Far to the south was a tiny, yet conspicuous pyramid of a peak that somewhow seemed to dominate everything around it.

We returned to our camp on the col full of plans for the next few weeks. It was like being let into an Aladdin's cave full of treasures with only a limited time to collect them. We packed up the tent and started back for Base Camp; Al and I pulling ahead of Mike, wrapped in plans for the next few weeks, almost forgetting the objective of the expedition in that excited anticipation of the climbs in front of us.

We both felt fit, seemed well acclimatized, and then Al, in sheer exuberance started running down the easy mountain moraine, stepped awkwardly, keeled over and fell. He tried to stand, but couldn't; his ankle was twisted at an extreme angle and by the time Mike Ward caught up with us had blown up into a puffy, bruised swelling.

We spent the next week, with various misadventures, getting Al back to Base Camp. He never complained, and although Mike warned him that he could sustain long term damage to his ankle, resolved to stay with us, to do what he could to help our recce. We went round to the northern side of the mountain. Al hobbled about, even managing to pick his way cautiously to one viewpoint, and cheerfully sat it out whilst Mike and I went further afield, snatching another minor, unclimbed peak.

Al wasn't just staying with us for the sake of appearances. He made a very positive contribution, particularly in the analysis of the data we had collected and the preparation of our report. He was also superb company, never showing any sign of depression or resentment when Mike and I set off on our mini-expeditions.

The recce formed a sound base for the main expedition. In 1981 we returned with a larger team of four climbers, Pete Boardman and Joe Tasker, as well as Al and myself, with a scientific team of four, who were going to monitor our levels of acclimatization, and two others in support. We were a four-man Alpine team with all the trappings of a heavyweight traditional expedition, but it made for good company and good conversation back at Base Camp.

Kongur proved a much tougher proposition than any of us had anticipated. The Kirghiz hat of a summit, that had hidden so coyly behind its outer defences, was linked by a knife-edged ridge to a tapering summit pyramid. On our first attempt we fled, daunted by its difficulty and the fact we had nearly run out of food. On the second attempt we were hit by a storm at the foot of the summit pyramid, spent three days incarcerated in what were little more than snow coffins carved in a thin layer of snow lying on ice and rock.

By the time the storm had cleared we were down to barely a day's food, but nonetheless went for the summit. It was good to reach it as a foursome and the view was even more magnificent than the one Al and I had enjoyed from Sarakyaguqi, just to the north of Kongur. To the west we could see the Soviet Pamirs. Mustagh Ata, like a massive extinct volcano filled the south-west and far to the south was the same pyramid that dominated the skyline.

Pete Boardman, who was fascinated by the topography of the mountains, took a bearing. It couldn't possibly be K2 and on our return to Europe he worked out that it was a peak called Karun Koh high above Hunza almost on the Pakistan-Chinese frontier. Nothing was known about it. There were no photographs, not even Eric Shipton had passed anywhere near it. Pete and I resolved to attempt it in 1983 after our expedition to the North-east Ridge of Everest in 1982.

In the event, I had no heart for Karun Koh in the immediate aftermath of the tragedy of the death of Pete and Joe high on the North-east Ridge of Everest. But then the lure of that unknown, unclimbed pyramid began to reassert itself and since I had seen it for the first time with Al, and had enjoyed that reconnaissance with him so much, I invited him to join me in 1984.

It was a mountain that could only be climbed as a joint venture with Pakistan climbers. We met our two climbing partners in Islamabad in the May of 1984. Ikram Khan was a major in the signals, had been a Liaison Officer on several expeditions and was obviously a good steady organizer. Maqsood, in his early twenties, had a woodcarving business of his own, had attended a climbing course in Chamonix and had an extravagant enthusiasm for the mountains. Their mountaineering experience was limited but they were immensely keen and delightful company. They also made all our preparations and purchase of local foods in Islamabad very easy. We were quickly and painlessly on the road bound for Gilgit, driving up the Karakoram Highway in the luxury of a mini bus crammed with all our expedition luggage.

Just three days later we had reached Markhun, a small Hunza village at the foot of the valley we were told led to Karun Koh, but on our arrival the mountains were hidden, with low cloud weeping a thin drizzle. We stopped at the army post just outside the village and the following day our porters arrived, a small gaggle of villagers to carry our 30 loads to the base of the mountain.

Our route led through a narrow gorge that opened into a broad high valley, paved with well-kept fields, which in turn took us through dense birch scrub on to the high pasture. It was a complete approach march compressed into a single day. Indeed we could have reached the glacier that same day but for the strength of local union regulations. The approach, which had only once been made the previous year by the Austrian climber, Robert Schauer, was now officially three full days. It was a concession that we were allowed to make it in one-and-a-half, paying, of course, for the full three.

Before long the clouds had lifted, revealing a treasure trove of unclimbed, unexplored peaks, soaring snow aretes leading to picture book summits, all in the region of 6,000 metres. But Karun Koh remained hidden, tucked behind a bend in the valley. We only saw it on the morning of our second day as we came round the shoulder. Robert Schauer had sent us photographs he had taken of the mountain. He had attempted it with just one partner, who, unfortunately for him, perhaps fortunately for us, had been sick. He had been able to do no more than look at it.

As we studied it for the first time it became quickly obvious that the photographs had been deceptive. It was by no means the easy push-over we had anticipated. Massive, yet shapely, the easier angled upper ridges seemed to drop into steep, avalanche- threatened slopes in their lower reaches.

We established our Base Camp on the lower part of the glacier — just four little dome tents and a cook tent — and the next day approached for a closer look. The more we looked, the harder the climb seemed. Our acclimatization became a series of recces, climbing on the minor peaks on either side of the glacier in an effort to get different views of our objective.

The key was its west ridge, but its lower part was barred by a series of pinnacles whose rock, we had already ascertained by our attempts at bouldering in the valley below, was singularly unsympathetic to climbers, being smooth and crackless yet crumbly. We thought we could perhaps get around the pinnacles by a series of long snow-slopes below them — but closer inspection through the binoculars revealed tell-tale gleams of ice.

Nevertheless, this seemed the only way. We had now been to almost 6,000m on a couple of occasions and it seemed time to go for it. We were worried about Maqsood and Ikram. They were immensely keen and helpful but lacked experience. Our mountain was much more serious than we had anticipated. Could they really cope with an Alpine style push on something so difficult? We deferred the decision and set out for the ridge. An easy but long approach up the side of the valley to the base of the ridge took us to a high cwm at about 5,800m. We set out the next morning for the neck of the ridge where it joined the main mass of Karun Koh. It was as we had feared; hard unyielding ice lying under only a few inches of unconsolidated snow. No place for comparative beginners. I put it to Ikram, and he took it really well. They were obviously disappointed but, at the same time, I suspect a little relieved. They turned back, wishing us the best of good fortune, while Al and I started up the ice. It wasn't steep, but it was nerve-racking, the ice having that steel-hard quality that only old Himalayan ice seems to achieve. Pitch followed pitch and we seemed to have made hardly any progress at all. The sun crept round the corner, scorching the backs of our necks and softening the snow still further. It had been Al's lead and as I came up to him on a tiny levelling at the base of one of the rock towers, we just looked at each other. There was no discussion — we had already established such a good understanding and were on the same wavelength as far as this mountain was concerned, that talk was hardly necessary.

'There must be a better way than this up the bloody mountain,' I suggested.

'I'd been thinking along those lines,' was the reply.

We just turned round, and slowly, carefully went all the way down again, getting back at about two that afternoon.

The others couldn't quite understand why we had turned back, but we did our best to explain that we wanted to find an easier route by making our way to the other side of the mountain. It would at least give them a chance of having another go.

We lay sweltering in our tiny two-man tent for the rest of the day, playing word games, chatting occasionally and getting together as a foursome for games of Min — a trick-taking game sometimes called Hunt the Lady or Black Bitch — that I learnt from Mo Anthoine whilst climbing the Ogre in 1977.

The view was superb. Looking south across the deep gash described by the Shimshal Gorge were some of the most complex peaks of the Karakoram. Just under that fashionable height of 8,000m, they have been neglected, but Disteghil Sar, Khinyang Chish and Yukshin Gardan Sar, are amongst the most challenging peaks of the Himalaya.

We set out before dawn the following morning, climbing the col at the foot of the west ridge and then dropping on to the glacier that led down to the south east of Karun Koh. We reached the confluence with another glacier leading up to its eastern flank as the sun hit the snow. We lazed through the heat of the middle of the day and set out once more in the late afternoon, picking our way through the labyrinthine ice-fall and plodding up the easy slopes of the upper glacier to reach a fine view point of the eastern aspect of Karun Koh in the early evening.

There was no sign of the easier line we had craved. The eastern ridge soared in a knife edge of rippling cornices, broken by the occasional rock step to a splendid pointed summit. It was beautiful but it'd be a pig to climb. We walked up to the col and looked down on to the glacier that skirted the north-eastern flank of Karun Koh. That seemed to offer no better prospect and anyway we were tiring from our switchback circumnavigation.

That night we slept under the stars, but the dawn didn't make the east ridge look any easier. We decided to return to the west ridge and give it another go. Two days later, weary but pleased with our little adventure which had been very much in the Shipton/Tilman tradition, we were back at Base Camp. Before long threatening clouds began to gather — it seemed we had used up our ration of good weather. At first we welcomed the storm. We needed a rest anyway and the west ridge could do with some more snow to cover that hard, smooth ice. But the storm went on and on and 10 days slid by with no sign of improvement. At least we had neighbours. An Austrian team had arrived, re-routed from K12 above the Siachen Glacier in the Eastern Karakoram, because of the unofficial war being waged by the Indians and Pakistanis. They were good company and enlarged our 'Min' school.

However, Al and I were now running out of time. We had always planned on a quick trip, and had commitments back home. The weather showed no signs of improvement and finally, in early July decided it was time to abandon our attempt. The Austrians sat it out and in early August, with an improvement in the weather, reached the top.

Yet it had been a good experience. I had thoroughly enjoyed Al's company. We had explored and wandered through a fascinating fresh section of the Karakoram and had seen many exciting mountain prospects. There was that nagging itch of ego that we hadn't reached the top, that if we had just pressed on we might have made it, but it was only an itch. In the five weeks we had climbed together there had never been either stress or serious disagreement. The really important thing was that friendships had been strengthened, not just between Al and myself, but with our two partners, Ikram and Maqsood.

23

A Winter's Tale

AID BURGESS

AN OLD RED mini van rattled south towards London. Christine, Carlos, and I were bound for Chamonix during the early days of 1979. I suppose that it could have been a pleasant journey but I was in disgrace and my face hurt like hell. Too many pints of Ram Tam Bitter had led to a broken nose and inflamed mouth the previous night — the joys of a farewell booze-up.

A short visit to Mick Coffey in his North London flat helped to kill the pain but also made me unable to drive in rush-hour traffic. I crawled in among the jumbled rucksacks with the disgrace ever deepening.

'Oh Monsieur, what happened?' asked a friendly motorist in France. His deep frown seemed to reflect my own visage. Did it really look so awful?

'A skiing accident,' I lied. 'In England, much ice.' My inflated lips struggled to get around clear pronunciation.

'Are you ashamed to tell him you have been fighting?' asked Christine reproachfully.

'No. Only that I lost,' said balloon lips.

The Bar National Brasserie contained the usual number of English skier-cum-climbers.

'Alan Rouse is working for Silvain Soudain,' I was told.

The restaurant 'L'Impossible' was owned by extreme skier Soudain who for some inexplicable reason seemed to hold the 'vagabond anglais' in high esteem. Rouse was there OK; lying down behind the bar in a vain attempt to rid himself of the previous evening's party hangover. It was well after midday.

His face seemed a little pained as he rose to greet us but that soon disappeared when he saw my plaster-covered face. A big smile spread across his face as I explained how it happened and how I couldn't have helped being involved.

'Yes,' he said with mock understanding, 'I've been going into pubs for 15 years and have never even seen a scrap, but they always seem to come looking for you.'

We were playing our old game. Me feigning innocence and Al feigning disbelief. We both knew each other too well to believe either of us would change.

I saw him every day in the Bar Nash where he would come with Gwen, his French girlfriend. Outwardly he had changed some of his life-style to satisfy her more civilized requirements but when we were together over a glass of frothy Stella Artois, the stories flowing as fast as the beer, a worried look would appear in Gwen's delicate eyes. Perhaps at these times she thought she saw tiny black pointed ears growing from beneath his dishevelled mop of hair. I'm sure that I represented a full-blown devil, complete with forked tail, come to transform her prince-charming. I did not need to try as midnight came soon enough.

Al had suggested that we ought to climb a route together and Carlos would also come along. As he and I had already made many ascents in the area, Al thought that we really ought to make a new one. He had spent years studying French guidebooks and had a large number of probables tucked away for such an occasion. The North face of the Pointe Domino offered something of interest — an area of unclimbed ice and rock about 2,000ft high and not even a summer route had been made there.

This relatively insignificant peak stands at the far end of the Argentiere Glacier, overshadowed by the high faces of the Droites, Courtes and Triolet. It would provide difficult climbing but because of its diminutive size would not be too serious. Anyhow, I didn't care what I climbed. Although I had known Al for 10 years, we had never made an Alpine ascent together so that route would be perfect.

The ski descent from the Grande Montets on to the Argentière Glacier is always interesting to such a shoddy skier as myself. Al with superficially adopted French arrogance pretended that it was easy but made the same number of craters as I. Carlos, who is American, looked on with strange disbelief that two well-known climbers could behave as such 'bumblies' and yet emerge with positive attitudes later in the pub. I explained to him that the world was full of imposters but that the key to success was positive thinking and a poor memory for shortcomings.

Rather than stay at the Argentière Hut we decided to ski past it and bivouac at the base of the face. As we shuffled along through pristine snow I became aware of how beautiful and wild were our surroundings. Of course it was forbidden to voice such thoughts but I could see in Alan's eyes that he was experiencing similar feelings.

In the night, the wind rose and the ground blizzards drove powder-snow into every crevice of our equipment. By morning our bivouac gear was so seriously iced over that without any discussion, we fitted our skis and descended to the hut. Alan was already a dot in the distance before Carlos had finished shaking his head in disbelief at the rapidity of English decision making.

Pure white plumes pierced the deep blue of the Alpine sky. Strong winds cleared fresh powder from all the surrounding mountains. We knew that the next day the winds would calm and made preparations for a speedy return to the face.

We approached the bergschrund as dawn began to lighten the eastern sky. Alan chimneyed up between a flake of ice and the overhanging ice-barrier. A 15ft high lip prevented him from reaching the easier slopes above. Alan began to explain how he did not use artificial aids these days and seeing that cheating was my forte I should finish off that particular section. Ice-axes driven horizontally into the snow provided shaky attachment points for foot-slings. He had very subtly just sandbagged me and it took 40ft of fresh air beneath my behind before I realized it.

An ice-slope led up into rocky terrain and Alan took over the lead. He balanced his way from one icy foothold to another. I fed the rope out very slowly while wishing that the weak winter sun would leap over the distant peaks and remove the chill from the still, dawn air. Carlos and I jumared behind.

I arrived at one tiny outcrop where Alan half-stood, half-hung from a rock-peg. He wore a down jacket because the shadows were lengthening and the cold deepening. A bivvy site I was told. Scanning the surrounding face I saw no such place but when he told me that I was lucky as I had the big ledge, I said nothing lest I should have to share it.

I sat on a one-foot wide snow-ledge and thought how horrible must be the predicament of the other two. A sling was passed across my chest and under my armpits. I could still slide off the 'big ledge'. Finally, with feet sunk into a hanging rucksack, I could doze for 10 minutes at a time.

It was a long uncomfortable night filled with cramps and aching muscles. As soon as I could see enough to pack my gear I was up and stamping out the rigours of the night. A rope hung down from the others and I jumared up to join them. I expected to see two weary faces but instead I saw smiles, almost sheepish grins. Both were lying down on hewn-out snow-ledges. The second sandbag of the route. Steep, firm snow lay overhead and I tried to kick as much snow down their necks as possible to gain revenge.

Then we were on the edge of a broad open gully and while Carlos led, Alan and I joked and told each other stories bordering on the bawdy and sometimes criminal. We discussed the potential of a book based upon a Rogues Gallery. Like young children, we laughed and sniggered, almost oblivious to the strugglings of Carlos or the serious nature of our environment. As we jumared the ropes we stayed together so that we could sometimes stop and share a joke or a quip. How ridiculously easy life was when all we had to do was climb. Light snowflakes drifted down but who cared. The summit lay near and it was good to be alive. Even as darkness overtook us while we rappelled into Italy there was no hint of panic. A small cave, a slot beneath an overhang, danced around in the beam of my headtorch. Just the place we needed.

Because I had had one poor night, Alan suggested that I take the inside while he fought with the spindrift on the outside. I did not argue.

It was claustrophobic in the confines of that slot and I fell asleep almost immediately. Alan had already disappeared into the depths of his own down bag and did not reappear until dawn's light called us into action. By not being able to descend easily down our ascent route we had committed ourselves to a long, long, slog down to join the Val Ferret valley which runs along behind the Italian side of the Grande Jorasses.

Without a bite to eat or even a sip of water, we arose and began the descent. Deep, fresh snow slowed us down a great deal but the remote and pristine surroundings were ample compensation for the strain in my legs.

We had been post-holing crusty snow for hours before finally hitting the tree line. With still seven miles to go to Entreve and the Mont Blanc Tunnel to Chamonix, we settled into a steady gait.

Alan told me of his Cambridge University days: formal dinners in penguin suits and less formal banquets where he had performed Aleister Crowlian antics before the tables of fellow mountaineers.

I told him of my naive clean-cut college days. He didn't believe me. I insisted it was true. We were role-playing once more. The miles were being gobbled up while we chatted. Fatigue dissolved as new stories were sought out: embellished, moderated and finally narrated.

Our goal had been a climb; an event. The bar of the L'Impossible restaurant became the next one. A ride through the tunnel in a French lorry; another mile or so to Chamonix Sud; and at 10pm, we dumped our rucksacks behind the restaurant door. The circle was complete, all we needed were a few more drinks.

24
Sandbagged

RICHARD HASZKO

THE INSISTENT RINGING of the telephone wore its way into my dream until the juxtaposition of fighting my way solo to the top of the South West Face of Everest with the third year drama class racing down from the South Summit on the 3.30 school bell became so ridiculous I was forced to wake up. Stumbling downstairs in dreaded anticipation I lifted the receiver: 'Oh, er, hello Richard, Al here. Look it's a really fine day and I fancy a good training walk. I think you ought to come along.' I knew that arguments or excuses were futile. Al had a way of making you feel mentally incompetent and physically useless, desperately in need of exercise — so much so that you inevitably went along with his plans no matter how far fetched.

Resigning myself to another long and doubtless painful day out I forced down some breakfast, hefted my sack and ambled round to Al's house . I was greeted by a scene reminiscent of a climbing shop after a bomb had gone off. There was gear everywhere, and in the middle of the room was Al, busily shovelling sand into a plastic bag, 'Oh hi, Richard.' He obviously mistook the look on my face as he said 'Don't worry, there's plenty of sand left for you.' I just groaned and stuck a bagful of the wretched stuff into my sack on top of a rack of nuts, two ropes and sundry other paraphernalia; all quite useless for a walk, but heavy. I knew if I could pick up my sack with anything resembling ease he would scoff, although why I needed a training walk when it was him who was going to K2 I never did understand. He did explain it once and I remember it sounded quite plausible, but then his theories always did. Before I had the chance to get the remainder of the sand, Scoop (Simon Wells), burst in with the usual mad gleam in his eyes. 'Hello Scoop. Look, there's some sand left. I reckon you should take it. That'll give you about 30lbs. I've got about 40lbs but I'm more experienced than you.'

Scoop also knew better than to protest, so mumbling something about training neurosis he prepared himself. At this point Pete O'Donovan, a born-again crag rat, called round. He barely had time to draw breath before being roped in. Fortunately for him all the sand was gone so he could come along just for the fun of it. 'We'll go over Bleaklow' announced Al, 'I've worked out a route. It's only about eight miles and it should be well frozen so it won't take long.' I sincerely hoped it wouldn't as it was already half past ten and the sun set at 4.30pm.

Minutes later we were in the car, on the way, while Al explained the logic of the day's bizarre activities. 'You see, the thing is I can't go running because of my ankle, and anyway I reckon a long walk with a heavy sack is much better training for expeditions because that's what you do in the Himalayas. You don't run anywhere, you carry loads uphill. Running doesn't prepare you in the same way, and it wrecks your joints as well...' This went on all the way, occasionally interspersed with comments on the evils of women, politics, philosophy, climbing, and whatever else entered his stream of monologues.

We parked somewhere up by the Derwent reservoir, the sun shining in a clear blue sky. Al gesticulated wildly at the map muttering something about '...Alport Castles, then go up Alport Dale to Bleaklow Head. From there we can head back east along the main Bleaklow ridge, and then drop down from Grynah Stones. Seven or eight miles, no problem.' Sneaking a glance at the map it was obvious the route was at least double that but my attempts to protest came to naught as Al levered himself into the straps of his sack and set off. Bent nearly double I shuffled along behind, trying to think pleasant thoughts and wondering how on earth I was going to survive the miles ahead of us. I consoled myself by remembering that Al was very proud of the fact he could weigh up someone's climbing potential and push them to realize it by a subtle mixture of cajoling, scoffing, and encouragement without ever making them get into positions beyond themselves. He'd done it with me numerous times, particularly when out bouldering, so I had developed some confidence in him. I trusted this would be one of those occasions.

It was with some sense of relief that we emerged at last from the confusing environs of the upper reaches of the River Alport and on to the edge of the Bleaklow plateau. Scoop brought out a chocolate bar while Al looked on disparagingly. 'I'm training my body to go without food and water,' he said, while helping himself to half the chocolate and most of my water. He was convinced that going without food for a day on the hills would help him outflank the rest of the field on K2, so he would never take any for a day out. However his resolve instantly evaporated as soon as someone else produced sustenance, so I always made sure I carried double. On this occasion it was Scoop's entire day's food that disappeared, as I pretended not to have any either in sympathy with the training objectives.

The break was over all too soon as we set off over the tidal wave of something resembling cow's muck which is Bleaklow. By this time we'd already covered 12 miles and the sun was dipping towards the horizon. Al didn't seem at all perturbed. He had a far-away look in his eyes and tramped on, no doubt dreaming of the day when he would stand on top of K2, and this lunatic escapade would be justified — another theory vindicated. Whatever, it kept him quiet for a while as we slowly climbed up to the pile of stones marking the summit of Bleaklow. The weight of Al's sack proved too much for the stones as they collapsed under him, so he had to remove it before joining us on top. The view was magnificent. To the north sparkled the bright lights of Huddersfield. To the west the Clwyd hills were clearly visible and on the far, far horizon a thin black line. 'Yes, that must be Snowdonia' affirmed Al. Like most of Al's great theories, loudly and confidently spoken, there was little real chance of dispute. He had the ability to convince himself, and those around him, of the most absurd things, backing up each idea with 15 minutes of increasingly intangible 'facts'. The trouble was that he was normally right, but however sound the theory, by the time he'd finished explaining it it sounded highly unlikely. I suppose it could have been Snowdonia but no-one was prepared to argue in case he started expounding on the bending of light rays when there was a temperature inversion. Anyway it was certainly a beautiful sight, but the gathering gloom and plummeting temperature reminded us that we still had a long way to go and our predicament was becoming serious. Benighted, no torches, a long, long way from home with one duvet, a third of a bar of chocolate, five ropes and around a hundredweight of sand between the four of us.

Emboldened by our success, or perhaps taking pity on Al, Scoop volunteered to carry his sand for the descent. Much to my astonishment Al agreed to this. I couldn't fathom this at all until Al explained with impeccable reasoning: 'Well, you don't carry heavy loads down mountains in the Himalayas, only up them so I don't need to train for that. Besides it might hurt my knees, what with the jarring, and anyway Scoop's going skiing soon so it'll be good for him.' So that was that. Three perfectly good reasons for shedding his load, any one of which would have been sufficient justification. I was dumbstruck and did not even attempt to pass my sack on to Pete. All I could do was try to sneakily dispose of a few pounds of sand while Al wasn't looking, wondering why I should feel vaguely guilty. I knew if he had spotted me he would have mocked and no amount of pointing out that he had no load whatever, would have made the slightest difference.

So on we plodded, now completely in the dark, me dreaming of pints of foaming beer, Pete lost in thoughts of potential injuries (he's something of a hypochondriac), Scoop complaining and regretting his rashness, and Al doubtless composing a list of the things he absolutely had to do tomorrow but should have done today. The descent was a nightmare as we stumbled through bogs, crashed into stones, and fell into icy streams, but like all nightmares it finally ended and we got back to the car in a warm glow of satisfaction already thinking of ways to exaggerate the story. Al's eight miles had turned into something like 19, so I never did trust his map reading again.

This was just as well because this was not to be the only training walk. Al really got into the idea of humping huge loads around the Derbyshire hills. About a month after the Bleaklow episode he conceived the idea of walking the Edale skyline and talked me into it when I wasn't on my guard. This time I studied the map beforehand and realized he was talking about something like 23 miles, starting up Win Hill and finishing on Lose Hill. We had the usual monstrous loads, a good 60lbs and Al's fierce determination to see us through. We started late, of course, Al probably believing that all winter routes must, by tradition, finish in the dark. We hardly spoke a word all the way round, Al relentlessly pushing on, me struggling to keep up. Of course, he didn't take any food but was quite happy to share mine telling me it was for my own good. Naturally we finished in the dark, Al still feeling relatively fresh and me completely shattered. That time it took us six and three quarter hours but we did it again later in the year, without huge loads, in under five hours, but somehow it was not the same.

These walks were stamina training and Al thought out a particularly vicious one for strength training. This was the very steep path up Win Hill from Yorkshire Bridge and the essence of the scheme was to put as many heavy stones as possible into a sack and then stagger to the top. If criminals were forced to do this as punishment it would be banned as cruel and unnatural, but we kept on doing it, eventually carrying up enough stones to build a hut. If nothing else, the silly walks made great material for an evening's tale spinning in the pub, one of Al's most favoured activities. These were usually followed by a 'soiree' back at his house, with a monster carry-out and a few friends passing the night hours trying to work out his problems, or planning the next venture, be it new routes on an obscure crag or constructing another ludicrous walk hard enough to temporarily, at least, disperse some of his restless energy.

Great days indeed.

This is a new version of an article entitled 'Three Men in a Bog' by Simon Wells and Richard Haszko which first appeared in High Magazine.

25

Post Mortem

TOM RICHARDSON

THE POPULATION OF Al's house could vary from up to three (those who lived there) to over 15 in any single 24-hour period. The balance being made up of an ever-changing number of famous, not so famous and totally unfamous climbers from around the world.

To me, at first, it was like living in a Who's Who of climbing. It was almost disappointing to realize that my heroes were, in the main, ordinary people.

On reflection, the thing that was really special about living with Al were the post-mortems. Post-mortems happened after most things; an evening's drinking, a day's working, climbing (of course), and arguments with present or past girlfriends. No day was complete without a post-mortem and no post-mortem was complete without it straying off into a variety of our pet subjects.

The discussions themselves tended to follow a scientific approach (Al might have described them as a common-sense approach). Their aim, as with science, was to create a new theory or to prove a law or principle. Favourite subjects included such things as:

'Why brown rice is bad for you'
'Why running is bad for you'
'Why climbing is good for you'
and what the role of women is/should be.

The best post-mortems began well after closing-time and went on until the small hours, or until the cigarettes ran out. On one occasion, Al woke me up when he came home at 3.30 in the morning. Events had to be analysed while the memory was still fresh.

We frequently disagreed with each other, in fact we nearly always did, but we also gained more than the words that were spoken from each other.

At our last such discussion before Al left for K2, he said:

'Tom, I think you're getting more like me and I'm getting more like you. I'll be turning into a brown-ricer next.'

I will never have a finer compliment.

26

Cragging

NEIL FOSTER

THE SHEFFIELD CLIMBING scene used to revolve around a series of pubs — one for each night of the week. Devoted followers of this ritual would troop via The White Lion, Noahs Ark and The Byron to reach The Porter on a Thursday night. This signified the highest turnout and by then the accounts of the previous weekend's deeds of daring had reached such levels of fine tuning, they bore no resemblance to the actual event whatsoever. Thursday night was also a traditional time for hatching plans for the adventures of the weekend ahead, the purpose, of course, being to provide the following week's entertainment.

Al was a master of this fine-tuning process, though he felt the need to practise nightly, lest he should forget how. The Friday following one such Porter purgatory session saw Al, myself and Richard 'The Retainer' Haszko blasting up the M6, bound for the Ben. This particular scheme revolved around the fact that Al, who was working for Berghaus at the time, had to get some winter shots of their gear whilst there still was a winter and before they stopped believing that he had actually already been out and taken them, only the postal service not being what it was...

Liking a challenge, Al shared the driving with himself, one foot up on the transmission tunnel, the other foot flat to the floor, with sustenance provided by a continuous stream of furiously smoked ciggies. Al was in his element. He knew the road by heart and this was critical as we raced for last orders in the Clachaig, (the route from door to the bar being equally familiar). Needless to say we made it and I woke with a throbbing head at about six the following morning at the reservoir car park beneath The Allt a' Mhuillinn. Not being used to such situations and feeling somewhat nauseous, I declined Al's offer of breakfast. This consisted of Tizer, chocolate and crisps, being the result of a deli stop in Lockerbie. Al then opened the boot to reveal a mountain of sparkling kit which we greedily donned, with varying degrees of success. I ended up with over-small Goretex over-trousers, over-large Goretex cag, shiny sack, crippling plastic boots and no gaiters. I felt like a real mountaineer and was determined to keep up as Al raced off up the glen.

Richard, who was a veteran of many such adventures (and a member, like Al, of the notorious Hunter's Bar Ramblers' Association), was more restrained, pacing himself steadily an ever-lengthening distance behind. To my great surprise, having avoided walking on hills for many years, I kept up with Al to the CIC where the commentary changed from pointing out buttresses, and the features of the hill, to explaining how he had secured a lifetime ban from the hut. We sat and waited for Richard, as Al had spotted some ice-falls just up from the hut, on which we could get the shots. Front-pointing up the melting, overhanging waterfall, wrestling with tools that seemed forever stuck, I must confess to wondering just what on earth I was doing there. Still, all this effort was rewarded on publication of the next Berghaus catalogue which had one of Al's photos of me, looking suitably convincing, gracing its pages. I must have looked convincing as the shot was captioned 'Al Rouse winter climbing on Ben Nevis — Photo Richard Haszko.' Cheers Al.

The work complete, I discreetly asked if we could go down, but Al would hear nothing of it, insisting on an easy route to the summit. The trouble with Al's idea of an easy route was the tortuous walk required to get there, right round to the far side of the North-East Buttress. Richard and Al raced off into the clag but I was more restrained, pacing myself an ever-lengthening distance behind. Having used up what little walking fitness I had, I arrived at the bottom of the route quite exhausted. Al's scheme had been for Richard and me to lead through, whilst he soloed up taking photos. However, our joint whimpering soon convinced him that the only way to get us out of this predicament with his reputation intact, would be for him to lead solo each pitch trailing a rope, whilst I brought up Richard, whereupon

Al would bring me up to his stance and then continue on up. This suited our worn nerves and jaded limbs perfectly, though our leader was obviously only playing, gleefully pausing only to offer some cruel comment at our humble progress.

By the time we topped out, the cloud had rolled away and we had a stunning view which was very lucky for my first (and only) time up there. Al said he had only seen the view four or five times in probably 50 or 60 times up there. By now I was suffering fairly severe dehydration, having had nothing to drink all day, as well as exhaustion from the walk. As we stumbled down, I mused as to why Al never fell over whilst I, following carefully in his footsteps, spent most of my time on the floor. Even on a day as tame as this, Al's total experience, confidence and skill had been only too apparent and highlighted by my own ineptitude. We never went on the hill together again. He had won that round convincingly, so I chose the more amicable Derbyshire Dales for the re-match.

Living with Al was certainly an experience. The chances of getting in some early climbing could normally be predicted by the aromas greeting me as I stumbled down the stairs. The smell of coffee and bacon frying was promising and the presence of a Peak guidebook augured well. In contrast, you could be greeted by the distinctive and familiar smell of simmering soup, complemented by other far more evil smells, and a bleary and drawn Rouse. Soup for breakfast was Al's tried and tested (though I am not certain it was ever proved) cure for a heavy night on the beer. Consequently Campbell's and Al had a steady business relationship.

Al had an intimate knowledge of our local Peak District crags, which had suddenly recaptured his imagination after several years' disinterest in rock-climbing. Al's energies were mostly directed into the quest for new routes, and to this end we spent many winter days wandering round poxy esoteric dripping Derbyshire backwaters, in search of the true potential of the crag. Having mentally climbed, named and graded all the routes, we would return nonchalantly to Sheffield to plan our campaign over a leisurely beer, whereupon Andy Barker and Paul Mitchell would inevitably steam in and steal our lines.

We did, however, have our share of the action, with Al

grabbing the exquisite Nicotine Stain on his beloved Burbage North and me leading him across the first free ascent of The Flying Blackberry on Dovedale's Bailey Buttress, whilst a host of reticent superstars watched in amazement at the obscurity of it all, from the more acceptable walls of Ravens Tor.

One evening in December '83 there was a party in Sheffield, and an air of excitement was evident between Al and Phil Burke who had been out in the Peak that day. I enquired where they had been but received little more than a wry smile. This was, of course, no problem with Al. You just had to ask him again, whereupon, after some vague oath of secrecy, I was excitedly informed how a modern classic at Millstone was half complete after much effort from an oft-airborne Rouse, most of it under the watchful eye of a lurking Fawcett. Ron had obviously succeeded in winding them up no end with his presence and taunting mocks, and I must confess seeing these two in such a state of nerves made me join in: 'It sounds like a stunning route' I said encouragingly. 'What a drag if Ron beat you to the top pitch.'

Expecting little more than an earlier than normal start, it was with amazement and total delight that I watched Phil depart in the early hours to go and doss beneath the route. I still could hardly believe he would be that eccentric, but as Al and I coaxed our hangovers up the path to Millstone at about nine the following morning, we were greeted by a multi-coloured Can Van, from which staggered Phil looking somewhat sheepish. I'm told you could almost hear the laughter in Sheffield when Ron was informed of this extreme behaviour. Anyway the sun was not on the crag yet, and as it was still bitterly cold, Phil and I were allowed to go to the Stoney Cafe for breakfast, whilst Al stayed on guard. This was a rare treat for me, a devoted cafe-goer, who was seldom allowed to attend my mecca when out climbing with Al.

Our return saw the route, Quality Street soon in the bag, and the same day I cleaned and soloed the superb arete of Winter's Grip, which a cock-a-hoop Burke had threatened to solo if I didn't get on with it. Ron wandered over at the end of the day, having put up The Crypt Trip on Stanage.

27
Pub Talk

JOHN GERRARD

AL HAD A way of putting things, speaking with such confidence that it was impossible not to believe him. Stopping Paul Nunn in full flow is next to impossible, but Al could.

Paul is something of an expert on industrial disasters. We were in the pub one night, as usual, having one of those silly conversations that happen after three or four pints. What was the death toll in the Tangshan earthquake? We all quoted various figures from various sources. Paul was talking a million or so. Al, unusually, was quiet, but smiling rather smugly: 'Actually,' he started, 'It was five million.' Paul questioned his source, falling into the trap head-first, as Al produced one of the greatest name-drops of all time: 'The provincial governor told me,' he said. Paul, silent, went for more beer.

There were times when Al could seem very correct. He grilled me with all the skills of a trained interrogator about my motives for wanting to start climbing again after a serious operation; very politely, very coolly, very probingly, and painfully accurately. He could take the same, dealing with his emotional problems in conversation, with clinical precision.

One subject was taboo. The film of the Everest West Ridge in winter trip has shot after shot of everybody but Al looking very dramatic. Al's big moment was at Camp 2, where, stricken with the runs, he was filmed in lingering detail trudging through the snow to relieve himself at the highest point ever recorded and seen on television.

28
The Bequest

BRIAN HALL

DEEP SLEEP, THE result of several beers and the long drive to Ullapool, was broken by a not too gentle kick and the white glare of a policeman's torch. Al and I thought we had found the ideal doss, on the covered balcony of one of the new wooden holiday chalets just outside Ullapool. The two policeman had different ideas and thought we were 'up to no good' and were going through their standard 'song and dance' routine; name, address, occupation (professional mountaineers eh!), car number, reason for being there, reason for living etc. Luckily they were sympathetic, the brutality of the inner city cop had not spread to the Highlands of North West Scotland. They left us in peace, and as usual Al was asleep in an instant. It was a bitterly cold, clear, February starlit night and I could not get back to sleep, instead I was left to ponder over the strange circumstances that had brought us to this remote corner of Britain.

Al and I had known Mick Geddes for many years, but in particular he was one of Al's closest friends. They shared a flat at Cambridge, travelled extensively in South America on the ill fated 'first trip to Patagonia', climbed in the Alps and made numerous significant Scottish winter ascents together. Recently Mick had settled down with his wife, Helen, near Aviemore but tragically he developed cancer and died in the autumn. Mick's death affected Al considerably and he often sadly reflected on how many of our contempories had died in their prime.

Mick's knowledge of winter climbing in Scotland was phenomenal; he had visited every Glen and Ben of the Highlands as a school kid, and with the help of this experience and a natural talent for ice-climbing he climbed many outstanding routes.

One particular day he was walking near Ullapool, in the area behind Seanna Bhraigh, at the head of Gleann a'Chadha Dheirg, when he spotted a large unclimbed north facing cliff. He was especially impressed by the 1,000ft gully splitting the highest part of the face. Like many cliffs in North West Scotland, they rarely come into condition due to the fickle nature of the Scottish 'Arctic' weather mixing unpredictably with the 'warm' Gulf Stream. On the occasion of Mick's visit the Gulf Stream had won and the climb was not in condition. He died without climbing on his virgin cliff.

Whilst in conversation with Al, Helen passed on this information along with the cliff's Grid reference. Over the early part of the winter it became an obsession of Al's to climb the route, and as soon as conditions looked promising we headed north.

We parked the car at the head of the forestry track, just before the gate through which leads the path to Beinn Dearg. It was still dark as we made our way steeply up the hillside on the left. As we gained height the dawn broke purple over the snow-covered heather and we became aware of an almost religious aura; we were on a pilgrimage to Mick's Highland Mecca.

It was quite a complicated walk, over a high plateau, through a valley, under a good-looking cliff dripping with 200ft ice smears, before arriving near the top of the cliff (we hoped). It was quite a long slog made worse as it was our first trip to Scotland that winter. It took about three-and-a-half hours, which seemed to pass quickly as we talked randomly of the good times we'd had with Mick; the second ascent of Orion Face Direct, first ascent of Route 2, attempts on the Croz in winter, Buenos Aires, Leeds and Cambridge. Locating the summit of the cliff and the descent gully was a puzzle and it was a matter of good luck (or fate) that we reached the cliff with ease in such a complicated and remote landscape.

The side walls of the descent gully, which formed the right-handside of the cliff were impressive enough, but nothing compared to the steep gully and walls in the centre. How climbers, particularly the canny Scots had not discovered and climbed here is a mystery though the fact that it had no name, is not on a 'summit' and is so remote, goes some way to answer this question.

On first inspection Mick's compelling gully line looked not too hard. In fact we almost chose as an alternative one of the lines up the side walls. But the gully was 'the' line so we geared up below it. It was quite a shock to be climbing, the brutal reality contrasted directly with the dreamy, flashback monotony of the walk-in.

The first pitch and the snow slopes above were relatively easy, but then the action started as the gully constricted and steepened. An ominous umbrella of ice which overhung the whole top section of the gully predicted interesting climbing higher up. Yet strangely there was no question of failure. Al instilled confidence — or was it Mick?

Al took his time on the first steep pitch which had ice thick enough to climb but thin enough not to protect. Perhaps he was too cautious but I could not criticize as it would be my turn next. Both of us were suffering from lack of ice-climbing that winter which caused panic at the steep unprotected climbing. Energy seemed to evaporate as slings, ice screws and tie-offs tangled with axes, and hands either went numb with the cold or throbbed painfully with hot-aches.

Several more pitches took us to the overhanging icicles of the top section of the gully. It was my turn to lead and it was not at all obvious how to break through this barrier. The main icicle in the back wall had not formed completely and for a while we were depressed as we talked of failure. Experience was on our side and a cunningly devious route was followed with difficulty up a thinly-iced overhanging wall to the right. Then, just as the ice ran out, a precarious ramp slanted leftwards through the icicles. This elegant crux produced a fitting climax to the day's climbing.

The too early northern night was soon upon us and hastily we stuffed our stiff, snow covered gear into our sacks and tried to find our walk-in tracks. After a false start and half-an-hour's walk in the wrong direction we got the compass out and soon found our tracks. We walked quickly and in complete silence. The snow was crisp and the world was a pool of yellow headtorch light. All was well at first but after half an hour I started to get this peculiar feeling, a tension, a strange desire to look behind into the hollow darkness from where we came. The feeling persisted and I looked back, there was nothing, but this did not satisfy my desire or quell the 'fear'. I looked back again maybe a dozen times. I could not resist the 'calling' of Mick, our third partner on the climb. The presence got stronger and I thought I should be frightened, but instead I realized I was smiling; I had an inner glow which made me feel happy yet sad.

The final steep descent of heather and tussock grass jolted reality and Mick was left behind. Yet as we reached the car we both gazed up the slope, as though to look at Mick, standing on top of the ridge. I had kept my feelings to myself all the way down yet at the car Al said: 'Did you feel something strange on the way down?' We both smiled and knew that Mick had been with us on the climb.

It was already nine o'clock and the ACG piss-up at the Kingshouse was in full swing. We drove like crazy to Glencoe and arrived before midnight for a memorable night of beer and bullshit. Neither Al nor I talked about the descent, our feelings were somehow very private.

29

K2 North-West Ridge

JOHN PORTER

I LOOKED BACK from Concordia and wondered why I was leaving. K2 was etched against a stainless blue sky. Not a single cloud, no hint of cirrus, and in every direction the solid bright colours of high mountains stood against the horizon. On the glacier, the warm air was working on the last of the drifted snow. Small streams glided across the ice, and vanished into crevasses. Thirty miles away at the glacier snout, the water reappeared, multiplied a million times. The rapids roared and leapt through the high desert. A hundred miles further, the Indus gathered its tributaries and forced a way out of the Karakoram, then on through the Himalayas before sprawling across the plain towards the Indian Ocean. The waters of summer were flowing at last. Like the water, I felt the passive hand of gravity. The wet tarmac of Heathrow mirrored the blankness of my mind. I knew only that weeks of hard work and missed opportunities were in the past. Chance might have been kinder to Al and I, but surely I could console myself that Al and some of the others would reach that unlikely summit seen so clearly from Concordia, perched on an arrow of ice and rock. For three weeks I lost myself in work and then the news came.

We had arrived in Base Camp towards the end of May. Al had assured us that the route, being on the north side of the mountain, would be 'refreshingly cool' after the unrelenting heat on the walk-in. When the temperature dropped to -20° at

Urdukass, and the snow continued to fall heavily most days, Al's quip became a byword. The weather had not improved much when we reached Base, but at least we were able to get to grips with the hill. Climbing provides relief after the uncertainty that creeps in during the long days of the walk-in.

The route we were trying was not our original objective. I have forgotten exactly when, but some years before Al had asked me to join an attempt on the South Face, Alpine-style, five members, probably climbing as a foursome, assuming normal drop-out rate. It had seemed a fine idea, almost achievable in a normal holiday. Within months of departure, we received permission for the NNW Ridge, a remote, technical and complicated route on the wrong side of the mountain. Then began the scramble for more members and money. Fullers Brewery came up trumps on the latter. Al and John Barry assured them that the team would quickly familiarize themselves with the product. After the various shuffles of members, we became 11: the Burgesses, Brian Hall, Phil Burke, Dave Wilkinson, Al, John and myself as climbers, Jim Hargreaves as master Base Camp organizer, Bev Holt as doctor and Jim Curran as film maker and sit-down comedian. The stand-up laughs were hard fought.

Al and I became paired almost at the beginning of the trip. Al's plan was to divide the climbers into two teams of four, and within those groups to split the obvious partnerships. The idea was a good one, but like many of Al's plans, it created its own problems. On the one hand we were supposed to be democratic. On the other, we all looked to Al to tell us what to do to prevent total anarchy. Inevitably, deals were hatched within the groups. Al's plan was to get everyone to work with everyone else, to avoid a situation where someone would fall behind early on, thereby losing their own mental grasp, and the team's belief, in that person's ability to get up. That had happened on Everest in winter to Al, and to other members. The core of the Everest team were here now on K2. It was a difficult and subtle plan to implement among a team of hardened individuals. Perhaps it would have worked had the weather been good, but it was doomed when the bad days began to out-number the good after only a week in Base. Competition went beyond the telling of jokes, and Al was perhaps more susceptible than anyone else to competition.

I thought about this long and hard in the weeks we spent together on the mountain. Many months later I looked back through my diary. Those distant jottings cursed the weather and our luck. I remembered lying in the tent at Base, reading or scribbling, trying not to laugh out loud at the team's unending flow of bullshit. It emanated half the night from the communal tent a hundred yards away, and echoed around the crumbling spires beneath which we had placed our camp. But mostly it was just hard work, climbing with the team of people I knew, or sometimes knew, best in the world. It was also an opportunity to climb with Al seriously for the first time, even though I had known him for many years. Despite the problems, we were able to make an impression on the mountain.

There was nothing exceptional about the climbing. What was exceptional were the surroundings, the greatest concentration of mountains in the world. The Karakoram may lack the individual beauty and the setting of other Himalayan peaks, but they create an impression of multitude and scale which adds up to a magnificent sum total. Al's plan to ski the eight miles up Savoia Glacier to the bottom of the NNW Ridge paid two dividends; first it saved time and effort, and second, it offered one of the most spectacular ski runs in the world. We reached Camp 1 on May 29th a week after arriving in Base Camp. Advance Base was set half-way up the Savoia Glacier and became a major staging point. At first it took a day to reach AB, and another day to Camp 1. By the end of the trip, the entire journey to Camp 1 took four hours. Al and I set all the ropes from the glacier up a 45° slope and through the small ice-fall above to reach Camp 1. On the first day up, a small windslab avalanche broke the surface just as we reached the safety of a rock buttress. During the weeks that followed, the slope changed and hardened with avalanche debris. It was the first danger zone, but seemed safe compared to the route beyond. In the ice-fall below Camp 1, we passed between two seracs that leaned menacingly, but they never moved. Their only danger was as a cause of heart failure in the race to get past them to the safety of the camp just above.

It took another three weeks to reach the ridge proper and to establish Camp 2 at 6,700m. These were frustrating weeks. First

Al Burgess's team went to stay in Camp 1 but returned after a few days with no progress. Brian Hall left the expedition with a damaged knee ligament. Al and I managed to get some ropes out, climbing in appalling weather even by Scottish standards, pushing five ropes a day up dangerous slopes that hissed and shuddered with coulees. It was never possible to climb for more than one day at a time. We snatched a few hours in between storms and spent the rest of the time lying in the tents talking of Al's favourite and least favourite topics; climbing, business, science and women. When we realized we were eating more than we were earning by staying high, it was back to Base, or drop down to AB to bring up a load. We spent more time high than in Base. For some reason both Al and I were sick in Base, and felt better on the mountain. The inactivity at Base seemed more depressing than on the mountain where you could at least sense the state of the weather higher up. On one sortie on the slopes above Camp 1, Phil arrived a bit late at the bottom of the ropes. Aid, Al and I watched him start up, 1,000ft beneath, only to be engulfed in a massive powder slide touched off by the fall of increasingly heavy snow. A white blanket filled the sky and Phil was lost in it. When it cleared, a small dot was descending back towards Camp 1. The avalanche had carried him several hundred feet, then spat him out at the bottom. We put up another rope, then tensely made our own way back.

In the middle of June the weather briefly improved. Our team was in Base on the morning of the 17th when we awoke to a still, bright sky. We set off for Camp 1 knowing that Al Burgess's threesome would be making the most of it and might reach the ridge that day. We were not long in Camp 1 when JB, Al and then Wilky arrived. The strained feelings that had been growing between the teams dissolved in a thanksgiving of progress and the prospect of good weather. A quiet evening spread across the massive west buttress of K2, seemingly for the first time in an eternity.

We were up at 4am the next morning. I had melted snow the night before, and was able to lie back and settle my aching head while the stuttering blue flames heated the pan. Al and I were halfway up the ropes when it became fully light. We carried good-sized loads now that we were fit. Al always seemed to carry just a bit more. I dropped my sack at the high point to take the lead. One pitch brought me to the ridge, to discover a knife-edge with a view vertically down to Sinkiang. I descended and then traversed several pitches across ice gullys and around towers before we landed on a broad col. Al was in great spirits. We looked up at the jumbled buttresses above that in profile had appeared a ridge. While Al explored, I descended to bring up my load, passing Aid and Phil on the way up. The others descended past me as I panted back up to the col. I stayed for an hour, climbing to a small rock tower from where I could look back down the route in the blinding white afternoon sun. I watched the others diminish downwards until they were lost in the harsh black and white world.

For the next few days, everything was climbing. The Burgesses went up to establish Camp 2, then Al and I took over the next day. We carried big loads and spent the afternoon transferring the dump on the col to the camp and making home improvements. There was never any need to discuss what to do or how to go about it. By this stage of the trip, we simply did things without wasting effort on plans. We alternated the chores of cooking, clearing and fetching snow, and making the effort in the morning, but never having to discuss whose turn it was.

The next two days were superb climbing days. We worked hard, pushing ropes to 7,400m and carrying up as much hardware and spare ropes as we could. The weather was perfect and the mountains began to fall away beneath us like a receding tide. A selfish scheme, born of the pleasure of being high, and pain at the thought of going down, entered our conversation. There was enough food at Camp 2 for a push to the top. We could see the great couloir that led to the north ridge only a few rope lengths to the left of our high point. Two days up and one down would do it. No more spirit-sapping rope fixing. A little voice inside kept saying, 'Go for it' loud and clear above the sounds of the tent flapping and the rasp of air entering tired lungs. But during the second night, Al developed a cough. In the morning, we again selected ropes and hardware for the sacks, and dismissed the food and bivvy tent. 'We'll fix for one more day, then go down for a couple of day's rest at Camp 1 before going for it,' Al told me, his voice a hoarse rasp that just got through above the creaking of boots and crampons. 'That will give us a chance to talk to the others and work out the teams for the first go.'

It was a decision that saved my life and postponed Al's death by a month. A massive storm broke. No further progress was made for the next three weeks. We all returned to Base and awoke each morning to the sound of snow scudding down the sides of the tents. On two occasions, we returned to Camp 1, but only to realize that we had been fooled by brief interludes in the storm.

But our problems were insignificant compared to others in nearby camps. Two Americans had been wiped out in a massive slab avalanche that fell down the couloir leading to the South-West Ridge. And during the same few days that Al and I might have reached the top, dramatic and horrible events overtook the Barrards, Michel Parmentier and Wanda Rutkiewicz. They reached the summit Alpine-style on the Abruzzi, but the Barrards perished in a storm and the other two made a miraculous descent. In that weather I doubt if Al and I could have found our way back to the top of the ropes on the featureless face above our high point.

Then another inner debate began. 'It's only a job, jack it,' said one side. 'It's only a mountain, think ahead,' said the other. The days moved past slowly. Boredom and doubt overcame my energy. Rather than kick against time and commitments, I let it take me away. I found myself standing at Concordia, looking back at K2. For a moment, I almost considered turning round and returning to the mountain. But I didn't and I am left with that image of Al and his tombstone, and a feeling of being stranded midstream.

30

K2 Abruzzi Ridge

JIM CURRAN

The 1986 British Fullers Expedition had two months of almost continuous bad weather attempting the North West Ridge of K2 and then, as a last resort, the Abruzzi Ridge. By the end of July, the bulk of the team had left for home and long overdue jobs.

Only Al Rouse remained for one final attempt. Film maker Jim Curran also decided to stay on at Base Camp until Al and his new-found partner, the Polish climber Dobraslawa 'Mrufka' Wolf returned. July 28 saw the departure of the rest of the team and the porters.

Al Rouse and Jim Curran prepared to move their gear across to the main K2 Base Camp. There, a strong Polish team were poised for a last attempt on the unclimbed South Pillar. Korean and Austrian teams were also attempting the Abruzzi as were Kurt Diemberger and Julie Tullis, who had been filming with a strong Italian expedition.

THROUGH THE FLICKERING heat from the bonfire, the last of our porters wavered out of sight down the moraine and on to the Godwin Austen glacier. Al and I gleefully fed the flames with paraffin. 'I feel like the headmaster on the first day of the holidays after the kids have broken up.' Al eyed my sooty face and hands dubiously 'You look more like the caretaker.'

I had expected to feel terrible as the others departed and envious of their imminent return to civilization. I had been looking forward to going for so long yet somehow was still here. But almost immediately the strains and tensions that had so obviously been affecting Al for the previous weeks dropped away. He became his normal boyish self again, bubbling with enthusiasm and self-confidence and I became infected with his change of mood. Despite the prospect of another week or 10 days at Base Camp, there suddenly seemed a real chance that something could be salvaged from the expedition. For now, Al could attempt the Abruzzi Ridge in the way he knew best; a fast lightweight ascent, unencumbered by the logistics and trappings of a big expedition.

That night, after we had moved our by now meagre possessions over to 'The Strip', as we called the main K2 Base Camp site, and camped just up the moraine from the Polish tents, I drifted off to sleep with thoughts of the film uppermost in my mind. If Al got up and the film that he, Aid Burgess and John Barry had shot was OK, I might yet get a decent documentary together. I realized that I was actually getting excited for the first time in weeks.

Next morning Al and I went back to complete the clearing up of our old site. It was a much better day and the barometer was rising. I half expected some, or all the others, to race back from Concordia but of course once the decision to go has been made, it is almost impossible to reverse. Al said that he and Mrufka planned to set out that night and get to Camp 1 the following morning. I took the opportunity to ask Al if he really felt all right after all this time at high altitude, for I had noticed in the last week or so a definite decline in my own performance. I had started 'Cheyne Stokes' breathing at night again and felt very lethargic. Al said, not wholly convincingly, that he felt fine — but added realistically that if he wasn't 100% he would find out very quickly. 'If I'm knackered we'll just jack it in straight away, and catch the others up.' It was typical Al optimism. How we could catch the others up having given them three or four days start on a week's walk was beyond me, particularly as I wanted to do more filming on the walk out. But Al's enthusiasm by now knew no bounds, and it seemed a pity to stop him in mid-flight. 'Four days up and two down,' he enthused, then mused on the possibility of an illegal descent down the North Ridge into China to meet up with the American expedition and then walk back over the Mustagh Pass. I drew the line at this latest fantasy, pointing out that apart from leaving me stranded at Base Camp, he could also end up in Outer Mongolia in a Labour Camp. Laughing, we returned to the Strip carrying rucksacks full of tinned meat for the Polish expedition we were camped with, who we knew would probably loath it.

That afternoon everyone prepared to leave in the evening. The Poles were off for a last attempt on the South Pillar. I had intended to spend the next few days filming down at Concordia but their leader, Janusz Meyer, asked me if I would keep radio contact with them, in particular giving weather reports from Pakistan Radio.

This gave me a reason for existence but also tied me to Base Camp. Later I saw him talking quietly and earnestly to Al, and gathered he was concerned that Al might be overestimating Mrufka's ability to keep up with him. The previous night Al had dropped some heavy hints that he was keen to join all the Poles on the South Pillar, pointing out that they would then gain, not lose a member, and they would therefore stand a better chance. This offer was not taken up. I suspect the Poles felt that given Al's reputation and access to the media in the West that in the event of a successful ascent, he would cash in on all the Poles's hard-won effort, which was fair enough. Or perhaps given the constant problems with language they didn't really understand Al's offer. Al didn't press it and the original plan was adhered to.

Late afternoon, and Al and Mrufka went through the time honoured ritual of adding and discarding bits and pieces from the their sacks. Al, as usual, paring the weight down to a minimum. 'We're not going to take a fortnight, you know,' he explained patiently to Mrufka. But he was acutely aware that given the problems of permission for the Abruzzi that he and Mrufka must be seen to be completely self-contained, and not rely on anyone else's equipment apart, of course, from the fixed ropes. He planned to walk up to Advance Base and snatch a couple of hours sleep then press on at first light to Camp 1 before the sun got to work on the easy lower snow-slopes of the ridge.

As dusk fell, we all had a huge meal in the Polish Base Camp tent, a good humoured affair with a lot of joking. Wojiech Wroz came in preparing to leave for the South Pillar, wearing his longjohns. They seemed far too big and he did a good Charlie Chaplin impersonation. Then at around eight, Al and Mrufka prepared to set off. Almost at the last minute Al suggested I came with them to Advance Base, at least, and possibly to Camp 1 to film. As all my climbing gear had already gone off with the porters, it wasn't a very good idea, and in any case we had already decided that my presence on the Abruzzi with cameras was likely to draw attention to an illicit attempt. But I wish we'd thought of it earlier. A few last minute modifications and they were ready: 'Take care Al, see you in a few days.' A quick, shy hug from Mrufka and they were off, their head torches bobbing up the Strip. I watched them for a long time before retreating to the warmth of my sleeping bag. The Poles left an hour or so later and we exchanged goodbyes through the tent wall. I slept well, with the irrational feeling that this time luck would be with Al and that in just a week's time we would be happily walking home.

I awoke to a brilliant, cloudless morning. Base Camp was strangely quiet. After the last hectic days that had passed I tried to work out who exactly was on the mountain, and what their likely tactics would be. The Koreans had always tried to man Advance Base and Camp 1 in all but the worse weather and now, presumably, would have a head start on the rest of the field, though the enigmatic and somewhat dour Austrian expedition would also be in evidence. They were the only expedition at K2 Base Camp I had not got to know at all. I found them, if not exactly unfriendly, then rather unresponsive and withdrawn. I never felt at ease in their company and without consciously thinking about it, tended to avoid the slight embarrassment and tension that I felt in their presence.

Kurt Diemerger and Julie Tullis had left on the 28th, ostensibly to return to Camp 2 to film and retrieve gear, but it didn't need much imagination to guess that they too would be sorely tempted to have one last try for the top. Julie had said only a few days earlier that she was homesick and had been away far too long. Also her book was due to be published and she had a lecture tour to prepare. I assumed that there was a degree of gamesmanship at work and never seriously doubted that given half a chance, she and Kurt would go for it. But as with Al, I couldn't help worrying about their physical condition. Having been to 8,300 metres once, and had an epic retreat, they had both seemed utterly exhausted on their return. Even after three weeks' rest I wondered if they would have recovered enough, physically and mentally, for another attempt.

Julie obviously had extraordinary depths of physical reserve and willpower to match, but there was also a disarming and slightly disturbing naivety in her belief that she and Kurt had an almost proprietorial right to climb K2. The more I thought about it the more I wondered just how everyone would relate, for it seemed unlikely that the four groups could simply ignore each other. If they could work together then there would be a formidably strong team moving up the mountain. Trailbreaking would be made easier and higher up much energy would be saved. But there was also the possibility of a 'Tower of Babel' syndrome developing. Human fallibility, language barrier, bruised egos and professsional jealously could all conspire to destroy the obvious unity of purpose that should exist. It was an intriguing situation and one, that from the safety of Base Camp, I could ponder at my leisure.

The day passed slowly. I had set the camera and tripod up, framed and focussed on the big serac on Broad Peak to film the next huge avalanche to peel off. Time and time again I had caught the middle or tail end of these awe-inspiring spectacles but never the whole of one from a tripod. Inevitably, with the camera trained on the likely break-off point, nothing happened. Later, I visited the Korean Base Camp where Mr.Kim, the Korean leader, told me with a smile and a wink that Al and Mrufka had slept under a boulder at Advance Base and had moved up to Camp 1. This was a relief as this seemed to be a tacit assumption from the Koreans that Al's presence on the Abruzzi was accepted by them at least. At seven I opened up to talk to Janusz and the Poles. Already Wojciech Wroz, Peter Bozik and Przemyslav Piasecki had gone straight up the South Pillar to Camp 2, whilst Janusz Majer, Anna Czerwinska and Krystyna Palmowska had gone to Camp 1 on the Negretto Col. Thus a day's gap had been opened within the Polish team and would be maintained throughout their climb. All seemed well and after filming a cloudless sunset with a wonderful afterglow on K2 and Broad Peak I slept, content once more.

The following days, the first and second of August, were similarly uneventful. No firm news came from the Koreans, the Poles seemed to be maintaining good progress, and I occupied myself with some of the location shots and cutaways that I needed for the film. But next day, on the afternoon of the third, I received a disturbing piece of news from the Koreans — that Al had spent the night at Camp 2 and had given up. Depressed, I walked up the Strip halfway to Advance Base with some cold drinks to meet them — what had happened? There was no sign of anyone and, puzzled, I returned to Base Camp, shortly to be given the news that Al was now at Camp 4. Try as I might, I couldn't understand how or why the Koreans had so clearly got the first message wrong. Communication with them was never easy as they were so anxious to show they understood, they would often answer any question with an answer that had nothing to do with the subject in hand. But if they instigated the conversation themselves it was much easier. Was it I who had misunderstood? Perhaps it didn't matter much anyway if Al was now at Camp 4 but even so, on his original schedule he was due to reach the top today, so was now a day behind. Even so, I couldn't help the first shivers of foreboding running down my spine even though there was no logical reason to be scared.

The morning of August 3 dawned with a cloudless sky once more but with the strange silvery luminosity in the atmosphere that had previously heralded a weather change, though sometimes not for a couple of days. But surely by then, with or without the summit, Al and Mrufka should be well on their way down?

The day wore on and I was gripped. The three Koreans were moving ever closer to the summit, and three of the Poles as well on their much harder route on the South Pillar were actually visible through a giant telephoto lens moving almost imperceptably towards the top. But still no news of the seven climbers lower who should have been taking advantage of the Koreans' oxygen- assisted progress by following in their footsteps, effectively hitching a ride to the summit. What was going on? Surely climbers with the experience of Al knew that a rest day at 8,000 metres was of dubious worth, for not only does the body deteriorate increasingly quickly at high altitude and any 'rest' would largely be negated by the strain on the body by staying there, but a whole day of food and, even more important, fuel was being used up. Al on his own reckoning must be very low already. Had they given up? The day wore on until just after 4pm when the Korean camp erupted with joy as their radio burst into life with the news that the summit had been reached. I joined in their celebrations out of courtesy, but felt great waves of apprehension flooding over me, made worse with the news that no one had followed the Koreans to the summit.

I was also worried about the Polish teams who had split up on the South Pillar. The three lead climbers were almost on top but below them Janusz Majer, Krystyna and Anna Czerwinska still had at least two days of hard climbing before reaching the summit. I had lost radio contact with the leaders, but talking to Janusz I realised that they were sounding increasingly tired and incoherent. I hoped they would make the sensible decision and retreat.

Early next morning, 4th August, I was awakened by Captain Neer Khan, one of the two remaining Army Liaison Officers who are supposed to accompany and look after each expedition. 'Jim there is some bad news.' Instantly awake, heart pounding – 'What's happened?' 'One of the Polish climbers Wojeich Wroz, poor chap, has most unfortunately perished in the night on his descent from the summit – the other two are now at Camp 4 on Abruzzi Ridge.' The Peter Sellers voice and language didn't conceal his very real concern and worry for his charges, even if he found it hard to understand their motives. At eight I opened up the radio to hear subdued Polish voices; the two survivors had at last made contact with Janusz and the girls. But I couldn't understand their conversation and failed to make contact to find out exactly what was going on at Camp 4. I just hoped that everyone would now abandon the mountain as the weather was all too clearly breaking down. Great feathery plumes of cloud were blowing in from the south and above that, were huge banks of 'mackerel' cloud formations. Across the glacier Broad Peak's twin summits were hidden in a sinister torpedo of cloud, though K2 remained clear.

The day passed somehow with one bit of reassuring news that Janusz and the girls had decided to retreat. That evening the Korean Camp was plunged into gloom and sadness as the news filtered back from Advance Base that Mohammed Ali, one of their high altitude porters, had been killed by rockfall below Camp

1. 'This,' I commented into my tape diary, 'is like living through a badly written novel.'

No more news of the others but I prayed that the two Poles descending the Abruzzi would have left their radio at Camp 4 for Al and Mrufka to use. But I could get no response that evening, nor the next, and it was not until the afternoon of the 6th August that there were any more developments. By now the storm had moved in with a sustained ferocity that I had not seen before, even at Base Camp. Inches of snow fell every night, above it would be continuous, and the constant roar of the wind high up was like the distant sound of the sea breaking against the shore. How could anyone survive?

But on the afternoon of the sixth the two successful Poles, Przemyslav and Peter returned shattered and still distraught at the death of Wojciech. Exhausted in the middle of the night of the third and descending with the three Korean summiteers he had apparently abseiled off the end of an unsecured fixed rope. The details were scanty and no-one had seen him fall. A long discussion with the Koreans that evening, conducted in broken English, with me attempting to explain to each group what I thought the others might mean, was fraught with problems. I hoped that eventually everyone understood what had happened and was aware that there had been some tension in the air.

Next day radio contact with Janusz and the two girls established that they expected to get down in the afternoon and at around 11 o'clock I spotted three tiny dots high above, descending painfully slowly; they too were alive and safe and a weight lifted from my mind. But underneath a great well of sorrow was building up, for Przemyslav had told me that Al and Mrufka had left Camp 4 at 6.00 on the morning of the 4th. They had last seen Al, with no rucksack and wearing his red one-piece down suit, breaking trail for the top ahead of Mrufka, Alfred Imitzer, Kurt, Julie and Willi Bauer. Hannes Weiser, after 100m had returned to Camp 4 with wet gloves and the chance of frostbite. What had happened? Had they all been avalanched? It seemed a bit unlikely. Or had they all failed to return to Camp 4? Again not very plausible. Were they all trapped and sitting it out at Camp 4? In which case they would be out of gas and food. Any attempt at descent in the storm would be doomed to failure, but after four or five nights at 8,000 metres their survival chances seemed minimal.

On the 9th, with all hope almost gone, I went up to Advance Base with a young Austrian climber, Michael Messner, (no relation of his famous namesake Reinhold). One tent, that of Kurt and Julie still stood. Michael returned but I spent a lonely night there scanning the ridge in the twilight and again in the dawn, for any signs of life.

Through a pair of binoculars Michael had left, I could see a great wall of powder-snow slamming horizontally into the rock buttresses and pinnacles of the ridge. Tearfully I said my farewells to Al, Julie, Kurt and the Austrians and returned slowly to Base Camp, pausing frequently to search the avalanche debris below K2, which was already a poignant rubbish dump of gear that had been swept down from above. Bits of old tents, sleeping bags, and ancient broken ice-axe that could have been silent testimony to some previous disaster, even on one grim occasion a human femur, all ended up on the glacier. But there were no signs. On the 11th I started the sad task of sorting and packing our gear and also that of Kurt and Julie, whose film equipment I could take back to civilization.

That afternoon a Pakistan Army helicopter arrived. Not as we hoped, and had requested, to search the lower section of the Abruzzi (the helicopter's height ceiling prevented a comprehensive search), but to buy clothing and scrounge equipment from the Koreans. No amount of pleading made any difference, and stacked with booty the helicopter clattered off towards civilization, leaving everyone boiling with rage and frustration at combined Pakistani intransigence and Army inflexibility. I felt the last ray of hope disappear.

In the evening in the Polish tent, drinking Kurt's home-brew lager, we drank a sad toast to those left on the mountain. As dusk fell there was a sudden commotion outside the tent and a porter sprinted past. What on earth...? Looking out a figure was just visible, silhouetted against the glacier stumbling and swaying towards Base Camp. Heart bursting with hope and apprehension, I rushed with everyone towards him. It was not Al and I felt guilty as my heart sank, it was the Austrian Willi Bauer. He was speechless with exhaustion and dehydration, and quite literally on his last legs. He was helped to a tent and fluids poured into him. At last in a whisper he managed to tell us that Kurt Diemberger was somewhere behind him and that Mrufka had left Camp 4 but had fallen behind. Julie Tullis was dead. Hannes Weiser and Alfred Imitzer had collapsed almost immediately they left Camp 4 and poor Al, delirious and drifting in and out of consciousness had been unable to move at all. All the information was fragmentary and obviously incomplete, but immediately Janusz, Krystyna and I got ourselves ready to go to Advance Base and see who, if any, were still alive, while Michael Messner and Przemyslaw Piasrcki prepared to leave later to climb to Camp 2 in search of Mrufka.

We arrived at Advance Base at 11pm and while the others started putting up a tent, I went off to collect melt-water and to look up the first long snow-slope of the Abruzzi Ridge, It was a moonless night but the clouds were thinning and a few stars were apearing in a gusty sky. Above me a repetitive noise could have been a loose rope-end flapping or melt water dripping, or someone descending. There was no sign of a light, but I set off kicking steps in easy angled frozen snow, my head torch by now very dim. The noise grew louder. Suddenly I almost bumped into Kurt, climbing down with painful slowness. 'Kurt — it's me Jim— you're OK — you're nearly safe.' He turned uncomprehendingly towards me. 'I thought I saw lights but I am imagining things' — then simply, 'I have lost Julie.'

The next day was spent getting Kurt down the glacier to Base Camp. Twice I thought he would die only hours from safety. Both he and Willi were horrendously frostbitten but Kurt's whole metabolism seemed about to fail. I took his pulse at his request and announced it to be seventy, which cheered him up. In fact I couldn't feel it at all. Later he tripped and fell full length on the flat ice of the glacier. I thought he would never get up and it took all my strength and persuasion to help him. At last more help arrived from Base Camp and on an improvised stretcher Kurt was carried the last mile or so, having undergone, with Willi, one of the most incredible survival ordeals in mountaineering history.

Unbelievably the helicopter failed to arrive that day and when one flew in the day after, it was only to pick up an Army officer.

Kurt and Willi, whose frostbitten hands were already infected must have felt their ordeal was in vain as they patiently sat it out, for every hour away from hospital treatment increased the chances of amputation.

Kurt and I talked of what had happened. He was understandably so devastated at the death of Julie it was not easy to talk about anything else, but bit by bit he described how he and Julie had arrived on the summit late on the 4th August. Julie had fallen on the descent, pulling Kurt 100 metres before he managed to arrest their slide. They had bivouacked in a snow-hole and made it back to camp by the next day where Al, Mrufka and the three Austrians were still holed up in a white out, and deteriorating weather that soon developed into a raging storm with wind speed of over 100mph and temperatures of -30°. On the morning of the sixth, their tent collapsed and Kurt went into Al and Mrufka's tiny bivouac tent, while Julie was taken in by the Austrians. With her eyesight impaired, a sign of cerebral oedema, Julie was sleeping for longer and longer and died ('softly' as Kurt put it) during the night of the seventh.

Out of gas so necessary for melting snow, Al's condition had slowly deteriorated and when on the morning of the tenth the surviving climbers realized it was now or never if they were to live, he was delirious and quite beyond help. Hannes Weiser and Alfred Imitzer only struggled a few hundred metres before collapsing and though Mrufka reached the comparative safety of the fixed ropes leading down to camps stocked with food and fuel, she too failed to make it. All this emerged in disjointed fragments. One detail escaped. I had somehow formed the impression that Al had failed to reach the top. It seemed a trivial, almost insensitive question to ask, but Kurt suddenly volunteered the information that Al had been the strongest on the 4th and had broken trail almost all day before the Austrians had caught him up just below the summit. Incredibly, just 100 years after K2 had been surveyed by an Englishman, it had received its first British ascent twice on the same day, first by Al and two hours later by Julie Tullis. Both had perished in their triumph.

Despite the difficulty of accepting Al's death and the endless wrestling with my own sorrow, some memories slowly re-emerged from the depths of my despair. I had known Al for 12 years, but our friendship really dated from 1979, when I had just spent Christmas with him and his French girfriend, Gwen, in Chamonix. Then Al, not the world's greatest teacher, had tried to teach me (equally reluctant to learn) to ski. It had been a hilarious, but almost complete waste of time in abysmal weather that on one occasion reduced us to snowploughing through slush and puddles in a public park almost in the middle of Chamonix.

After that our paths crossed frequently. After Gwen's tragic death in 1980, Al returned to Sheffield where he quickly put down roots. In 1981 we were both invited to China by Chris Bonington and Michael Ward, Al to climb and me to film on Kongur, at that time one of the highest unclimbed peaks in the world. Al, amused but secretly rather flattered at his acceptance into the 'establishment' felt obliged to underplay the seriousness of the undertaking, commenting when asked if the team anticipated any problems that: 'We might have to use a rope.' Consequently it became a mountain that the British climbing scene could never take seriously.

Kongur was the first occasion I had spent any appreciable time with Al and we both shared the same sort of self-deprecatory humour as well as finding it almost impossible not to exercise it on others; Chris perhaps, inevitably, being the prime target. Al would propound absurd theories that we would totally laugh out of court. The expedition brought us together and on the subsequent film Al, with Chris, did the lion's share of the commentary with Al's blithly whimsical and apparently off the cuff commentary working well against Chris's earnest enthusiasm.

After Kongur, Al had become a close friend: both of us found in the other a confidant for our hopes and plans. We even climbed a bit together on the gritstone edges and limestone tors of Derbyshire. If Al dropped his standards and I raised mine we could occasionally enjoy ourselves on the rock, both of us rambling on about the imponderables in our lives, jobs, money, women, all at times proving either unsatisfactory, elusive or both.

I was under no illusions that it was our friendship more than my skill as a film-maker that had brought me to K2. As on Kongur we tended to share rooms and tents and could unwind in each other's company. In the end, I knew I could not leave him for his last and greatest climb. As on Kongur, when Michael Ward and I had waited with mounting anxiety for Chris, Peter, Joe and Al, I was happy to do the same again. But this time, it hadn't worked out. 'Al — you were supposed to come back — I can't just walk away without you.'

Alone in the one remaining tent, I looked out at K2 clear and bright against the black of night. The memories would release themselves in time: our trip to Jersey with Gemma, Becky, Cass, Hilary, Ian, Viv, Richard and Bill. The hilarious day we went to 10, Downing Street to meet Denis Thatcher, then only days later Al Harris's funeral. And again, the day on Bamford Edge when Al had soloed an absurdly hard arete, a new route. On Kinder's Northern Edges with Richard Haszko and Tom Richardson, Al had climbed a route no-one could begin to follow. He had knelt at the top for what seemed like hours, so drained of nervous energy he couldn't stand up. Walks around the Peak with Al, in all seasons... now all over. Not many places in far away Derbyshire I thought, where memories of Al would not abound. The day only months before watching Al, Rab and Martin trying a boulder problem Al had invented. Rab eventually succeeded, to Al's chagrin. 'Al, you can't just leave all that,' I kept thinking. Fortified with Polish sherry, I at last fell into a broken and miserable sleep.

The next day a few porters arrived, and after the usual insane scramble to get their loads packed and carried, Kurt called me over to his tent to say goodbye. (It was to be two more days before a helicopter arrived for Kurt, Willi and the Korean doctor who was looking after them so well). Tearfully we embraced.

Above, K2, now free of cloud and brilliant in the dawn sun, towered over us. As I left and started the long walk back, the mountain loomed compellingly behind me. Strangely it appeared to grow as I walked away. But as I stopped and turned for the last time at Concordia where the great glaciers of the Karakoram meet, cloud once more covered the summit. As I looked, the clouds parted and impossibly high in the sky, the black summit rocks momentarily appeared, then slid away into the mists.

A fuller account of the climbs and tragedies on K2 in 1982 appears in 'K2, Triumph and Tragedy' by Jim Curran.

Notes on Contributors

Geoff Birtles: Born in Sheffield in 1947. He began climbing at the age of 14 and progressed to become involved in several waves of rock-climbing development particularly in the Peak District and North Wales. In 1966, at the age of 19, he wrote and published a rock-climbers' guide to Stoney Middleton and has since contributed regularly to mountaineering magazines, books and journals. He founded, published and edited Crags Magazine from 1976 to 1982 when he transformed it to High Magazine. Geoff is married with three young children, still living in Sheffield on the edge of the Peak District, and remains a keen climber and activist at several adventure sports.

Chris Bonington: Britain's best known climber. Born in Hampstead, 1934, educated at University College School, London, leaving in 1952 to do National Service, at the RAF College, Cranwell. Transferred to the Army and completed training at the Royal Military Academy at Sandhurst and commissioned in the Royal Tank Regiment in 1956. Spent three years in Germany and then two years at the Army Outward Bound School as a mountaineering instructor. During this period he started climbing in the Alps and went on with Ian Clough to make the first British ascent of the North Face of the Eiger in 1962 and 23 years later climbed Everest himself via the South Col at the age of 51. Apart from his outstanding climbing record he achieved considerable success at leading expeditions, most notably Annapurna South Face in 1970 and Everest by the South-West Face 1975.

Adrian Burgess: Has been climbing for over 20 years. Born in Holmfirth, Yorkshire. He is 37 years of age and identical twin brother to Al Burgess. He is married to an American and lives in Colorado. His expedition experience ranges from Alaska to Patagonia and includes Himalayan expeditions, five of which were in winter.

Rab Carrington: Born a Cockney (1947), bred a Glaswegian, Rab has been a well established member of the British climbing scene for over 20 years. He was Al Rouse's main climbing partner throughout the 1970s. Most of Rab's major climbing exploits are covered in this book including his ascent of Jannu, a fine example of the modern Alpine-style approach to Himalayan climbing. He now runs his own company manufacturing specialist down clothing and sleeping bags.

Greg Child: Australian climber now domiciled in the USA. He has climbed extensively throughout the world and has achieved success at both rock-climbing from the big walls of Yosemite to the Himalayas. He was a member of the same expedition as Alan Rouse when they climbed Broad Peak. He is also noted as one of the world's best climbing writers.

Michael Patrick Coffey: Mick Coffey (Tiger Mick) is a Safety Engineer in the Petro-Chem/Construction industry and lives in Killarney, Country Kerry, Ireland. He has climbed extensively for over 20 years in Europe, USA, Canada, South America and the Himalayas. His record is impressive and he has a number of first ascents and early repeats of difficult routes to his name. Tiger Mick was a notorious member of the group of anarchistic climbers loosely based in North Wales during the sixties and early seventies. It was here that he became a close friend and admirer of Al Rouse.

Jim Curran: Is one of Britain's best known and most accomplished mountaineering film makers. He has 27 years climbing experience in Britain, the Alps, Peru and the Himalayas. His films, which have won numerous awards at international film festivals, include: 'Trango', 'The Bat', and most recently 'Kongur', a documentary of the first ascent of Mount Kongur in China with Chris Bonington and Al Rouse. He is at present senior lecturer in Foundation Art Studies at Bristol Polytechnic, though his home is in Sheffield. He wrote a book entitled 'Trango. The Nameless Tower', which tells the story of the first ascent of the most impressive rock spire in the Karakoram. He was a member of the K2 expedition when Al Rouse died.

Leo Dickinson: Born in 1946 and educated at Rossall and the Blackpool School of Art, where he took both second- and third- year prizes for photography. He began rock-climbing in the Lake District and North Wales while still at school and spent his first alpine season in 1966 in the Dolomites. Two years later he met the Welsh climber Eric Jones, who had just escaped from a fall while attempting to solo the Bonatti Pillar. Dickinson was 24 when he persuaded Yorkshire Television to finance his first film, an ascent of the Eiger's notoriously dangerous North Wall. Eric Jones was to accompany him on that venture, which resulted in the prize-winning film that established Leo Dickinson's reputation.

Neil Foster: Started climbing on the North Lancashire quarries and outcrops around Carnforth, crags local to his home at Brookhouse in the Lune Valley. His climbing progressed via the Lakes to his favourite area, the Yorkshire Dales. He pioneered a number of new climbs here, most at Malham Cove, to which he wrote the recent guidebook.
Like many climbers looking for a degree course, the venue was more important than the subject and in 1981 he went to college in Sheffield. He met Alan Rouse soon afterwards and they climbed together extensively on the local Peak District edges and in Wales. They climbed a number of new routes together, the best probably being Make It Snappy at Gardoms which is still unrepeated at the time of writing. Neil lodged with Alan from 1984 until Al's death in 1986.

Mick Geddes: By the age of 17 had climbed all the Munros. Went to Cambridge where he climbed extensively with Al Rouse and introduced him to the rigours of hard Scottish winter ice-climbing. Sadly Mick died of cancer a few months before Al went to K2.

John Gerrard: Born in London 1943. He started climbing seriously in 1961, graduating from Harrisons to Wales with Al Harris. Moving North in 1963, he was active developing Derbyshire Limestone (1st ascent Prow, etc) and in the Dolomites. Following a road accident he retired from serious climbing. He has retired from teaching early but still keeps in close contact with the Sheffield climbing community. He is currently researching a book on J.W. Puttrell.

Brian Hall: Born in 1951 in the English Lake District and trained as an Ecologist. Started climbing at 16 and is now a professional climber and fully qualified mountain guide. Climbs at a high standard on both rock and ice, especially in the Alps and Greater Ranges. Three expeditions to South America with many difficult ascents in Patagonia, Bolivia and Peru, including Cerro Stanhardt, the last major Peak to be climbed in Patagonia. One of Britain's leading Himalayan mountaineers with seven expeditions to Nepal and Pakistan, including Jannu, Nuptse, Everest in winter, Makalu, Baltoro Kangri, Ogre and K2. Particularly important were the first Alpine ascent of Jannu and the first ascent of the North Face of Nuptse.

Richard Haszko: Richard is 37 years of age and lives in Sheffield, working as an occasional teacher and lecturer. He has been an active climber for 20 years with experience in the Alps, California, Japan, the Himalaya, as well as most of Britain. He was a frequent partner of Al's on many of his climbs and 'walks'.

Dennis Hay: Born Liverpool 1952. Went to Birkenhead School and Nottingham University, graduated in Geography in 1973. Since worked variously as teacher, labourer, manager of cycle routes project in N. Wales and recently as Senior Research Fellow in Dept. of Economics at Reading University. Co-author of two books on European urban trends and problems. Currently Research Manager for the College of Estate Management also in Reading. Still an active, though moderate, mountaineer. Participated in two small Himalayan expeditions.

Fred Heywood LRSC: Employed as a Chemist at Shell UK Oil's Stanlow Refinery. Chairman of the Gwydyr Mountain Club and club representative in the past to the Wales and Lake District committees of the BMC. Climbed regularly with Alan at the start of his climbing career in Wales and at Helsby and the Breck. Climbed with Alan on his first Alpine routes and several Scottish winter climbs. Fred designed and helped build the climbing wall at the EPIC centre at Ellesmere Port which Alan opened in 1985.

Nigel Lyle: A fellow under graduate and one of Al Rouse's main climbing companions during the Cambridge years. Known as Pubes to his friends he broke his leg after a fall on the Bonatti Pillar and subsequently had it amputated. Despite this he continued to climb, achieving leads of Hard VS standard.

Brian Molyneux: Born 8th November 1947 at Kirkby, Lancs. Brian was introduced to hill-walking by his parents at the age of six, started rock-climbing at 16 and joined the North Wales based Vagabond Mountaineering Club at 18. Here he teamed up with Peter Minks and later with Leo Dickinson and Alan Rouse for an eventful climbing and drinking career. In 1967 he made his first climbing trip abroad to Norway and since then has climbed extensively throughout Europe in both summer and winter. With Leo Dickinson he has worked on several mountain films, including 'Matterhorn North Face in Winter', 'Eiger Solo', 'Extreme Ice Climbing and Extreme Skiing' as climber, skier, stuntman, assistant cameraman and safety officer. He is the hardwear buyer for the Ellis Brigham Mountain Sports Shops chain and is based in Liverpool.

Paul Nunn: Has had climbing experience throughout Britain and the Alps and has made new climbs in the Arctic, the Caucasus, the Pamirs and the Himalayas. He is a director of 'Mountain' Magazine and author of 'Rock Climbing in the Peak District' (Constable) and 'Climbing' (Unwin Hyman), as well as contributing to other climbing guides, 'Hard Rock', 'Classic Rock', 'Cold Climbs', 'Extreme Rock' and 'High Drama'. He is Vice President of the British Mountaineering Council. At 44 he is married, has two daughters and is Principal Lecturer in Economic History, Sheffield City Polytechnic.

Nick Parry: A school companion of Al Rouse's with whom he began climbing. Though he never achieved the same high standard as Alan he remained a dedicated climber and maintained his friendship with Alan over the years.

John Porter: Born in the USA, John came to Britain to take a degree at Leeds University and made his home here. Began climbing in his teens in the States with a number of hard climbs in the New England Hills before graduating to the bigger faces of the Rockies. While at Leeds he made numerous hard routes in the alps and in 1977 organised the first East-West expedition with the Poles during which six new faces were climbed in the Hindu Kush. Other expeditions include first ascent of the S. Face of Changabang, Peruvian Andes, Everest in Winter etc. He works as an Economic Development Officer in local government.

Tom Richardson: Is a freelance trainer: a one-time lodger/apprentice of Al's who lives and works in Sheffield. On occasions he has been accused of being a climber and a vegetarian, both of which he vigorously denies.

Susan Elizabeth Rouse: Born May 1954. Obtained a First Class Honours degree in Mathematics from Bedford College, University of London in 1972, followed by a PhD in Theoretical Nuclear Engineering from Queen Mary College, University of London. Taught Mathematics at The King's School, Worcester from 1978 until 1986. At present teaching at Framlingham College, Suffolk.

Doug Scott: One of Britain's best known mountaineers. Along with Dougal Haston, he became the first undisputed Briton to climb Everest in 1975 via the South-West Face. His early interests included big mountain faces and he is the author of the book 'Big Wall Climbing'. In the British Isles he made the first ascents of Parliament House Cave on the Hebridean Island of Harris. He is Britain's most prolific Himalyan climber.